ROUND ABOUT
MIDDLE THAMES

Glimpses of Rural
Victorian Life

ROUND ABOUT MIDDLE THAMES

Glimpses of Rural Victorian Life

Alfred Williams

Selected from the writings of Alfred Williams
by Michael Justin Davis

ALAN SUTTON

Alan Sutton Publishing Limited
Phoenix Mill, Far Thrupp, Stroud, Gloucestershire

Alan Sutton Publishing Inc.,
Wolfeboro Falls, NH 03896–0848, U.S.A.

First published 1982
Reprinted 1992

Copyright © in introduction 1982 Michael Justin Davis

British Library Cataloguing in Publication Data

Williams, Alfred
   Round about Middle Thames
   1. Villages—England—Thames River Valley
   2. Thames River Valley (England)—Social Life
and customs
   I. Title   II. Davis, Michael, *1925–1991*
   942.5'7081'0924   DA670.T2

   ISBN 0–86299–032–7

Typesetting and origination by
Alan Sutton Publishing Limited.
Photoset in Bembo 10/11.
Printed in Great Britain by
The Bath Press,
Bath, Avon.

CONTENTS

Dedication

For Jack Maisey

LIST OF ILLUSTRATIONS

Photographs in roman type, *drawings in italic type*

ACKNOWLEDGEMENTS

In compiling this book I have received great encouragement and help from many people, and to all of them I wish to express my gratitude. The "Friends of Alfred Williams", through Marjorie Leigh, Joan Jefferies and Jack Maisey have been a source of informed enthusiasm; and I am also much indebted to Leonard Clark for *Alfred Williams, His Life and Work*, a book on which I have relied. I have received invaluable help from the Swindon Reference Library, where Roger Trayhurn has given most generously of his time and knowledge; and from the staff of the Local History Library in Oxford; and from the Marlborough Branch of the Wiltshire County Library, where the staff has been extremely kind and patient. I am particularly grateful to the librarians of those libraries, and to the following who have given me most generous personal help: David Brown, of the Ashmolean Museum, Oxford; Jim Glover, of the White Horse Bookshop, Marlborough; Beverley Heath; Denys Hodson; E.G.H. Kempson; John Steen; David Wilson; and Jonathan Stedman and Nicholas Hodson, photographers, whose expert help in reproducing old photographs I particularly value. To them all, I offer my profound thanks, and above all to my wife, who has constantly helped and encouraged me with her unfailing devotion, wise comments and practical skills.

For permission to reproduce photographs and maps, acknowledgement is gratefully made as follows: to Jack Maisey JP for the photograph on page 22; to the Packer Studio, Chipping Norton, for the photograph on page 41; to the University of Reading, Institute of Agricultural History and Museum of English Rural Life for the photographs on pages 81, 107 and 137; and to Oxfordshire County Libraries for both the maps and for all the other photographs.

The tailpieces, from old pictures, have been drawn by Martin Roberts, to whom I am especially grateful.

INTRODUCTION

Alfred Williams was a villager who spent nearly all his life, from 1877 to 1930, in the place of his birth, South Marston, near Swindon, in North Wiltshire. He was a farmer's boy, until the prospect of poverty drove him to become a factory hand. His heart was always in the countryside and in the true way of life which he believed the traditional villagers had lived and the oldest could still remember. Appalled by the false way of life imposed by industry, Williams rebelled against the railway factory in Swindon where he worked, and wrote about the village life that he loved. He knew that traditional village life was doomed. Even though he could not halt the march of progress, at least he could record for posterity a rich heritage that he saw being destroyed.

He wrote two works specifically about the Thames valley above Oxford, and the present book is compiled from them. The first seven chapters of it are derived from *Round About the Upper Thames,* which he wrote in 1914 and 1915, and the last five chapters are derived from *Round About the Middle Thames,* which he wrote in 1923 and 1924.

In these prose works, Williams wanted 'to leave', he declared, 'a permanent record of the language and activities of the district in which I find myself. . . . What I had in view was nature and life. I have tried to depict the beautiful and the actual. Above all, I wanted to describe how people spent their days and nights, in what employments, recreations, and amusements. In a word, I wished to show how they lived.'

Williams aspired to success as a poet. By the end of 1911 two books of his poetry had been published and he had, indeed, achieved some acclaim. However, poetry brought him little money and so he decided to write prose. His subjects were to be those areas of life that he really knew about: farm, village, factory and countryside.

His father was Elias Williams, a carpenter and joiner who came from North Wales to South Marston, a village about four miles from Swindon, then a rapidly developing railway town. Elias Williams was not only an excellent craftsman, highly skilled in structural carpentry and decorative woodwork: he was also interested in architecture and poetry. At South marston he lodged in Rose Cottage, the home of Joshua Hughes, a tanner and smallholder, whose wife, Ann, had opened a school for the village children of mothers working in the fields. Elizabeth Hughes, the younger daughter, was a very beautiful girl. Elias Williams courted her for two years and they married in 1870.

Their home was to be Cambria Cottage, which they built, with a carpenter's shop, on part of Joshua Hughes's meadow, called The Hook. Elias also rented a timber yard in the nearby expanding town of Swindon, where there was plenty of work for a building contractor. Elizabeth bore Elias many children. Bess, their eldest daughter, records that the first son was born at Rose Cottage, and then six more sons and four daughters at Cambria Cottage. Owen Alfred was born on 6 February 1877. He was the youngest son, the seventh. Four boys and four girls survived infancy.

According to Bess, their father was a very good carpenter, joiner, bricklayer and architect who could work from his own plans, and he 'might have had hundreds of pounds where he had not a penny, because he developed the drinking habit.' Their mother 'was a clean and smart housewife' who bore a child annually for eleven years. Every year there was less money to feed and clothe the children, so their mother 'took in needlework and plied the trade through the midnight hours, while waiting for our father' to return, drunk. He 'would go to bed without a word, and carry a knife and put it under his pillow.'

Bess recalls one 'Sunday noon. A hot meal had been cooked and covered close till our father returned from the inn. When he arrived he was in such a strange and awful state that he said not a word; but, taking the covered dishes of food he bashed them against the wall, breaking food and dishes, and which caused us younger ones to burst into tears of fright. He then went back to the open door and stood facing us, throwing what money he had left into the room. Mother said nothing. She was nursing the youngest. . . . When father had gone, mother dished up one of her large "spotted dogs" . . . a roly-poly currant suet pudding. And we had one course only, that dinner time.'

The marriage lasted ten years. It finally broke when Elizabeth discovered a paper falling from Elias's 'trousers pocket, proving to be a notice of occupation by a bailiff, of Cambria Cottage, at which he turned coward and fled.' Bess goes on to say that her mother 'met our father's creditors — whose deficits were for timber — bricks — iron-mongery . . . not a penny owing on her side for food, physic, coal or clothing. . . . She would have paid all father's debts if she could: she felt the shame of it. . . . Father went first to Nottingham. . . . He did not send regular payment for our upkeep, nor enough.'

Elizabeth and her eight children, evicted from Cambria Cottage, were given a home in Rose Cottage by Grandmother Hughes. Alfred Williams, aged three when the marriage broke, continued to live there until he married. He was, according to Bess, 'a very passionate personality. . . . His self-control was wonderful. And so were the diligence and resourcefulness of their mother. She took on the job of newsagent, and after putting the children to bed, 'circuited the village' with her eldest son 'for company (in winter) to distribute *The Swindon Advertiser. . . .* After a time the *North Wilts Herald* appeared, and mother became agent as well, for those' at fourpence a dozen. She also 'started a confectionary business, and made ten shillings to £1 weekly profit. Bess 'used to be taken when old enough to help carry the sweets' from the wholesale manufacturer in Swindon. Food 'was cheap then; and mother pocketed any pride she had and went yearly gleaning at corn harvest: and we always had a sack of flour.' But cash was essential too. 'School money had to be found; for seven years a pile of ten pence went every Monday morning. Not till baby Ada's last year or two at school did free education come.'

Alfred went to the village school with his brothers and sisters full-time until he was eight. Miss Deacon, the school mistress, singled out the Williams children for their diligence and politeness. The education they received was very simple and limited. In later life, Alfred criticized more complex types of schooling. But he must have learned extremely valuable lessons from his mother, a woman who 'often composed poetry while working in her garden, but did not stop to write any,' as Bess records. 'To take a walk with her was an education. She always pointed out some fresh beauty of nature. We did not walk by road if we could travel through the fields.' Alfred Williams's love of nature shines out in all his writings: it was fostered by his mother, and so was his delight in poetry.

Soon after his eighth birthday he became a half-timer, spending only part of the day at school and the rest of it working on the local farm of Launcelot Whitfield. Bess had started working there half-time when she was nine. 'We were so fond of the fields,' she writes, 'that to work in them was a beatitude to us! And every little helped in the house-keeping. . . . The public must have wondered why Alfred began as a farmer's boy at such an age. Our mother remarked sadly once to me, when she had read a paper report of his achievement: "No-one knows he ever had a mother". Yet, it was her genius, her great endurance, her wonderful will-power that equipped him to achieve.'

Alfred later wrote that he was very happy as a half-timer working in a gang, 'pulling weeds and thistles from the wheat. At other times we scared birds, tended pigs, and worked in the hayfield, or at corn harvest.' At eleven, like other children of his age and circumstances, he left school and became a full-time farm worker. His love of flowers, animals and birds was intense, and he learned a lot about them. Although he made few young friends of his own age he enjoyed going for walks with his sisters. The family was happy and united, and Alfred had plenty of interests. He was fascinated by all sorts of machinery: trains enthralled him. Several engine drivers gave him short rides on the nearby Great Western Railway line to London. For a dare, he had, at the age of ten, lain down between the metals of the track and stayed there while a long train rumbled over him.

In adolescence, he joined in more readily with boys of his own age, and shared their sports and pastimes. He also met Mary Peck, when he was fourteen, and he became fond of her. She had come to South Marston to help her married sister. Bess described Mary as 'a winsome and witty girl'. Alfred was increasingly restless, however. Several times he tried, although under age, to join the Navy. Pay for farm-hands was meagre. His elder brothers, Edgar and Henry, were earning much more at the Great Western Railway Works in Swindon. When he was fifteen he decided to join them, and the three would walk the four miles to Swindon and back daily.

Alfred began his factory work as a rivet hotter in 1892. Soon after, he became a furnace boy in the stamping shop, where metal articles were stamped out between dies under steam hammers. He enjoyed the arduous physical challenge of heavy factory work with its violent processes, and he was completely dependable. In 1893 he became a drop stamper. Although he accepted the responsibility of being chargeman of his gang, twice he refused further promotion. He would not become foreman, because he did not wish to give orders to others or sacrifice any of his individuality.

Harry Byett, who knew Alfred Williams well, described his appearance as a young man: 'He was well over medium height, spare of flesh, had squarish, angular features, powerful lower jaw; dry, wrinkled and almost colourless lips generally parted in a pleasing smile, revealing pale gums and a perfect set of well-tended, gleaming white teeth. Blue-grey, far-seeing eyes which looked straight into yours, proclaiming sincerity, and forbidding aught else in his *vis-à-vis*. Light brown hair, short cropped from time to time, as necessitated by his hot, sweating work as hammerman. Fair complexion, perfectly upright figure, head erect whether walking, standing or sitting, imparting a military bearing and a sense of invincibility when confronted with obstacles.'

In his spare time, Williams continued to roam the countryside, and he gained a local reputation for knowledge of nearby sites and customs. He took up painting: some of his pictures he sold in the neighbourhood. He also showed an interest in politics, at first as a Liberal, later as a Tory. His thirst for knowledge and for self-expression was remarkable. In 1897 he began reading English literature in earnest during his spare time, and would not waste a minute of his dinner hour.

Despite the exhausting demands of full-time factory work and his long daily walk, Williams began a four year course in English Literature with Ruskin Hall, Oxford, in 1900. Baffled by the numerous Latin quotations in the books he had to study, he determined to learn that language. 'Beginning with the books of Caesar,' he declared, 'I afterwards became bolder, and dipped with delight into the wonders of Cicero, Ovid, Sallust, Horace and Virgil.'

When he was twenty-four he became engaged to Mary Peck, although he was regarded by her family as a poor match. They were married in Hungerford in October, 1903, and after a honeymoon at Torquay they made their home in Dryden Cottage, very close to Cambria Cottage.

Every room was soon in use as a library, because Williams was reading for London Matriculation in his spare time and now learning not only Latin, but Greek and French as well. 'I used to print a troublesome Greek word on the toe of my boot in the morning,' he later recalled, 'and allow it to remain till the evening. Never mind what your workmates think or say. They may deem you eccentric, but you know what you are doing, while they do not.' He learned astonishingly fast and crammed his days with study, rising at four a.m. and eventually going to bed at midnight, besides cycling to and from Swindon and doing a full day's work as a hammerman at the railway factory. His eyes began to suffer, and he accepted his doctor's advice to stop studying at night, but continued to study by day at every possible moment.

His wife Mary supported him in all his labours. 'She is,' he wrote, 'indispensable to my pursuits. While she knits I commune with my gods. We lead a simple and quiet life.' Harry Byett once asked her:

'Do you ever help Alf in his work?'

'Yes,' she said, 'by keeping quiet.'

At the factory, Williams was scrupulously careful not to allow his studies to encroach on his work as a hammerman. 'When learning Greek,' Byett writes, 'he made a practice of chalking a few Greek characters or words at the rear of his steam drophammer.' He would catch sight of them in passing and so they would become automatically impressed on his mind. Rather, however, than chalk up these few characters during the time of his employers, he reached his work early, and did so before starting time at six o'clock in the morning.'

Life in the factory had by now become soul-destroying for Williams. The coarser men persecuted him. An official who regarded the chalk marks as pretentious ordered their effacement. However, Williams continued to draw his Greek characters and, when the official had thick grease daubed on the drophammer, Williams wiped the grease off and inscribed his Greek in white paint. 'Men and boys in the shop,' Byett writes, 'were encouraged by the official to do any mean thing to annoy, even to the extent of throwing water over him.'

Away from the factory, Mary guarded her husband jealously against all disturbance. As Leonard Clark, Williams's biographer, writes: 'She was no scholar herself, but sympathetic to all he undertook: her nature was so finely drawn that she understood the urge of all his strivings. Hers was not an enviable existence, yet she looked upon her task as a privilege. . . . The brief companionship of their evening meal, when he poured forth all the happenings of the day, and dwelt upon his aims and desires, was her greatest joy. He would have liked to have given more time to her, but it was she who unselfishly pressed him on to his goal.'

Every Sunday they went for a country walk together. He continued to study nature with an intense delight which, despite his solitary character, he was able to share with the village children. They regarded him as someone special; and in response to their friendly greeting — 'Hullo, Mister Willums!' — he would talk to them quietly about animals or birds, or teach them poetry. Alfred and Mary Williams never had any children of their own.

Besides studying, he had begun to write. In 1904 he completed a lyrical play, *Sardanapalus,* and in 1907 two of his poems were published in an anthology. One of them was highly praised by an eminent author, Sidney Colvin. Three prose articles by Williams about his own methods of study were also published, in the *Young Men's Magazine.* In 1909 two more of his poems were anthologized, and the *Daily Telegraph* critic acclaimed him as 'one of the most remarkable men in Wiltshire, if not in England' — fulsome praise which amused Alfred Williams. This year, however, he aroused the interest of Lord Edmond Fitzmaurice, an important figure in Wiltshire life and a member of the Government, who became his patron and helped foster the publication of the first book of Williams's poems, *Songs in Wiltshire.* Meanwhile, Williams discovered the works of Richard Jefferies, the Wiltshire writer remarkable for his power of observing nature and writing about it in a poetic and philsophical way. Williams, intensely excited, felt that he had found a kindred spirit in Jefferies who had lovingly described the landscape of north Wiltshire, and had died ten years before Williams was born.

Thanks partly to Williams's friends who bought copies of *Songs in Wiltshire,* and especially to the Swindon enthusiast, Reuben George, who tried to sell copies wherever he went, the expenses of publication were covered, but only because Williams worked very hard as his own travelling salesman and spent £30 out of his savings, mostly on railway fares. The book, a collection of love songs and nature poems, was well received. Life, however, was far from easy for Williams: and his health was suffering. He wrote to William Dowsing, a poet working in the Vickers factory at Sheffield: 'What with being assailed with internal fatigue, with fag in the worst form, with poor health generally, with the worry of keeping myself together at all cost, with increasing duties at the forge, the utter lack of sympathy, and enmity of one and another, I very often feel most unhappy. My strength seems very often to be exhausted. But it is useless to feel faint. You must march forward or fall to the rear. There is no room to turn back.'

In April 1910 he was invited to a gathering of 300 poets and their descendants at the Holborn Restaurant, in London. He met the *Daily Mail* reporter there. Williams was invited to read his own poetry aloud, but he could not stay to do so: he had to catch the late train back to Swindon, to be at his steamhammer next morning on time.

Williams worked extremely hard to get his second volume of poetry published. It appeared in November, 1911, with the title *Poems in Wiltshire.* There were some translations from Greek and Latin, and one from French, and some tributes to friends, but most of the works were original nature poems. The book was praised in *The Times* and other papers, and as well received as *Songs in Wiltshire*. Williams, however, had contracted to sell half the edition of 500 copies himself, and he stood to lose money.

Realising that ill-health might force him to give up factory work and turn to writing for a living, he decided to write a book in prose. By October, 1911, he had completed *Life in a Railway Factory*, a bold, unvarnished account of his own experiences and observations. This important and provocative book remained unpublished until Williams's digestive and cardiac trouble made his doctor insist, in 1914, on Williams leaving the Great Western Railway works. If the book had been published earlier, Williams would have lost his job.

Meanwhile, in the spring of 1912, he began a book about village life, 'making use,' he said 'of my own early experience on the farm, and portraying local character.' The first draft, completed in only ten weeks of his spare time, he entitled *A Wiltshire Village* and sent to Fritzmaurice. 'No composition', Leonard Clark writes, had ever given Williams 'greater release or pleasure than this honest and unadorned story of the life that went on daily in South Marston.' Fitzmaurice praised the manuscript and, in July, Duckworth accepted it for publication. 'The motif of the work', as Williams told Fitzmaurice, 'is to give a picture of rural life — an unvarnished one — as I have lived it,' and also 'to sketch the locality — an unknown corner of north Wilts. — and call attention to the farm labourer's lot.' To William Bavin, a schoolmaster friend and admirer, Williams wrote: 'Whatever I have written I have seen, though what I have described is chiefly in the immediate past.'

While waiting for the publication of *A Wiltshire Village,* Williams prepared his third volume of poetry, *Nature and other poems,* a collection that includes some large-scale works, notably 'The Testament', his longest poem, which he considered 'to be the best for thought and nature feeling.' Very few of his fellow workmen bought his books of poetry, however, and this was a bitter disappointment to him. he had put all his life savings into the three volumes, and he was now so poor that he considered emigrating.

Nature and other poems was published in October, 1912, and was even more highly praised than its two predecessors. John Bailey, in *The Times*, hailed 'another collection from the Wiltshire poet' and praised its combination of 'fine taste and culture with rugged simplicity.' The *Athenaeum* compared Williams with Cowper, a poet renowned for simple, natural verse. No longer was Williams patronisingly praised as 'The Hammerman Poet' or 'The Harmonious Blacksmith': his achievement as a nature poet was taken seriously and aclaimed.

A Wiltshire Village was published a few weeks later. The reviewer in *The Times* 'found it a gentle and continuous delight' and praised the 'wonderful little descriptions. Here is a vivid portrait that will seem to many like that of an old friend — Jemmy Boulton, the carter. . . . We know and loved him ever so many years ago.' Harry Byett pointed out later in *The Swindon Advertiser* that Williams's 'dialogue, wonderful pen pictures of his characters' and his anecdotes all reflect, 'incidentally, some of the history of the period.' Much of the book's value, Byett claimed, 'lies in the fact that every word is absolutely true, and is therefore history. This feature will be the more appreciated as time goes on.'

In South Marston itself, the 'old-fashioned, agricultural village' that Williams had described, the book — which uses no fictitious names — was not generally resented. Some villagers even complained to Williams that they and their relatives had been omitted. The vicar, however, perhaps objecting to Williams's statement that the 'sermons are long and the minister severe', publicly burnt two copies of the book because it was 'too disgusting to read', and preached against the author (who was present in the church) on a number of Sundays. Williams, though deeply hurt, managed to ignore the affair.

The book sold well, and in a few months he was writing a successor, based on weekend visits in the late summer of 1912 to neighbouring villages 'from Wroughton to the Blowing Stone all along the downside' as far as Kingstone Lisle in Berkshire. This attempt 'to depict the life and characteristics of the agricultural classes in that region', he told Fitzmaurice, would 'not be stylish literature but I hope to preserve a lot of interesting matter.'

He was also working on a fourth book of poems, *Cor Cordium,* the contents of which he described to his younger sister, Ada. 'Half the work shows my evolution from a *doubting* to a *trusting* state in religious belief, and the other half are love poems.' *Cor Cordium* was published in October, 1913. The book, his highest achievement in poetry, was much admired and it sold well. As always, Williams was very grateful to his friends: 'I despair of getting any local support except among those who know me personally.'

Villages of the White Horse, published a month later, describes a score of villages set in twenty miles of downland. The villages were accessible by bike from South Marston, and Williams had done his research with vigour and enthusiasm. 'As to the persons and "characters" that figure in the pages, I have made a point of introducing them exactly as I found them, rough and plain, frank and hearty, honest and homely,' he wrote in his preface. 'I am proud of every single one of them. Some of the dialect and narrative may appear a little barbarous to those of refined tastes, but I can assure them it is all accurate and characteristic.' The book was highly praised by critics as a record of 'real rural life'. One reviewer commended its 'simple strength of style, its sweetness, its fine balance, its sanity of outlook, its flashes of rollicking humour, its informativeness.'

Williams set to work at once on a book about the Upper Thames valley 'and the villages and small towns there'. In February 1914 he was ill in bed with 'violent pains below his heart' which prevented him reading and writing, but by the end of the month he had finished about half the first draft.

The pains persisted. His doctor warned him to give up factory work or 'become a confirmed invalid'. In 21 years, smoke from the furnaces had ruined Williams's digestive system, and he could no longer endure the double strain of work as both hammerman and writer. Williams had come to hate all aspects of the factory, but he knew that he could make very little money from his pen. *Villages of the White Horse* was selling slowly, despite good reviews. He finished the first draft of *Round About the Upper Thames* four months before he finally left the Great Western Railway factory on 3 September, 1914. He was aged 37, his health was broken, but he was determined to earn a living from market gardening and writing.

The outbreak of the Great War deeply shocked Williams, but it brought out his patriotic belief 'that in the end our glorious Britain will prove triumphant, both in overthrowing the German master and in showing the world how it is possible, by honourable politics and right dealing, to advance the real civilization and the lasting welfare of humanity generally.'

By April 1915, Williams was less hopeful than he had been about his market gardening which, indeed, never proved successful. His faith in his writing, however, continued unabated. While *Round About the Upper Thames* was being serialized weekly in the *Wilts and Gloucestershire Standard*, he was cycling round the villages of North Wiltshire and the Vale of the White Horse, on both sides of the Thames between Oxford and Malmesbury, listening to all the folk-songs that he could, and writing down the words of them. The music was not his concern. His aim was to publish a representative collection of the lyrics, because he believed that they embodied the real life of the Upper Thames Valley. By the middle of May, 1915, he had collected more than 300 folk-songs. His expeditions to find them gave him great pleasure and helped to restore his health.

His next book to be published, in 1915, was *Life in a Railway Factory*, which he had finished in 1911. 'This is,' Williams told a friend, 'rather a disagreeable book, both to myself, and I expect it will be, to some others. However, it had to be done, and done without respect to anything besides the truth. . . . I shall offend many, I daresay, and unintentionally: but . . . if I had not treated life in the factory boldly I should have done better not to have written at all on the matter.'

Life in a Railway Factory caused something of a sensation. *The Daily Chronicle* hailed it as 'a book of revelation', *The Times* commended it as pure literature as well as a social study, but the *G.W.R. Magazine* criticized the author for bias and a 'bitter spirit against the management.'

By March 1916 Williams had cycled nearly 7000 miles to collect folk-songs from the 'dreamy villages, and the placid and seemingly imperturbable folks of the countryside'. Before the year was out he had volunteered as a gunner recruit for the Royal Field Artillery and, in an adequate state of health, he had been accepted.

Williams became a highly efficient gunner. After postings to Ireland and Scotland, he sailed for India in September, 1917. His experiences aboard the troopship and while serving in India he described fully and with great zest, both in letters home to Mary and in prose accounts which he hoped to work up for eventual publication. He found India enthralling. Whenever he had any leave, he explored as much of it as he could. He even considered settling there with Mary when he was demobilised, but the pull of England proved too strong and he returned to South Marston in 1919.

He and Mary gathered building materials from a tumbled-down lock, exhausting themselves with the hard physical work, for the building of a new and substantial home. They called the house by the Indian name 'Ranikhet'. There Williams resumed market-gardening and set about teaching himself Sanskrit. He and Mary were very poor and very independent. He revised his manuscript of *Round About the Upper Thames,* sent it to eight publishers who rejected it, but finally placed it with Duckworth. They published it in 1922.

The book, an extension of Williams's work on life in South Marston and villages of the White Horse, covers roughly the first 25 miles of the river's course, from Thames Head to Radcot Bridge, and 'embraces portions of three counties — Wiltshire, Berkshire, and Gloucestershire.' His theme is the old way of life whose passing he deplored. From the 50 or so villages and hamlets that he had visited, he concentrated on about 20. The book wanders, like the river itself, and Williams pauses and elaborates whenever a character, a place, an anecdote or a custom catches his fancy.

Reviewers liked the book and praised Williams for his research and his presevation of a vanished way of life. Sales were slow, however, but improved and persisted. Williams himself hawked the volumes from door to door: he managed to sell 120 copies. Duckworth agreed to publish *Folk Songs of the Upper Thames,* much to his delight. He reckoned that he had cycled more than 13,000 miles in 19 months to gather the 600 lyrics, about 260 of which went into the book.

He was working hard at his Sanskrit, and leading a very frugal life. Royalties on his books were meagre: two small meals a day were all that he and Mary could afford.

In 1923 he decided to write another book about the Thames valley. Its scope would be the region of the river between Faringdon and Oxford, and its title would be either *Round About the Middle Thames* or *Villages of the Middle Thames.* By June 1924 he had written a dozen chapters and gained much satisfaction from the expeditions he made from South Marston to gather material. 'If, after 50 miles of cycling, and much interrogation, I discover a quaint custom, or a curious item of information, or see a new bird by the river, it gives me no end of pleasure.' He finished the book in August, decided after all to entitle it *The Banks of Isis* and submitted it to Duckworth for publication.

Duckworth rejected it because their book of Williams's *Folk Songs of the Upper Thames*, published in 1923, was selling badly. Basil Blackwell, too, declined *The Banks of Isis*. It has never been published in book form.

In 1925, however, Williams persuaded *The North Berkshire Herald* to serialize it. The newspaper's narrow, cramped columns and small print were ill suited to the rambling, leisurely, meditative chapters that Williams wrote out of his powerful love for the river, the meadows, trees, flowers, birds and animals. He included many descriptions of landscapes and buildings, and outlines of history. Only short extracts from passages such as those have been included in *Round About Middle Thames*: this selection focuses principally on people in the living world that Williams himself knew or that they described to him.

'Since my object,' he wrote, 'was to portray as much life as possible — not its sufferings and tragedy — I have made free use of persons, and these not fictitious, but real, who inhabited the villages within the memory of those yet living, believing that such records can never become stale or valueless, and that here, as elsewhere, a little fact is more convincing than a goodly array of fiction. It was in support of this that I have retained the account of Squire Archer of Castle Eaton, and have given the extraordinary list of worthies of the villages of Blunsdon and Hannington, with the prevalent beliefs in sorcery and witchcraft.'

Williams's pen-portraits in *Round About Middle Thames* are full of life. They do, however, lack the intimacy and pathos of his descriptions of some of the old people of South Marston, which were included in the selection, *In a Wiltshire Village* (1981). That book, with its loving description of Mark Titcombe (about whom Williams was also moved to write a long poem), and its compassionate account of Nellie Kempster, and its jovial portrait of Dudley Sansum, shows an emotional involvement that is absent from this book, *Round About Middle Thames*. The variety and scope of this more recent selection does, however, show the astonishing breadth and intensity of Williams's interests. He was fascinated not only by people and places, but by how things worked and how they had evolved. He brings a wealth of experience and enthusiasm to his chosen topics, and his mature prose has a fine, confident ring. Editorial changes have been confined to a little simplification of style and a little re-punctuation.

Williams's heroic struggle to earn a living was unremitting. He finished his last book, *Tales from the Panchatantra*, a translation from the Sanskrit, shortly before he died, starving, in 1930. His services to literature were rewarded by a Civil List Pension, but it arrived too late: he was already dead, and his devoted widow, Mary, was on her death-bed. The living memorial to them both consists of his vivid celebration in prose of the people, region and village life that he knew and loved.

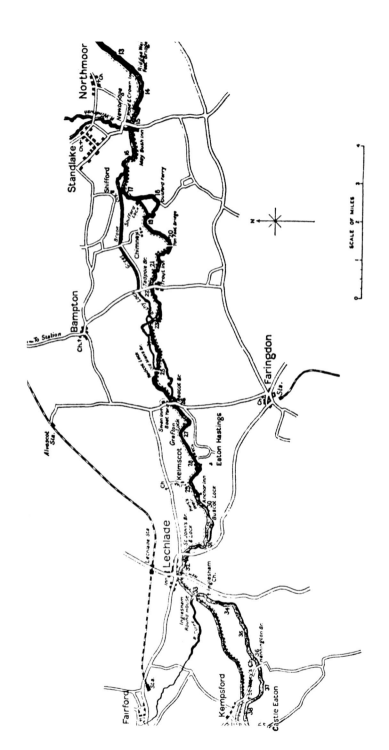

from Salter's Guide to the Thames, 10th Edition, 1904

SCALE OF MILES

N

Northmoor
13
14
Ridge's New Foot Bridge
Ferry & Crown In
15
Newbridge
Standlake
Ch.
16
Maybush Inn
Shifford
17
Duxford Ferry
18
Shifford
Br.poor
Chimney
19
Tadpole Br.
20
Ten Foot Bridge
Trout Inn
21
22
23
Bampton
Ch.
To Station
24
25
Radcot Br.
26
Swan Inn
Boat Yard
Grafton
27
Eaton Hastings
Faringdon
Sta.
Alvescot Sta.
28
Kelmscot
Ch.
29
Anchor Inn
30
Buscot Lock
31
St. John's Br.
& Lock
Lechlade
Ch.
Lechlade Sta.
32
Inn
33
Inglesham
Ch.
Inglesham
Round House
R. Coln
34
35
36
Hannington Br.
Castle Eaton
Ch.
37
Kempsford
38
39
Fairford
Sta.

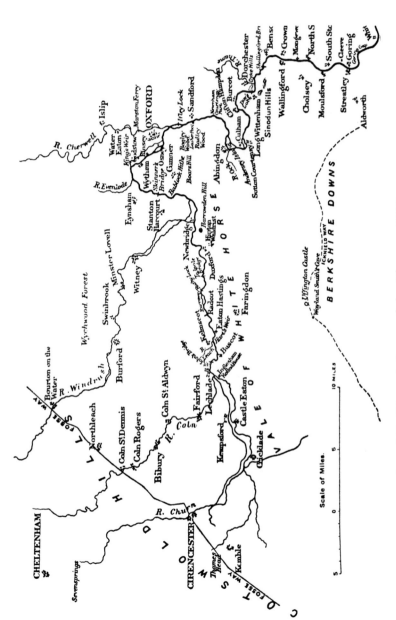

from J.E. Vincent's Story of the Thames, *1909*

Alfred Williams, aged about 30

Chapter 1

THE THAMES VALLEY AND HIGHWORTH

"Ther', ther', ther'. Pat it down. Pat it down. A little bit more on the fer far corner. Put on a thunderin' good load but don' strain the 'osses. We be in for a wet un to-morra, as sure as thy name's Jack Robbut."

"Aa, zur. The owl' zun bin a-zuckin' an't up all th'aat'noon awver Castle Yetton yander."

"An' the cows be moonin' about, an' the martins be clawss to the ground, an' tha's a sure zign o' casulty weather, as my owl' faather used to zaay."

"Aa, an' the dew's a-vaallin', an' this aay 'll soon be as wet as muck, an' the rick's a-yettin now, an' us shan't a done bi doomsday if ya don't look sprack. Go farrud, bwoy, an' pull towwerd a bit. Coom e! Gip now!"

"Lar! dwunt chaestise the poor craturs, maester. The little mer's a-tired. A bin in the shafes all day, ver' nigh."

There were six toilers engaged with the waggon gathering up the hay. First were the two pitchers — always considered the principal men of the field; next was the loader; then the two rakers, Jin, the fogger's wife, and Aaron, the odd man, and, last, the youngster to lead the horses, and feed them with handfuls of sweet hay from the wake. A small green elm bough, cut from the tree, was hung over the mare's forehead, half veiling her eyes, to protect her from the troublesome insects. In the middle of the field, beside a haycock, was a large wooden bottle containing the ale, with a tin cup turned upside down over the handle of a spare fork thrust into the earth to render its whereabouts visible.

"Hello! Jin. Hast thee found thy tongue? Wher's thy man got to to-day?"

"A yent very well, zur."

"Aw! Wha's the matter wi' he, then?"

"Got a naesty cowld on 'in."

"'Ev a bin to the chimist?"

"Ae! A went to Hyvuth tha smarnin', awhever. Tha told un a'd got the — I caen't tell 'e what tha zed."

23

"What is it?"

"I caen't tell 'e. You'd oni laaf at ma if e was to't."

"Come on. Out wi't."

"I caen't zaay't."

"Yes, tha cast."

"Tha telled un a'd got the infli—zummat."

"The what?"

"The infliwinzy cowld. Yellacks! I zed you'd oni laugh at ma."

"What! 'Ev a bin sleepin' out under the aay-cocks agyen? Thee must kip un a-twhum o' nights, Jin."

"Lar! Chent no use to tell 'e nothin'. A takes no moore notice o' I than a crow do o' Zunday."

"Tell tha what, Jin. Go down to the kitchen, an' missis ull gi' tha a bif bwun. Bile 'e up wi' some suety dumplins. That'll cure 'is cowld, as sure as God made little apples!"

"Sartintly, zur, an' thenk 'e. Tha's what I'll do, when us a done."

"An' 'ow's that you byent 'elpin' yer father wi' tha ship to-night, artful? Ood you sooner be along wi' tha 'osses? What be us to make on in, Dannul?"

"'E don' keer for tha 'osses. It striks I 'e's a-veerd an 'em. 'E can get an wi' tha ship tha yezziest."

"Aa. 'E's like I. 'E can 'andle the ship better when tha bin under the pot-lid. Never mind, sonny. Tha't be a man now afore thi mother!"

Enter, by the gate, a rustic, with a note in his hand.

"Be you the maester?"

"I be zummat, awhever."

"Was to gi' ya this, then."

"Wher' d'ye come from?"

"Hyvuth."

"Wha's yer name?"

"Mister Ferris."

"An' wha's yer maaster's name?"

"John Whitful."

"Well! You can tell Maaster Whitful I'll meet 'e at 'Annington, bi the Jolly Tar, at two o'clock to-morra."

The hayfield was situated about half-way between Lushill and Castle Eaton, in the valley of the Upper Thames, near to where the four counties of Wiltshire, Berkshire, Gloucestershire, and Oxfordshire come into conjunction. A hard road ran through the field, bordered by a high hedge on one side. Here the beautiful wild rose, shell-pink and creamy-white, hung in luxuriant trusses and clusters from the top of the hedge down to the ground, shedding a soft radiance, and emitting a faint tea perfume.

Running along at the bottom of the field was a deep ditch, like a brook, one of those made to conduct the water readily into the Thames, and relieve the river in flood-time. On one side the tall taper top of the rick, nearly completed, was visible in the farmyard; on the other the stately tower of Kempsford church rose above the elm-trees and peered majestically over all the valley round about.

Now a large dark cloud, like a bat, with head distinct and wings outstretched, rose slowly out of the west, covering the sky, and causing the interiors of the elms to show blue-black. The moist night wind, laden with the warm scents of the hay and the stronger smell of the ricks heating in the farmyard, came puffing up from the river, and the haymakers hung their rakes on the hedge and left the field, the rumbling of the heavy waggon echoing loudly down the road in the twilight.

The Upper Thames Valley, roughly speaking, comprehends the whole of the ground between the base of the Cotswolds and the northern extremities of the Wiltshire and Berkshire Downs, running from Swindon to Wantage. This tract of country is more commonly known as the Vale of White Horse, since it is dominated by the huge chalk hill upon which the ancient figure of the White Horse is graven at Uffington. But the actual bed of the Upper Thames, or Isis, is really much smaller in extent, and covers no more than half that ground. This begins near Cirencester and continues eastward towards Oxford, bounded on the north, past Burford and Witney, by the Cotswolds, and, on the south, by a low ridge of stone hills running in an almost direct line from Purton, past Highworth and Faringdon, to Cumnor and Hinksey.

The waters of the Thames, in the neighbourhood of Inglesham and Lechlade, are augmented with the addition of several tributary streams that flow down from the north and south, draining the localities through which they pass. The principal of these are the Coln, the Cole, and the Leach. The Coln is a swift-flowing trout stream rising in the Cotswolds and joining the Thames at the Round House, near Inglesham church. The Cole has its origin at the foot of the Wiltshire Downs, and flows by way of Sevenhampton and Coleshill; and the small river Leach, also a trout stream, bubbles out of the rock near Northleach, twelve miles distant to the north-west. Of these tributaries the Coln is the most beautiful.

The origin of the Thames is said locally to be in the neighbourhood of Cricklade, which error may easily have arisen since the river is not usually identified until it reaches the vicinity of that small town. This view of the inhabitants is quaintly and tersely expressed by the old man who keeps the tiny shop at the top of Blunsdon Hill, overlooking the valley, and to whom I applied for a glass of refreshing drink after climbing up the steep slope one broiling day in midsummer.

"This hill is very steep, and the sun scalds like a furnace to-day," said I.

"Yes," he replied slowly, and then galloped away with: "This is Broad Blunsdon 'Ill, Noth Wilts. You be close to Gloucestershire here. All this below is the Thames Valley, and you be jest come through Cricklet. The Thames rises in the meadas close to Cricklet, an' runs away, an' gets bigger an' bigger, an' jines the sea at Greenwich, an' don' mix wi' the salt water for miles out, an' the skipper ull tell 'e when you gets into salt water."

Everything about the valley — pasture, tillage and crops, vegetation, birds, and animals, the keeping of flocks and herds, work, business, pleasure, recreation, the whole life, in fact, is governed by the river, that operates in a hundred ways, openly and secretly, determining all things, and whose decrees are absolute and irrevocable. The invisible processes of draining, flushing, and exhalation go on year after year, producing a luxuriant growth of plants and foliage, unequalled on the hills and plains, or thirsty downlands stretching away to the south. On the hottest day of summer, when the down air is exceedingly dry, the whole valley will be full of vapours exhaled by the river. They float like a sea over the warm fields, enveloping everything — a spiritual food for leaf and flower, an invisible heavenly dew for the nourishment of Nature's garden; and at night the thick mist rises and condenses on the leaves of the trees and hedgerows, and makes the meadows "sopping" wet, and so waters and feeds every form of vegetation. The existence of vapours may have something to do with the prevalence of thunder-storms in the vale, that develop along the course of the river in the summer months. The hills on the one side and the river-bed on the other attract the greater part of the summer rains, leaving the inter-mediate region comparatively bare and dry.

There is a delightful irregularity in the course the Thames takes. The lines of willows and poplars, which the stranger immediately concludes to mark the course of the river, are often some distance from it, standing along the margin of a small brook, or back-water. Even the hawthorn clumps are not infallible evidence of the river's nearness, but may be ranged along some half-dry course in the field. Very often one happens suddenly upon the river, when one felt certain it was a mile or two away in another direction.

Two series of small towns, villages, and hamlets are scattered throughout Upper Thames Valley. Of these some follow the course of the river ; others are perched upon the stone hills running parallel with the stream at a distance of four miles to the south. Beginning with the river, a few miles from its source, are Ashton Keynes, Cricklade, Castle Eaton, Kempsford, Whelford, Fairford, Inglesham, Lechlade, Buscot, Eaton Hastings, and Kelmscott; along the ridge, and winding to the south-east towards the Berkshire Downs, are Blunsdon, Stanton Fitzwarren, Hannington, Highworth, Coleshill, and Shrivenham.

Of these the hill villages are the more ancient, having been occupied long before those were built by the river and in the level bed of the valley, while, in fact, all the country below was dense forest and swamp, swarming with big game and wild-fowl. At Blunsdon, besides its Roman ruins, the remains of an ancient camp or prehistoric village exist, high above the valley; Roman and British occupation is evidenced at Watchfield, Coleshill, Stanton Fitzwarren, and Highworth.

Haymaking, probably in fields west of Marlborough Road, Oxford, between 1900 and 1910

Old Aaron and Daniel, the haymakers of Lushill, are sceptical when mention is made of prehistoric times. For the physical features of the earth and the fossil remains discovered in the quarries, and ofttimes built into the walls of their houses, they hold Noah's Flood responsible. They believe that stones and minerals grow, and affirm that the sarsens in the meadow get visibly bigger year by year: some of them, they say, are as large again as when they were boys. They are, moreover, positive that bones grow when they are buried in the earth, and that the skeleton of a man or animal will ultimately be enlarged to very much more than its original size. They consider that the prehistoric camp at Blunsdon was made by Oliver Cromwell. The first hunters, according to their idea, were Robin Hood and his merry men. The earliest battles fought were those between King Alfred and the Danes; and they believe that man sprang direct from the Biblical Adam — there can be no doubt whatever about all these things.

But neither Daniel nor Aaron is given to deep and speculative thinking. They love, most of all, during haymaking, and at dinner-time, sitting beneath the thick hedge, fragrant with blossom, or around the trunk of the shady elm or willow beside the sunny river, to talk about past toils and conquests in the field, or divers experiences here and there. Daniel's chief diversion is to tell of the suspicious old farmer who always took a loaded gun to bed with him; the Inglesham Ghost, that appeared in the shape of a black dog, or old Bet Hyde, the witch of Cold Harbour; while Aaron's forte is the unromantic tale of John and Sally, first told by the local roadmender.

John worked on the road for many years, and Sally was his wife. By and by John got old and tired of his work. John said to Sally:

"Zally, I thinks I shall gie mi job up."

"Well, if 'e caan't get on wi't, a know, John, gie 't out," Sally said.

John said: "I'll gie mi nowtice in to-marra."

"Aa, zo do," said Sally.

In the morning John went to master. "I must jack it up, maester. I caan't manage it no longer."

"Well, if you caan't manage it, John, you must gie 't out," said master.

John went home to Sally. "I chocked it up, you!" exclaimed he.

"Aw right, Jacky. We shall get on zum'ow, mun."

The next day John walked about and seemed very miserable.

Sally says to John: "Whyever dossent make thizelf contented?"

"I caan't, you! I must get another job."

"What should 'e like to do, then, John?"

"Thinks 'e should like to go to school agyen."

Sally says: "I'll go an' zee schoolmaester about it."

This she did, and said to him: "My owl' chap wants to come to school agyen, you!"

"All right," said the schoolmaster. "Tell John he can come; we'll see what we can do for him."

Accordingly John went to school. When he came home at night Sally said: "'Ow dist get on at school?"

"Didn't get on at all, you."

"'Ow's that, then?"

"All the bwoys pinted at ma, an' called ma girt 'ed, an' thick 'ed. Byen a gwain ther' na moore."

The next day John was as miserable as before. "Zally," says he, "I ull go an' ax gaffer to let ma go back to mi job agyen."

"Well, zo do, if tha cassent make thizelf contented," replies Sally.

Then John went to master and told him about it.

"Yes, John," said he, "you can go to your work again."

John went back with the shovel. Passing along he saw something lying on the road. When he came to it he found it was a small leather bag. John said to himself: "This'll do aw right vor Zally," and took the bag home.

"Now, Zally, I got zummat var tha. This'll do djawwsid [deucid] well to kip thi candles in. Durzay thee cast awpen in, Zally, but I caan't."

After dinner Sally opened the bag, but did not tell John what it contained. It was full of money and notes.

The next day John was out on the road again when a traveller came by. "Old man, how long have you worked on the road?" said he.

"Aw, zum time, you," John replied.

"Did you find a bag?"

"Aa-a!"

"Where is it?"

"Too-am. I gied un to Zally to kip 'er candles in."

"Could I go home and have a look at it?"

"Aa-a! smine t'oot."

They went home together.

"Zally, this vella wants to zee the bag what I vound."

Sally produced the bag.

"Looks very much like my bag. How long have you worked on the road, old man?"

"Aw, gwain in vifty year an' more."

"And when did you find the bag?"

"The vust day I started to work on the rawd."

"Well, that can't be mine, then," said the traveller, and took his departure.

"Aa! but 'twas the zecond time as I worked on the rawd, Zally, ye zee," John said afterwards.

The town of Highworth is perched upon an eminence, half-way between the Cotswolds and the Wiltshire Downs. The hill commands a series of pleasing views. To the south, ten miles distant, are the exquisitely graven downs, with ever-varying hues from the gleaming chalk fallow-land to the tender green of the corn springing, the bright yellow charlock, or vivid red of the poppies, purple sainfoin, or autumnal gold of the wheat crops. Eastward, opening out from behind high avenues of elms, is the charming valley of the Cole; to the west, through a gap in the stone hills, is a view of the Cotswolds beyond Cirencester; while, stretching from west to east, by the north, in an unbroken panorama, is the Thames Valley and hills beyond, extending to Cheltenham, past Witney, and into Worcestershire.

Four main roads lead from the hill town, in as many directions, and connecting it with other towns situated to the right and left, at various distances. Each road, where it climbs the slope, bears the name of a particular hill, as though there were many of them, while, as a matter of fact, there is only one. But accurate localisation is a characteristic of rural people: every slope, angle of the road, field, dell, uncommon tree, or other outstanding feature is given a name, to ensure its immediate identification, and also to provide some small pleasure for the nominators and inhabitants at large.

In prehistoric times the site of the town was occupied by a British village. When the Romans came, they used the hill as an outpost for the observation and defence of their territory along the Thames; then it fell into the hands of the Saxons, who built a high wall around it and called it the "High warded enclosure," from which the name of Highworth is derived. The Danes seized upon it for strategical reasons; later it was a Royal Manor, and when the town grew and became commercially important it was presented with a Charter and styled the Borough of St. John.

The church is of Norman foundation. The building bears witness to several architectural periods, but is chiefly Perpendicular in style. In the stonework of the tower is a round hole, caused by a shot from the cannon of Oliver Cromwell, when he besieged the church after the battle of Naseby. Here he was defied by a garrison of troops, under one Major Hen, for three hours, at the expiration of which time the gallant defender "took down his bloody colours," and surrendered, handing over prisoners and arms. The missile that struck the tower is preserved, hanging in chains within the church. The common report is that the shot was fired from Blunsdon Hill, three miles off, but Cromwell's cannon were not sufficiently powerful to inflict damage at such a distance.

There is a charming confusion in the arrangement of houses and shops in the principal street and about the market square, which is in pleasing contrast to the formal and monotonous regularity observed in more modern towns. The roofs are an extraordinary medley. Some are very high and others low, with gable end towards the street, or sloping sideways, or having an end wall covered with stone tiles overlapping. These are narrow and pointed, those are broad and square, with an indescribable outline, and nearly all have tiny gables and windows inset, quaint and picturesque. The chimneys are tall and rakish, with parts added at different times, and they possess a certain gracefulness of outline.

There were two high wooden galleries in the church. In one of these, opposite the parson, sat the musicians, who provided harmony for the worshippers. Their instruments were: the violin, the key bugle, clarionette, baritone, bass viol, the "horse's leg," and the big wavy trumpet, commonly called "the Serpent," from its resemblance to that beast. A difficulty was often experienced in getting away with a hymn, as the two clerks were at loggerheads, and could not suppress their rivalry, even within the sacred building itself and during the service. "Peggy" Tawnley, the weird little woman, accounted a witch, started the singing; there was no surpliced choir, trained with hymn-book and psalter. "Peggy" also made pilgrimages to the village churches, and led the singing; that duty devolved upon one of the congregation. The churchwarden's aged aunt undertook the pulling of the "ting-tang" before the services; the paupers from the local workhouse stood or sat upon the floor, up the middle of the nave. The tunes were arranged to suit the instruments, and the Serpent had pieces specially composed for itself, and called "Trumpet Notes," they style of which is indicated in the following refrain:

> "Soon shall the trumpet sound:
> Soon shall the trumpet sound:
> And we shall rise, shall rise to immortality;
> Shall rise to immortality."

At Harvest Festival the people of Highworth observed a partial fast, and ate nothing more sumptuous than a rice pudding. The special harvest chant used at the church ended with the words:

> For mercies on the home, and for comforts on the hearth,
> O happy heart of this broad land, praise the God of Harvest.

The vicar — a plain, outspoken man, and a friend of the people — attended the domestic feasts — weddings and baptisms — and frequently entertained members of the congregation at his house. There the tables were laden with homely fare and an abundance of the nut-brown liquor. "Now, gentlemen, we've nothing to drink but beer! Pass round your jorams," the parson would cry, and the company responded with alacrity.

Markets and fairs were held periodically. There was a large assemblage of shows and booths, with boxing and wrestling, comic acting and plays, such as *The Tragedy of Maria Martin,* a ghost piece on the subject of *Hamlet,* and another play called *The Flying Virgin.* In the booths was step-dancing to the tunes of "Charlie over the Water," "The White Cock Hen," "Triumph," and "The Old Woman tossed in the Blanket," with entertainments by the strolling Ballad Singers. A tribe of gipsies, thieves, and fortune-tellers attended the fair, and were soberly engaged making money in one way or another. On the morrow — called Tib Day — they got drunk and disgraced themselves, and were promptly hurried off into the gaol hard by and confined there. The town possessed its markethouse, and it also retained its "Jury" and public Ale-taster down to the year 1850, or thereabout.

For a long time the old Bull Inn was remarkable for a large human skull that had been dug up with skeletons near by, and which was preserved upon the shelf among the mugs and bowls as a curio. But giants did not only exist in olden times, for it is said of a local corn merchant, one John Hall, who lived in the town fifty years ago, that he was as big as four ordinary men; that in conversation his voice could be heard half a mile away, and that his grave was wide enough to hold a fat ox. Over the breasts of some of the skeletons large flat stones were laid, which caused the local wits to suggest that they had been placed there in order to prevent the corpses from walking in their last sleep.

"Ther's nar a road neether comin' in, ner it gwain out o' Hywuth, but what carpses laays at," says "Old Jonathan." He dwells in the most ancient cottage in the town, and is tended by a middle-aged deaf-and-dumb daughter, who is unable to communicate with her father except by the primitive methods of nodding and pointing. He is aged ninety-two, is minus an eye, and very grey, but he is of robust health and indomitable spirit. As a young man he worked with the masons at London, and walked to and fro at week-ends, covering the distance — seventy-eight miles — in about twenty-two hours. He had many experiences on the road, and was often robbed of his earnings and forced to beg his food on the way home. The roads were very rough at that time. The railways were not made, and the stage-coaches and waggons passed him regularly on the way. He often stepped aside to view executions at different places. At one time the death sentence was for farm firing, and at another for "sheen-breakin' "; the hanging took place in the open, before a crowd of spectators. He reckoned to walk nine hundred miles with one pair of boots.

The industries of the town were important. The principal were : bell-casting, soap and candle making, saddlery, coach and waggon building, rope-making, and straw-plaiting. The town was also noted for the excellence of its wooden ploughs. Of the industries nothing now remains but the rope-making and coach-building.

The coach-building yards have long been famed for the excellence of the work made, and especially for the high quality of the wheels. It is astonishing to learn the great age of some of the vehicles in for repairs. Here is a waggon nearly a hundred years old, with wheels still more ancient, and which are good for another century, if the coach-builder is worthy of belief. The boxes of the wheels are nearly two feet in diameter, and the spokes are secured with round oak pegs, invisible from the outside. It was by these signs that the age of the wheels was proved; none of that pattern are made nowadays. A peculiarity of the waggon is that it has wooden axles, which run inside narrow liners within the box, and the farmer, who has looked in to inquire as to the progress of the work, says it is the most easily running vehicle he has ever known. He has no waggon less than seventy years old. He still calls the more recently made of them — exactly threescore and ten years in age — his new waggon; a little paint and a few slight repairs are all it has needed up to the present. The coach-builder used to accept payment in kind for his work. At one time he made a new cart for a sack of flour and a side of bacon; at another he exchanged a waggon for a quantity of corn, cheese, hay, or straw, and so helped the farmer out of a difficulty.

The local squire was noted for his eccentric behaviour. It is said that when he had done anything amiss privately he used to walk about the streets wearing a halter around his neck, with the rope trailing on the ground, as a token of self-abasement and humiliation.

On one occasion he lent his half-peck measure to a neighbour, who omitted to return it. Thereupon the waggish squire paid a visit to the town crier and had the matter published abroad. The next day the townsfolk were startled to hear the following announcement:

"Lost! Mr. Crowdy lent his half-peck measure to an unknown man. This is to give notice that if the said unknown person doesn't bring it back, Mr. Crowdy will never lend it to him any more."

At that time there was a "wise man" of Highworth, who was given to star-gazing and fortune-telling. Meeting him one day, the squire thought to have a joke at his expense.

"Well, and what have you been dreaming about now?" said he.

"I dreamt I was in hell," the other soberly replied.

"Ho! Ho! And what was it like there?" asked the squire.

"All they that had most money sat nearest the fire," the dreamer answered.

"Is that all?" the other inquired.

"Not quite," said the dreamer. "I walked about and found a beautiful golden seat and was going to sit down when somebody took hold of my shoulder and said: 'You mustn't sit there! You mustn't sit there.' 'And why not?' said I. 'That's reserved for old Crowdy of Highworth,' the other quickly answered."

When the squire died his spirit returned and continued to haunt the drives, as is seriously believed by the townspeople. Sometimes he appeared holding the shafts of the coach and drawing that noisily up and down the yard and before the house; at other times he walked the streets at midnight, with the halter around his neck, and struck fear into those who happened to be abroad at that hour. At last it was decided to lay the ghost. The Vicar, bailiff, and jurymen were approached, and one dark night they set out for the squire's house — locked up and deserted — and attempted to carry out the rite. But it proved a difficult matter, for the spirit was sulky, and resisted the efforts of the parson to pacify it. Finally, however, it consented to be laid on one condition, namely, that it might be allowed to enter a barrel of cider and remain there. So they proceeded to the cellar, where stood a large barrel full of apple juice. Someone took out the bung, the spirit entered, and the hole was securely stopped up again. Then the mason and his men were fetched out of their beds and the door of the cellar was bricked up; that was the last ever seen or heard of the squire's spirit.

"Peggy" Tawnley, accounted a witch, was believed to be half-man and half-woman. She used to be dressed in a tight-fitting black jacket with big green buttons and a blue gown, and she wore a quaint little bonnet on her head. A good many folks discredited the tales told about her, but her strange and sudden disappearance seemed to confirm the report of her being a witch. One Saturday night a rustic saw "Peggy," who stopped him on the road and tried to bring him under her spell, but without avail. He accordingly left her there and went on up the hill; but when he got to the town, behold ! there was "Peggy," down on her knees, scrubbing her doorstep. By that he knew for certain that she was a witch, so he ran up to her, and was about to give her a good kick, when she coiled herself up like a football and went rolling down the hill and was never seen after that night.

Another local "character" was the old apothecary. Every Lent he used to sit on the step of his door, clad in sackcloth and ashes, doing penance for his sins committed since the last Easter.

John Drew, the shoemaker, was a religious man, and a Methodist preacher. He had a big business, and employed several apprentices, whom he kept at work till a very late hour at night. At last the apprentices became dissatisfied and contrived to find means of redress.

Once every week the shoemaker went to Hannington to preach in the little chapel at night; his way back lay beneath a dense avenue of elms that made the road very dark. They agreed to wait for him there and accost him out of the darkness. Accordingly, as the old man was coming home late at night and passing beneath the avenue, he was suddenly hailed in a loud, deep tone of voice from the trees above his head.

"John Drew! John Drew!"

"Speak, Lord, for Thy servant heareth," replied he fearfully.

"Don't keep your apprentices at work so late nights," said the voice.

"No, my Lord ! I won't, never more," he answered, and, proceeding on his way, reached home in safety.

The next afternoon, before tea-time, he called his apprentices together and told them how, as he was coming home from chapel the night before, the Lord spoke to him out of heaven and told him not to keep his apprentices at work so late nights. "And now, henceforward, all you young men will go home at six o'clock," said he.

Another Highworth preacher was giving his congregation a few points on geography.

"This earth of ourn," said he, speaking in a solemn tone of voice and clutching the pulpit rail, "is a round — let me see, what shall I say?" "As round as a 'oss's 'ed," shouted someone at the rear, very irreverently. "Aa-a! as round as a 'oss's 'ed," repeated the preacher. This caused the congregation to smile, when someone on the other side quietly interposed with: "You couldn't mean 'is 'ed, could 'e, John?" to which the other promptly replied: "No; I meant as round as the *eye* in a 'oss's 'ed."

The first foot-bridge on the Thames

Chapter 2

SHRIVENHAM, WATCHFIELD AND COLESHILL

On the road south-east of Highworth is the entrance to a magificent avenue, half a mile long, leading to Warneford Place, out of sight behind densest foliage of elms and beeches. The entrance to the avenue is barred with a high gate, for the road is private.

Immediately within the gate is a pretty lodge with quaint windows, porch, and tiled roof. The high elms provide perpetual shade and overarch the wide road to the far bank, where a tall grey stone informs the traveller that he is seventy-six miles from London. The under-keeper lives at the lodge. Here he is close to the preserves and breeding-pens and the woods at the rear, and is able to see all who pass that way and prevent trespassers from encroaching upon the plantations or crossing through the avenue.

Below the lodge gate the road drops steeply down into a winding dell through which the small river Cole flows on its way from the towering downs to the Thames near Lechlade. A small wood of beech and poplar covers the slope on the right-hand side, and extends beside a rich green meadow rendered luxuriant with the waters of the river, that overflows its banks every winter. Across the river, on the opposite slope, is a large rambling farmhouse, and, by the water's side, a stone cottage, all that is left of the ancient mill. The water, through being bayed up to form the mill-head farther down, is almost motionless. Some of the pools are deep and swarm with roach, but there are shallower parts to which the old heron delights to come, watching in silence for hours by the bank, by and by to seize on his prey and carry it off to eat in the open field.

Shrivenham, or "Shrinam" — as it is called by the rustics — lies a little outside the actual Thames Valley. The river, with its broad sunlit face, deep shady pools and currents full of silent whirling eddies, is seven miles off, and the blue line of the Cotswolds is effectively shut out behind the lofty avenues away back on the road. Southward rise the

36

graceful, sweeping downs, with their hues of green and yellow, gold, crimson, or purple, varying according to the season of the year, the time of day, the light or shade, the cultivation of the slopes and the arrangement and disposition of the crops. To the right is the exquisitely shaped Charlbury Tump, and, east of that, the Russley Down, looking like a mighty heave of the sea or a huge green wave for ever about to break upon the shore, with the "One o'clock bush" showing against the skyline. Straight in front is the mysterious-looking beechen clump surrounding Wayland Smith's Cave ; to the left is the towering hill of the White Horse — the classic spot of the neighbourhood — with the graven outline showing clearly on the western slope and the huge fortifications frowning over the wide vale beneath.

The village is ancient, and, besides being of great beauty, it was noted for the sturdy characteristics of its population, from the fighting Lord of the Manor of Beckett adjoining, down to the old archdeacon of the church and the hardy farm labourers. While Lord Samuel Barrington, "Admiral of the White," in command of H.M.S. *Achilles,* was battering the French and sinking their ships at St. Lucia, and the archdeacon, in his capacity of local magistrate, was giving practical advice to would-be litigants at his house, the village teams of gamesters, trained to perform creditable feats with the single-sticks, and great in the wrestling contests, were slashing away at their inveterate enemies and breaking their heads at Ashbury, Uffington, or Stratton St. Margaret. The large tattered white flag (captured from the French battleship *St. Florentine*), discoloured with age and full of shot holes and rents, hangs in the roof of the chancel at the church, and the village gamesters are immortalised in Judge Hughes' account of the White Horse Revels of 1857.

At the entrance to the village are the remains of the pound, formerly used to confine lost or straying cattle. The ancient stocks, the terror of evil-doers, stood near. The last offender to sit in them was a carter of the village who had stolen saffron to give to his horses.

The church stands back from the street. Its style is "debased classic," and it is almost square in shape. The interior is chaste and pure. The inner walls are of chalk — obtained from the downs — beautifully prepared and shaped into squares. This is of a soft milky white, and, though it has stood for centuries, it looks clean and new. The chalk stone receives and reflects the light from the numerous great windows; the interior is never dark or dull while daylight lasts. Several fine brasses, including one to the memory of Disraeli, adorn the walls of the aisles and chancel, and a tablet records, in a poem, the virtues of fame of Samuel Barrington, Admiral of the White and General of Marines, who died in the year 1800.

> He, when his arm St. Lucia's trophies boasts,
> Ascribes the glory to the Lord of Hosts.

The archdeacon was a tactful man, very courteous to and popular with the villagers. Besides being magistrate he was skilled in the laying of spirits; it is still told how he laid a notorious one single-handed. The parson at a neighbouring village used always, in walking, to jerk his heels up so as to touch his thighs behind, and he urgently advised all his parishioners to do likewise, in order to exercise the muscles of the legs. Another habit of his was to walk backwards, which he sometimes did for a mile or more ; and he often lay on his back on the floor of the cottages and gave an exhibition of acrobatic feats before the astounded villagers.

The quaint old sexton, with wooden leg and piercing eye, knew every stone of the church tower and could tell the names of nearly all the dead buried in the churchyard. He was noted for his aristocratic tendencies and lack of sympathy towards the poorest of the villagers. When they were filling in the grave of one well-to-do the earth was thrown down lightly, but when a pauper came to be interred he hardened his heart against the corpse, and, setting the example himself, told his mates to "Hit it in!"

The village, though small, can boast of a fair. This falls in April, and though it is insignificant now, it was once a more considerable event. Any cottager, by placing a thorn bush outside his door, could see ale on fair-days. When the rustics had been served with a short measure of ale at the inns they bit the earthenware cup into small pieces. Brandy was periodically smuggled into all the villages around the downs by "commercial travellers" and packmen. They carried the spirit in bladders concealed in their bundles of calicoes and woollens, and regularly sold it to the cottagers.

After the fair came the feast and revels, which lasted a week. Every cottager, to start the feast, on the first day of the week cooked a quantity of food in the boiler — a gammon of bacon and ten or a dozen plum puddings — so as to be in a position to entertain his friends and kindred from the villages round about. The revels began on Monday. There were skittling and bowling, grinning through the horse's collar, dancing, boxing, back-swording, wrestling, cock-fighting, and prize-fighting. It was not uncommon to have a fatal accident at the games, but that was looked upon almost as a matter of course, and the law concerning a death was not as stringent then as it is now. Though the inhabitants of a village seldom interfered with one another they banded themselves together against outsiders ; thus the men of Shrivenham, Watchfield, and Highworth met and fought every week on the Sabbath.

Bull-baiting was also indulged in from time to time in the village and throughout the locality. First a strong rope, six yards long, was fixed to the ring in the bull's nose and the other end secured to a stake driven into the ground. Trained dogs were now set to worry the animal, that went nearly mad with rage, leaping from side to side, while the owners of the dogs stood near to catch them as they fell after being tossed by the bull. Sometimes the bull broke the rope and fiercely charged the crowd ; more than one spectator met his death at the game. It was the rule to "bait" a bull before slaughtering it for food. It is even said that the baiting was required by law, but for what reason is not evident, unless it was to ensure a better bleeding of the carcass.

It was customary to hold a public harvest-home at Shrivenham. This was kept in the park, after all the corn was gathered in. Lord Barrington and the local farmers contributed and provided food, tea, and ale. There the rustics regaled themselves and afterwards indulged in sports and games. Before hiring a man the local farmers used to take him into the barn and require him to lift a sack of wheat from the floor standing in an empty bushel measure. Many of the labourers could accomplish this feat with one hand.

Besides the ancient whipping-stocks, the village had a place of incarceration called the Blind House, used for shutting up offenders until such time that they could be removed to the central stations and gaols at the county towns. The "blind houses" were dungeon-like places, built without windows, having merely small apertures secured with stout iron bars for admitting air and light. The prisoners were usually relieved of their handcuffs and allowed the liberty of the cells, though sometimes they were kept chained and only permitted to lie down on a straw bed upon the floor. If a villager had indulged in too much of the nut-brown liquor and became troublesome he was quickly placed in the "blind house," there to stay according to the pleasure of the local magistrate. It was a common practice for the prisoner's friends to visit the "blind house" after dark and carry ale in a pot. This the inmate was able to drink by sucking it in with a long pipe or straw through the aperture.

Drunkards were also put in the stocks and made to sit in them from sunrise till sunset, exposed to the jeers and laughter of the rest of the villagers. Though the prisoner was under the supervision of the constable, he was not debarred the privilege of receiving food from sympathisers. In the afternoon the cottagers' wives brought provisions — bread and butter and a mug of tea — but alcoholic drinks were forbidden. If the boys had been guilty of stealing apples and were taken they, too, were put in the stocks and given a few stripes. Sunday nutting in the copses by juveniles was also punished in the same manner.

A modern mansion, Elizabethan in style, occupies the site of the old manorial residence. The lake before the house contains a small stock of fish — roach, perch, pike, and a few eels. The greedy pikes play havoc with the other occupants of the water. They devour everything they meet with in the pool, and finally prey on one another. Besides eating other fish, the pike devours frogs, rats, snakes, eels, young ducks, moorhens, and other wildfowl. One reason why moorhens and wild ducks leave the lake to breed in the spring is in order to be out of the reach of the voracious jaws of the pikes when they begin to move ; half the broods of little ones would otherwise be swallowed as they swam about in the water. Accordingly, if the tame ducklings stray into the lake, the keeper, or one of his men, gets into a boat, and, armed with a large wooden spoon made for the purpose, lifts them out of the water and carries them ashore.

An otter recently had her litter of five on the shores of the lake and was allowed to go unmolested. She had travelled up the small stream from the Cole, making her way under cover of darkness. The green woodpecker nests in the fir plantations; the local name for this is "the gallibird."

The inhabitants of every locality have special means of foretelling the weather. Alongside the Thames it is held that a fine evening with mist denotes fine weather, and a dull evening with mist denotes wet weather. The condition of mist on the downs, and especially around White Horse Hill, indicates to the occupants of the country below what the weather is likely to be. If the morning mist hangs over the hill that is a sign of wet, but if the summit is clear and the mist is drawn along in lines about the base, that is a sure sign of a fine day.

> "When the mist goes up the hill
> Then the rain runs down the drill,"

the ploughmen say. "Now, chaps, the owl' White Oss is a-blowin' 'is bacca off this mornin'. We shall ae't wet afoore night," cries the carter, and before the afternoon is over the rain pelts down in torrents and drives the toilers home from the fields.

"Missis," said old Ike Giles of "Fyas" to his young wife one day — who secretly kept her mother in food — "I caan't make out why our mate bill is so high. A gets 'eavier aitch wik. Whatever becomes an't all?"

"Why, our Jack" — the under-carter who lived in — "is sich a one to et," said she.

"I'll jest ev 'e in to dinner along o' I to-day, then, an' see what a does wi't all," the farmer replied.

This frightened the good wife; so she saw the youth and explained the situation to him, and urged him not to have any lunch, in order to be the better able to eat an extra big dinner.

"Lar, missis," said he, "if I don' 'ae no lunch I shaan' want no dinner!"

When dinner-time came he was brought into the kitchen and placed next to master: a mug of ale was set beside his plate. He fell to and devoured three platefuls of meat and vegetables, to the consternation of old Ike.

"When bist gwain to drenk thi beer?" inquired he presently.

"I never thinks o' drenkin' till I 'aaf finished mi dinner," the other responded.

A neighbouring squire was a notable "character" and much given to

Rickbuilding, probably near Chipping Norton, Gloucestershire, between 1910 and 1920

out-of-door sports, especially hunting and hare coursing. He was a giant in stature, and he weighed thirty stone. According to local accounts he was a thorough blackguard, proficient in the use of oaths, but very good-natured. No one ever applied to him for help and was refused, and he made many generous gifts of food and clothes to the poor round about the neighbourhood. A farmer dwelling near detested the squire, and often took him to task for his uncivil behaviour, but he laughed loudly and passed off the other's remarks good-humouredly.

"Whenever you die you'll go to hell," the farmer insisted.

"Bent gone to hell yet!" said the squire, with a laugh, meeting him one day on horseback.

"But you're on the way, right enough," replied the farmer.

By and by the squire fell sick and was like to die. When the end seemed to be drawing near he went into a trance, and all thought he was dead. Thereupon the usual offices were performed, and the old woman of the village began laying him out. Presently, however, the supposed corpse revived, and the squire sat upright on the bed. He cursed and raved and ran off, just as he was, and, seizing his gun, shot hard at the old woman, who quickly scrambled out of the way and barely escaped with her life.

It is said by the villagers that when the squire died and came to be buried the coffin and body were so heavy they had to be removed on rollers.

Farmer Jonson used to bet heavily and attend the principal race meetings in the country. He was tall and square-shouldered, with big, round belly and fat, chubby head, and he always wore a suit of big check and carried two crab-sticks, one in each hand. Being pestered with rats, he periodically hunted them indoors with ferrets and shot them in the kitchen and dining-room, ofttimes shivering the crockery ware to atoms and filling the house from top to bottom with the reeking smoke of the powder. His temper was not of the sweetest. There was a near neighbour to whom he had not spoken for thirty years. One day, however, on approaching the farm, the horse shied and overturned the high cart, and he was thrown into the ditch and pinned beneath. His inveterate enemy happened to pass that way at the same time, and, seeing his condition, went and released him from his unfortunate plight.

"So you thawt you'd pull me out them, Robbut!" said he, laughing.

"Aw, aa! thawt I'd better spake to tha to-day, maester," the rustic replied.

The Lord Craven lived at Ashdown Park, situated over the hill to the south of Shrivenham. One day he was walking down the hill into Ashbury and came upon a short, fat farm-boy lying on his belly in the road, and working his arms and legs about like a frog. When the noble lord drew near the youngster began:

"As black as a rook,
As black as a raven,
As black as the devil,
And so is Lord Craven."

"Ho! Ho! What's that? What's that?" cried Craven, stopping short and raising his stick to strike the youngster. Then the artful one began again:

"As black as a rook,
As black as a raven,
As bright as the sun,
And so is Lord Craven."

"Well done, boy! Well done, boy!" cried Craven; then, taking a crown piece and a half-sovereign from his pocket, he laid them on the palm of his hand and said:

"Here, boy! Have which you like."

"I wunt be covechus, I'll 'ae the little un," the youngster replied, and promptly pocketed the golden coin.

On another occasion the old lord addressed his valet, who also acted as jester, after being dressed previous to coming down to dinner.

"How do I look?" said he.

"As noble as a lion, mi lord," answered the valet.

"You've never seen a lion," said Craven.

"Yes, I have, mi lord," replied the other.

"Where did you see it, then?" said he.

"Down in Stubb's yard," answered the valet.

"You fool! That was not a lion. That was a jackass," replied Craven.

"Can't help it, mi lord. You're just like him," the valet answered.

After the line was laid to Hay Lane a rustic went on the platform in smock-frock and top hat, wanting to go to Shrivenham. When the train came in he saw it was crowded with "fine folks," and came to the conclusion it was not for him: he could not think he had to ride with such grand people. After the train had left he quietly asked the porter when the next would be in.

"To-morrow morning. Why didn't you get in this one?" answered he.

"I didn't like to get in wi' the fine gentlefolks; but s'pose you'll let me walk!" returned the rustic.

The story is told of the Irishman — a navvy — who came to the local railway station one Saturday night wanting to travel to Bath, and found the last train gone.

"Well," said he, with an oath, alluding to the line or the train, and turning to depart, "I thramped it before he was born and I'll thramp it again."

Watchfield lies to the north-east of Shrivenham, on the edge of a large tract of open country that extends beyond Faringdon to Abingdon. The village is small and compact. Of its past history very little is known, though it is held by the inhabitants that a great battle was fought on the site in olden times.

It is not often that a church is stolen, but that was most certainly the fate of the ancient church of Watchfield at some time during the latter half of the eighteenth century. It is said that the small building, left in the care of the parishioners, and sadly needing repairs, was sacrilegiously pulled down at night by the churchwardens and the stones carted off to make cowsheds and to fill up the farmyards. It is also related that the impudent churchwardens continued to report to the bishop that the church was in good condition for twenty-two years after it had been demolished. By and by, however, the truth leaked out, but before steps could be taken to punish the guilty churchwardens each died a violent death. One was found below a bridge with his neck broken, and the other was struck with a "thunderbolt" in the hayfield.

Beyond the village the road is open, and the way lonely. Here we are on the stone, as is evidenced by the colour of the cornfields and the great profusion of wild flowers. Immediately we leave the clay for chalk, or brash, we are made aware of a complete change in the flora and vegetation. There are fewer flowers upon the clay than are to be found on chalk and brash, though certain kinds, such as celandine and crowfoot, are seldom found off the clay. On the chalk and brash there is less vegetation, a smaller quantity of leaf and stem, and more blossom. The corn, also, yields less straw but a heavier ear. The elms are richer and tougher grown upon clay. They appear to thrive very well upon brash, but the wood is short and brittle.

No birds ever venture to eat the berries of the bryony, for they are poisonous, though the village children obtain both the long green vines in summer and the chains of brilliant ripe berries in autumn and make them into wreaths or wind them about their bodies. The bryony is also known as the mandrake, and its roots are still sought by herbalists and used for medicinal purposes. These roots are thought closely to resemble the human body; it is common for a rustic to dig one up and exhibit it to strangers.

"Yellacks! dist ever zee arn like that afoore? Yer's 'is yed an' body, arms an' legs, navel an' all an't, as plain as any mortal thing you ever zet eyes an. A oni wants life put into 'n an' a'd walk about."

"Code! en 'e naeterral! As naeterral as I be, that 'e is," the other replies.

Near the wall of a farm on the roadside is a large board containing the words: *Dangerous Bog*, warning off pedestrians and others who might be led on to the greensward where they would be swallowed up in a pit of bluish mud concealed from the eye with a covering of treacherous green turf. Higher up the dell are several other of these bogpits which are probably relics of the primeval swamp, witnesses to a condition of things once general in the hollow of the valley. In depth they are nearly twenty feet. No draining would carry off the water, for that is far below the river-bed, and the hottest summer has no effect upon the surface of the pits.

One Sir Charles Wetherell formerly resided at Warneford Place. He was noted for his eccentric behaviour and especially for his slovenly attire. It was said that no Jew would have given five shillings for his wardrobe. He had a seat in the House of Commons, where he debated with energy. He never wore braces, and while he was addressing the House he kept pulling up his trousers at the waist, that promptly slipped down again, to the amusement of members present.

While walking in the grounds of Warneford Place one day he met a tramp going to the house, who stopped him and asked him if he thought it was of any use to try the place.

"Oh, I should go and try. You might get something," said Wetherell, and, walking round the house, he met the tramp at the door and gave him a sovereign.

At another time his butler asked leave to spend an evening with a friend.

"A friend. Ah! Then I think I will come with you, for that is what I have never had in my life," said Sir Charles.

Many ridiculous things happen in the villages and are talked about and laughed at there, but are unknown to the outside world. There is the tale of a villager whose wife sent him to the little shop for needles, cotton, and thread. The old fellow, being unable to read, and of weak memory, was forced to repeat the names of the articles aloud upon the way to the shop. As he was passing down the hill repeating the words, "Needles, cotton, thread. Needles, cotton, thread," he stepped on a slide that the children had made in the road, slipped, and fell upon his back. In the confusion he forgot his needles, cotton, thread, and went on his way and burst into the shop, crying: 'Rasm, pitch, and tar! Rasm, pitch and tar!"

A few years ago the village choir was out "Christmasing" at the farmhouses. On going across a paddock in the darkness one of the number stumbled and fell over a donkey that sprang up with the chorister on his back and scampered off with him. The choirman thought he was being carried off by the Evil One, and cried: "Please, Mister Devil, put me down! I'm a religious man and a Psalm-singer."

"Maester, maester," cried the farm-boy one day, rushing into the kitchen in a state of great excitement, "the caaf got 'is yed droo the gyet an' caan't get un out agyen!"

"Get the zaa, bwoy. Get the zaa, an' zaa 'n out," the farmer answered. Thereupon the boy got the saw and started to saw off the calf's head.

"Dang the bwoy! Why dissent zaa the gyet?" the farmer cried. Then, turning to his wife, he said: "Never mind, missis, we shall hae plenty o' bif now."

John, the carter, is in a desperate hurry this morning, for he has a lot to do, *i.e.* "to shave an' 'ev a nap." Some farm-hands never use a looking-glass for shaving, but lather their face and shave with the razor as they walk about the stable.

"Amber," a clumsy young foxhound, was the squire's dog and a great favourite with the village children, though he was clownishly mischievous and committed many depredations. One day he came running up the street carrying by the cloth a large pudding made in a basin, which he had taken from the table of a cottager. At another time he stole a baby out of the cradle and was making off with it, carrying it by the waistband.

Sometimes, when a young calf dies, novel means have to be adopted in order to induce the mother to change her domicile or to get her to market. Recently, when the dead calf had been skinned and the carcass disposed of, the cow refused to budge, and the boy had to put the skin over his head and shoulders and walk on before; then she followed him. On another occasion the boy had to ride concealed in the high cart and cry "Bar-r-r," now and then, before the bereaved cow could be prevailed upon to leave the farmyard.

"Martha, our Jack" — the donkey — "bin an' jumped over the girt 'igh wall an' got out o' the pound. Fust a put 'is far fit up, then a draad back a bit an' over a come, right into the road," said the villager to his wife one day. But the donkey did not leap over the wall: it was lifted over by a couple of yokels intent on a little amusement. Perhaps the jest is of a more senseless, or even of a cruel kind, as when a pair of villagers raided a cottage one Sunday at dinner-time, seized the pot, full of food, and hung it high in an elm-tree and left it dangling there at the end of a rope.

Belief in ghosts dies hard in the hamlets and out-of-the-way places of the countryside. Besides the spirit of the hunting squire, laid in the fish-pond at Sevenhampton, there was another notable local one that refused to be laid without the sacrifice and offering of human blood.

The village of Coleshill, which bore the proud title "The Flower of Berks," lies along the western slope of a graceful hill immediately opposite Highworth, two miles away on the skyline. To the foot of the hill comes the river, winding round the small dell, as though it knew in the beginning that there would be work to do and a mill to turn at some future time.

Coleshill House, visible for many miles in its setting of elms and beeches, stands near the top of the hill overlooking the vale towards the faint blue downs. This is a moderate-sized mansion, built in the year 1660, to the plans of Inigo Jones, and representing that architect's skill at its best. A mysterious and jealously guarded tradition is associated with the house, though particulars of it have leaked out and are known to the villagers and others in the locality around. It is said that, concealed in a secret chamber in the inner parts of the house, is the embalmed body of a baby or of a young woman, which has been preserved there for several centuries, and upon the preservation of which the luck and security of the house depends. So long as the embalmed body remains, the house and property are assured to the family in possession, but should it ever be stolen or removed from the room in which it is concealed, then the luck of the house would fail and the estate would pass into other hands. Some, eager to shatter the romance of the embalmed child, say it is a wax doll, and not a human body, that is concealed in the secret chamber, but the belief of the villagers on the point is not to be shaken.

The villagers are very proud of their church, and consider it to be of great antiquity. "Sir," says the sexton enthusiastically, "this church is one of the howldest in the land. Why, the Romins builded this church, sir, when they was about 'ere, as I've hallus bin told bi they as hought to know." Doubtless there are those who would not be inclined to favour the view, but village people cling to their cherished opinions.

The sexton of nearly every village comes in for attention, and it is well-nigh impossible to overlook him. Sometimes he is made the subject of a rhyme, or he is famed for his shrewd wit and humour, or he may be remarkable for his oddness, or for the sharpness of his temper. In a village close at hand the sexton was a cobbler, and was celebrated by the cowman in the following lines:

> "As I walked along and looked over the wall
> I saw the sexton diggin' a hawl,
> A left-handed cobbler just backwards at work,
> He wore his waistcoat a-top of his shirt.
> Between the living and the dead,
> That's how the sexton got his bread."

Another used to sleep and snore loudly during the sermon, and sometimes he woke up and shocked the worshippers with irreverent expressions, or disturbed the service by hurling the coal-hammer across the church at the children talking and laughing in the gallery.

Here at Coleshill the sexton — whose name happened to be Sexton — used to imbibe too much of the homemade liquor, and when he came to church he was incapable of performing his duties and made inexcusable blunders. Accordingly he was dismissed and the village blacksmith preferred for the post, but he was soon afterwards removed. A carter near Coleshill bore the nickname of "Blackbird," which he received in consequence of his having fallen asleep at church one Sunday morning. Half-way through the sermon he began to snore, and very soon the people were startled with a loud cry of "Come idder, Blackbird!" The carter was dreaming that he was in the field ploughing up the wheat stubble.

There was never an inn at Coleshill, so the villagers were forced to provide ale for their own use. Accordingly, they grew their own barley, threshed it out at home, or in a barn lent for the purpose, made their own malt, gathered wild hops from the hedges, and brewed their own beer in the cottages. This they did in a large copper pot of twenty gallons hung from chains over a wood fire. The vessel — named the "Parish Kettle" — was given to the villagers by the Lord Radnor, and was used alternately by the cottagers. His Lordship also paid the duty on one sack of malt per annum for each labourer on his estate.

The ancient game of back-swording was practised at the feast. At one time two heads were broken simultaneously, which was a very rare occurrence, and a notable event. A swaggering professional back-sworder, unbeaten with the sticks, used to visit the feast and overawe the local men with the "cocksureness" of his attitude and behaviour. At last a young carter determined to make a supreme effort to humble his pride and carry off the prize of thirty shillings offered by the champion. Accordingly, when the swaggerer cried out: "Will any young gamester come upon the platform?" the carter responded: "Yes, I ool," and leapt nimbly upon the stage. Seizing the single-stick firmly, he turned to the crowd and cried: "Well, gentlemen! What be I to do wi' this owl' man? Be I to break 'is 'ed or no?" "Ef 'e ool be obstinate, go at un," they cried, whereupon the young carter began fencing, and presently broke the head of the old gamester, who wept at his disgrace and never more showed himself in the neighbourhood. After that the carter was pressed off to fight against the French at Waterloo, and on returning to the village he introduced the game known as "Prisoner's Base," or "Crossing the Line," which was for some years popular with the youths of the countryside.

Old Lord Radnor, although a stern man in some respects, had the welfare of the village at heart, and did his best to provide employment for the workpeople and keep them in a prosperous condition. The clothes he wore about the farms and grounds were extremely plain, and his old white top-hat and threadbare coat were more fitting for a beggar than an aristocrat.

He was rather eccentric, and he caused some amusement around the neighbourhood by reason of his singular behaviour and his weakness for wanting to know how he was regarded by his workpeople. On the passing of the Reform Bill he entertained the rustics to dinner at Coleshill House and feasted them on the lawn to commemorate the event. He ran about in the marquee carrying the plates of meat and shouted loudly to the carvers to cut thick slices "Now, Pinnegar," cried he to a farmer who was carving, "put that knife into it, and give the men some victuals, and don't be frightened of a bit of meat."

He had a bullock killed once a fortnight and five sheep every week for use at the house, and he gave the inferior parts and gallons of good soup to the villagers.

It greatly amused old Angel, the rustic, to learn that his lord and master sat in a chair on runners in front of a fire on the hearth and had a long staff with a spike and "cruckle" (crook) on the end of it to push himself farther back or draw himself nearer to the fire.

One day he came upon some men sorting over a pile of stones.

"That's a nice little job, men. I think I could do that," said he.

"Come on, then, an' have a go, if you wants to," said an un-suspecting workman, who took him to be a stranger at one of the farms.

Thereupon Radnor threw off his coat, and began to load the wheel-barrow with stones. Very soon he began to question them. "What sort of a man is this old Lord Radnor?" said he.

"Oh," said they, "ther's two ways to take un — the right way er the wrong way. If you takes un the right way you'll find he yent much amiss."

"Oh, I'm glad to hear there's a bit of good about him," he replied, and, giving them half a crown each, he put on his coat and departed.

While he was presiding at Faringdon Police Court a case came forward in which a poacher was the defendant. He pleaded not guilty.

"What were you doing in the wood?" asked Radnor.

"I only went in to cut a stick, my lord," replied the defendant.

"How would you like me to go into your garden and cut a cabbage?" promptly returned Radnor.

While he was talking to two labourers one morning, several others, dressed in Sunday best, went by on their way to Highworth Fair.

"H'm! Looks as if they are going to enjoy themselves," said he. Then, putting his hand into his pocket and taking out a crown he gave it to the men and continued: "Well, you go and enjoy yourselves then, but don't drink too much of that beer."

He used to declare to one of his tenant-farmers that every pheasant reared on the estate cost him a pound, and he was furious when a party of young sportsmen, whom he had invited to Coleshill Woods, went out and shot nine hundred birds in one day around Badbury Hill.

His desire to know how he was regarded by the villagers exposed him to certain dangers, and he did not always escape scot-free. Meeting with an old woman who was gathering wood in the field one day he addressed the usual questions to her.

"And whose field might this be, my good woman?" inquired he.

"Aw! this belongs to owld Lard Radner," she replied.

"Ah! And what sort of a man is he?" asked Radnor.

"A crafty, covechus owld bagger, as ull never be satisfied till 'is mouth's chock full o' dust," she answered spitefully.

"Ah! Is that so? Good-day, my good woman," said he, and went his way.

The next morning the old woman was sent for to the house, and was met at the door by Radnor, who gave her a sovereign and a bundle of clothing. "I'm very sorry to hear such a poor account of Lord Radnor. I didn't know he was quite so bad, and I hope you'll think a *little* better of him in the future," said he to the bewildered dame.

Notwithstanding Radnor's fair reputation he was severely handled once or twice at the Cricklade elections; the last time he appeared there his carriage was smashed, and he was fortunate to escape without injury.

One of Lord Radnor's tenants was a rich farmer who was noted for a remarkably keen eye in looking up and down the drills. He was driven everywhere in a small carriage drawn by two horses, and he crossed the rough ploughed land or young crops at any time of the year. If he found a small portion of land missed by the drill he discharged the carter and put him on again within the hour.

One day he was arranging with Moses, the day man, about the hoeing of a patch of beans.

"Now, Mose! What ca'st do this for?"

"Aw! I don' know, maester. What can you gie?"

"I'll gi' tha 'aaf a crown" — *i.e.* an acre.

"Aw! Aaf a crown. Well, I'll show 'e 'ow I can do't for 'aaf a crown. Like this, look!"

Here he put the handle of the hoe between his knees and dragged it behind him up the drills.

"Daal! That wunt do. I'll gie tha sixpence more," said the farmer.

"Must still trot wi' the 'ow, maester," Mose replied.

"I'll make it another shillin'."

"I'll gie one blow yer an' another ther'," Mose answered, indicating his meaning with the hoe.

"S'pose I must gie tha five shillin's," said the farmer.

"Tha's more like business, maester. Now I can do't, an' do't well," Mose replied.

The village of Coleshill was unmolested with witches, but it is said that one Robert Polebrook, who lived not far off, was in league with the Evil One. Robert had been cowman for the greater part of his life, and when he got old he left the herd and did a little odd work on the road. He it was who went to Longworth Lodge, that was haunted and deserted of its tenants, at midnight, and attempted to carry off a table for use in his cottage. Clutching the table, and hoisting it upon his shoulders, he succeeded in getting it outside when a terrific contest began. The table struggled violently and overthrew Robert, who got up again and tried hard to master it, but the table hopped and jumped about around him and struck him on the head once or twice and finally overpowered him, and he was constrained to carry it back to the Lodge and replace it in the room. The operation took him all night to perform; he just managed to get it over by daybreak and on his way back home met the shepherd coming to work.

But the old fellow was cheerful at times, and sang merrily as he pushed his wheelbarrow along the road or clipped the edges of the green turf:

"My pack at my back, and they all wish me well."

Often in winter, when it was bitterly cold and the snow fell, he would be out at work, whistling cheerily, with no hat, and only half dressed. One morning, when the snow was falling in thick, heavy flakes, Robert was out stone-breaking, with his hat tossed in the hedge, full of snow, and his clothes nearly buried on the ground. Then Brown, the fogger, came past on his way back from breakfast.

"Good morning, John Brown! Very muggy warm this morning, John Brown!" said Polebrook.

"Aa, 'tis, Robbut, an' thee't very zoon be buried out o' zight, 'ammer, stwuns, an' all, if thee dossent lave it an' get along whum wi' tha," the cowman answered.

When at length the old man became very sick and felt that death was drawing near he addressed a final entreaty to his lifelong friend and neighbour. "Betty," said he, "plaaze to put the owl zythe an' shart-'andled hoe into the coffin wi' ma, for I dwunt know what tha'll put ma at when e gets to t'other country. I'll lose a bucketful o' sweat wi that owl' hoe."

After he was dead his two sons, who lived afar off, came with a waggon, put up the coffin first, then piled the furniture of the cottage, the garden tools, wheelbarrow, and clothes-props on top and carted them all off together.

The first lock on the Thames

Chapter 3

INGLESHAM, OLD ELIJAH, BUSCOT AND LECHLADE

Before the days of the old Lord Radnor the Cole was crossed by a ford and the road was diverted from its original course in order to approach the bridge. Even after the bridge was made the carters continued to use the ford. The horses were accustomed to wade through the river and to take a drink of water, while the carters liked to wash the wheels of the waggons or to soak them if the weather was hot and dry.

Fording the river at deep water was dangerous, however, and accidents occasionally happened. One day a Cheap Jack with his stock of jewellery was being driven in a coach to Highworth Fair and came to the river, that was swollen with recent rains. The driver thought he would take the ford and drove his horse into the river, but the current was strong, and the coach was washed downstream and smashed against the bridge. The Cheap Jack escaped by climbing through the window and clinging to the roof of the battered coach. "I'm a ruined man, but save my life!" cried he to the villagers who had assembled to give assistance on hearing of the accident.

When the workmen were clearing a flam out of the river in order to make the bridge they found embedded in the sand several human skeletons, probably the remains of gipsies, which had been disposed of secretly. The old Lord Radnor's French valet is said to have been buried on the roadside. This was in accordance with his private wish: he objected to being interred with the Protestant villagers.

While the carter was at plough one day near the river the front mare of the team stumbled and her fore-legs sank into the earth up to her knees. Upon examination it was found that she had stepped into a stone coffin buried just below the surface; though the field had been in cultivation for untold years no one had made the discovery before. Inside the coffin were the bones and dust of a corpse, and a small urn full of ancient coins, which were claimed by the bailiff of the farm, while the carter received the bones for his share of the booty. These he carried home with solemn care and reverence, intending to keep them, but the house was immediately disturbed with ghostly sounds and unaccountable happenings, and the carter was compelled to leave the cottage.

Many attempts were made to unearth the coffin but to no purpose; even the two strongest horses on the farm could not move it from its low bed. Then the carters were doubly assured of the supernatural agency and declared that the coffin was never intended to be moved. Accordingly it was left in the field, where it still lies beneath the yellow wheat stubble. I have been confidentially informed of an old farm labourer — a very quiet and unobtrusive individual — who is said to possess a sackful of ancient gold and silver coins which he dug up with skeletons in one place and another.

At one time the sermons at the church lasted an hour, and the parson frequently criticised the farmers' methods of cultivating their land and took them to task about the couch. He told them that sin was just like couch, and if any of the congregation did not know what that was they could see plenty of it by just going outside and looking over the wall into farmer Gosling's field.

Beyond the mill the stream, that before had been but a few yards wide, assumes greater dimensions and puts on the dignity of a real river. Here its course is more open and direct. The willows and poplars have been left behind and the hawthorn clumps are fewer and smaller in size than they are farther back towards the head. A great part of the charm has gone, too; the sweet mystery of the pools beneath the boughs is laid bare and the spell is broken.

Of fish there are not so many, except in the pools lower down, and where the water has been bayed up for the mills. Being confined with the flams and shallows they fall an easy prey to the heron, and also to the otter, that leaves the deeper water of the Thames and works its way up to the stream's head under cover of the bushes and reeds. The otter also plays havoc with the wild fowls, though it is often discovered and shot by the farmer whose fields lie alongside the river. A favourite lurking-place of the otter, by day, is a hollow withy tree; the farmer's dog occasionally scents out one there. If it is disturbed and surprised out of the water it is easily taken. The shortness of its legs prevents it from running away, though it is very fierce when attacked by the dogs.

Below Coleshill the course of the river is interrupted and the water turned aside and led away at right angles to meet the Thames a mile above the original junction. This is effected by means of a strong wall built across the bed and provided with a hatch to regulate the water for the cattle in the meadows beyond. The bed was dug out and the course so conducted as to procure sufficient fall for the water to turn the wheel of Inglesham mill. This was done centuries ago, when Inglesham — at this time a ruined place and almost deserted, except for the very ancient and interesting church — was a prosperous and flourishing village, proud in its position alongside the undulating Thames. But evil days fell upon the place and brought about its overthrow; only a heap of ruins remains to mark the site upon which the village formerly stood. The site of the mill is marked by a set of hatches and a broad pool — formerly the "whirly hole."

Numbers of eels pass the hatches every year and many are trapped on their way through the gate. The miller used to take eels by means of a "twig budget"; that is, a bent willow wand with a long net attached. This was set through the hatch and the eels fell into it and became entangled. After taking them from the net, in order to keep them alive until such time as they should be required for the table, they were put into a large perforated box, which was placed in the pool and kept there, secured with a rope. Hundreds of eels are taken at the weirs on the Thames and sold at a shilling a pound by the lock-keepers: an eel-pie is a favourite and highly esteemed dish in the Thames Valley.

In the midst of the withy bed alongside the stream — once the site of the miller's house and garden — is a pit-like place, formerly used as a fish-pond. At one time every miller had one, and sometimes several small ponds and wells in which he stored live fish according to their kind. If anyone was ill, or otherwise in need of a fish diet, instead of resorting to the angle he merely applied to the miller, who, with the aid of a net fixed on a pole, obtained a fish from his pond and sold it to the applicant. Now the dry pond, overgrown with dense bushes and reeds, affords a cover for the great old fox that leaps out at your approach and bounds across the meadow, several times stopping and turning round to watch your intentions before he gallops off and disappears through the thick hedge into the green field beyond.

Out in the meadows alongside the river the haymakers are busy. Here the mowing machines, drawn by stout horses, are going round and round the piece, tinkling merrily, while the tall grass, full of sorrel and crowfoot, staggers and totters for a moment and then falls, to be finally disposed into neat rows by the swath-board, that fetches the cut over.On the other hand are the machines tedding the half-dried grass or waking up the hay; beyond, the loaders are busy gathering it up from the field and hauling it into the farmyard to place it upon the rick.

Quaint old Inglesham church lies off the main road, but a few yards from the Thames. The building dates from the twelfth century: in the year 1205 it was given by King John to the Monks of Beaulieu, in the New Forest. Its length is no more than forty-nine feet. It has north and south aisles, with trans-Norman and Early English features, and a little bell-cot at the west end. Part of the original oak of the roof is yet intact. Built into the walls are several crude figures of great antiquity; the old hour-glass, used formerly by the preacher to regulate the length of his discourse, is preserved, a relic of days long past and of methods no more to be employed.

Below the church, shaded by a group of Lombardy poplars, is a building called the Round House, guarding the entrance to the old Thames and Severn Canal, which was once a great highway for those trading between the ports of London, Bristol, and Gloucester. Here, too, the Coln, flowing from the stony Cotswolds, is received into the Thames. Broad meadows, the home of the fritillaries, and dotted with clumps of hawthorn, stretch alongside the river. The tall spire of Lechlade church rises beyond the grey stone bridge and above the clustering roofs of the houses in the town.

The canal, with its once broad and deep channel and elaborate system of locks, after being in use for over a century, is neglected now. Its construction was formerly looked upon as a great engineering feat. Hopes were entertained of an endless period of usefulness and prosperity for the waterway; but the possibilities of the steam-engine had not then been entertained, nor could any foretell the wondrous inventions and revolutions to be effected throughout the globe within less than a century from that time.

The Round House is much frequented by tourists and holiday parties during the summer months. The very name of the place excites a pleasing curiosity. Formerly the house was occupied by the lock-keeper, who superintended the traffic passing through the gates and received the tolls. Now the old blacksmith has taken up his abode there and lives in semi-retirement. He still keeps a small tin of borax, begged from the bargeman who piloted the last load through the locks, in memory of that event. Some of this he occasionally uses for welding steel tackle, such as grains of forks and pickaxes.

Spinning and weaving, though not on a large scale, were carried on in the cottages at Inglesham in olden times; agriculture was the principal industry alongside the Thames banks and round about the valley.

Old Elijah, the "Grand Old Man of Inglesham," lives in a house fronting the road and overlooking the Thames opposite Kempsford church, three miles away, the grey tower of which rises magnificently above the dark tree-tops and beats back the strong rays of the morning sun. His widowed daughter tends him in his age — he is nearly ninety-five. The farmer has assured them the use of the cottage at a nominal rent as long as they have need of it : their anxiety for the future is reduced to the minimum.

Seeing the old man outside, I addressed him, standing near the gate.

"I'm come to have a chat with you," said I.

"An' very plaazed to zee 'e. I likes a bit o' good company," returned he.

"Oh, sir, he's very dull of understanding!" cried the middle-aged daughter, appearing in the doorway.

There was no need of the apology. A man of ninety-five, and a rustic, of no school education, who can talk intelligently for hours about the farm, the passing of Laws and Acts, electioneering, historical events, and great national movements, who can explain many of the phenomena of the heavens and describe the equinox, discuss local topics, from the old Priory of St. John to the British village on Badbury Hill and the Hannington "Liberty," and finish up with singing a score of songs remembered for sixty or seventy years, is not dull of under-standing.

As a matter of fact — I tell it as a confidence — Gramp thought at first I was a curate come to make the usual call and was inclined to be formal, but when I had discovered myself as a very common sort of mortal he became friendly and familiar. Gramp is really a splendid figure — a delightful and congenial soul. He is of medium height, is broad and well made, and as erect as many a man at sixty. His head is massive and his features are typically English, with heavy brows, expressive eyes, aristocratic nose, and clean-shaven lips and chin. His long, silky, snow-white hair hangs nearly to his shoulders and adds reverence to his appearance. Every day, when it is dry and fine, with his feet inside a pair of large slippers, and gripping a stout stick in his hand, Gramp walks down the road to the old pound and chats with his neighbour. When it is wet and cold he sits by the fire, hat on head, and smokes his pipe, or hums over the airs he learned as a youth.

Until he was over ninety Gramp gathered flags and bulrushes from the river and made baskets, chair-bottoms, and other articles. He also made the hassocks in use at the quaint little church by the Thames' side. He would have gone this year and got more rushes, but his daughter would not allow him to walk so far; accordingly he has to be content with looking over the garden or sitting and thinking about old times. One of the men with whom he worked on the farm as a boy fought at Trafalgar and amused them with his tales of the battle. When the fight was at its hottest a Sergeant of marines was very despondent.

"Oh dear," said he, "we shall never see England nor the old folks any more, for we can't stand this much longer."

While he was thinking of death, a jolly tar came running up from below and shouted: "What cheer! What cheer! Duck for dinner! Duck for dinner! There's hundreds on the water," and, looking over, they spied scores of wild fowls that had got in the way of the guns, being washed against the ship's side and seized by the sailors.

Another local recruit fought at the battle of Waterloo. During the battle he got cut off from his company and was isolated and surrounded by the Frenchmen, but he fought and killed seven of them single-handed before he himself was overpowered and slain.

The scarcity of men and the difficulty of obtaining recruits at that time is well known. The sum of thirty pounds was paid to volunteers, and Gramp had heard it said that a bold sergeant sat before a drum in the market-place, upon which was placed thirty sovereigns in gold, and that every time he beat the drum the coins sprang into the air, which feat was practised in order to attract the attention of the rustics and induce them to enlist. Towards the end of the war local farmers sub-scribed the sum of fifty pounds and gave to a villager to procure his enlistment. Before he had got far on his journey peace was proclaimed, and he came home with the money and did no more work for two years.

Gramp has seen many great floods in the Vale. "The water ull cut out o' that owl' Thames an' bust out o' the bank, an' be all over everything in 'aaf a' hour, an' zumtimes be gone agyen in forty minutes," he says. He remembers when there were many more weirs on the Thames than there are now, and when the stream was navigable up to Cricklade. "But the sprengs be wakened in thaay owl' 'ills, an' ther yent so much water comes down as 'twas when I was a bwoy," he tells you. The winter of 1788–89 was unusually severe. The frost lasted continually for thirteen weeks, and the Thames, in many places, was frozen to the bottom. This Elijah had learned of his grandfather, and the matter was also celebrated in a short lyric sung by the fiddlers who came to the feasts:

"The frost began in eighty-eight
And ended in eighty-nine."

Now the summer is over. All the haymaking is done. The ricks have been tucked and thatched. The mowing machines and horse-rakes have been gathered together and safely stowed in the sheds, and the fields are green with the fresh young aftermath. The sun, that looked down day after day from an almost tropical sky, strikes not so fiercely now. In the evening the mists thicken.

Already the steam-plough is at work in the field, breaking up the dry, stubborn soil and preparing it to receive the seed, when the kindly rain has fallen and powdered the surface of the earth. The huge engines, one on each side of the field, are puffing and panting alternately, rocking, trembling, and straining like giants to draw the mighty cultivator that staggers and stumbles, jumps and jolts, and plunges headlong on its rough course across the patch. How hard the ground is! How fearful the effort required to force a way through it! And how doggedly the green-painted wizard persists in the toil! The dense black smoke and cinders shoot high into the air. The bright, smooth piston-rod shoots in and out like lightning, and the heavy fly-wheel whirls rapidly round, enveloped in a halo of light. The heavy steel cable, well polished with trailing the implement, flashes like silver in the sunshine. At one time this is straight and taut. Now it leaps into the air, now plunges down, lashing the earth furiously; now it sways to and fro sideways, jerking and tugging, and now it lies prone on the earth, half the length of the patch, its glittering, snake-like coil creeping silently along the surface of the ground. A cloud of brownish dust encircles the plough, half concealing the steersman perched upon his iron seat. He holds fast and grips hard on the wheel and pilots the machine skilfully from end to end.

Now the first engine stops, for the plough has reached the end, and the other begins, steadily at first the ponderous implement turns clumsily round and goes plunging back across the piece. Meanwhile the vacant engine takes advantage of the respite to go forward several paces and patiently awaits the plough's arrival on the other side. The driver leaps down from the engine and pours oil into the lubricators, or chats with the farmer who has come out to see the finishing up of the work, for there is not much more to be done. A few more journeys and several half-turns complete the ploughing; then the engine farthest from the entrance turns round and rushes powerfully across the rough piece, leaving the implement to follow behind and plough out the tracks of the ribbed wheels. This is no sooner done than with a bright flash and a sharp clap overhead the heavens break and a light thunder shower falls, causing the heavy wheels to skid round and bringing the engine to a standstill, with the machinery in full motion.

Formerly a bridle-track though green fields led to the Thames, wide and deep at this point, and travellers and others wishing to go by that way were ferried across into the Gloucestershire town of Lechlade. At length, on the completion of the Canal, the inhabitants decided to build a bridge over the stream and to construct a hard road in place of the green track. Accordingly, after many difficulties, the work was completed. The huge span of the bridge was made and a pike house built to take tolls from those crossing into the town. The amount of the toll was fixed at a halfpenny, and the bridge came to be known far and wide as the Ha'penny Bridge. There is a local tradition to the effect that when the bridge was about to undergo the first severe test the master mason ran and climbed one of the high poplar-trees at the Round House and declared that if the bridge gave way he would leap into the river and be drowned.

Below the bridge the river, that was flowing serenely down the green fields, suddenly turns and forms a double loop, sweeping majestically round and afterwards resuming its course between lines of silvery willows. Running beneath the road is a long tunnel to assist in carrying off the water in flood-time; several other shorter arches, made for the same purpose, support the highway. Pools of stagnant water, half concealed with tall flags and rushes, lie around and below the arches throughout the summer and afford a secure refuge for the water-fowl. Here also the otters love to come and fish in the shallows and chase the half-grown pikes that were borne out of the river during the floods and left behind when the waters sank.

The frequent rising of the water in the winter has washed the mortar out of the stones in the wall and left many deep holes running within. In these crevices a colony of sand-martins have their lodging and rear their offspring, out of the reach of mischievous boys and others, who are unable to climb down the wall and interfere with the eggs and young.

The village of Buscot, though insignificant in size, is famed throughout the Upper Thames Valley. This, in the first place, is owing to the beauty of its surroundings, its woods and grounds, and, secondly, by reason of the remarkable energy and prodigality of a

The lock at Buscot Weir

former occupant of the mansion in the park, whose name became familiar for many miles around. The doings of Squire Campbell, of Buscot Park, were told far and near, and many people came to the little riverside village in order to obtain employment at one or other of the great works he took in hand. He brought into cultivation hundreds of acres of land that before had been useless, dug lakes and reservoirs at the cost of many thousands of pounds, and turned what had been a wilderness into a beautiful and fertile paradise. Money flowed like water, and the workmen were as the squire swore he would have them to be, "as thick as flies"; there was no limit to the outpouring of gold till the Crimean War arose and ruined the well-intentioned but imprudent speculator.

Formerly Buscot had its medical practitioner, who did something for suffering humanity, as is proved by his records unwittingly left behind, in which we read the frequently occurring and significant phrase: "For bleeding old Betty Martin, one shilling." With the doctor's records is preserved a leather label formerly nailed to a package consigned to the Vicar from London "By Waggon to Oxford. To be forwarded by Caravan No. 1." The road through the village is one of the chief highways from Gloucester to London and was regularly traversed by the heavy lumbering waggons and stagecoaches.

The grey church stands but a few paces from the river's brink, upon a small terrace sufficiently high to prevent its being flooded after the heavy winter rains. The building dates from the twelfth century, though little of the original survives. The interior is simple.

To-day the church is strewn with cuttings of flowers and leaves and is generally untidy, for it is being decorated for Harvest Festival. All the morning the farmers' wives have been employed arranging fruits, flowers, and vegetables in the windows and twining the golden corn around the pulpit and choirstalls. In the corner is a sheaf of wheat with heavy ears; here the pure white and bronze chrysanthemums mingle with the Michaelmas daisies. Vegetables are piled upon the floor, while orchard fruits are set in the windows; a large home-made loaf is fixed conspicuously upon the lectern. One thing alone is wanting to the picture, that is, a large shock or stook of a dozen or twenty sheaves set up in the middle of the church or a heap of threshed grain.

A water-wheel, twelve feet high and sixteen feet wide, stands on the river. The weight of this is over twenty-five tons, and it has a driving capacity equivalent to twenty-one horse-power. It is fitted with a number of iron shell-like blades; the water, flowing swiftly down a chute beneath a heavy cast-iron plate, rushes upon these and forces them round, enabling the wheel to revolve four or five times a minute. Alongside is a shed containing powerful pumps which are operated by means of a system of cogs and gear. The teeth of the cogs around the great wheel are worn as thin as pennies, for they have been in constant use for twenty years. A special Act of Parliament was needed to sanction the building of the wheel on the Thames; upon its continued exertions depends the success and welfare of all the farms on the estate, which would be deprived of water if the pumps were stopped.

A spirit factory stood on the bank of the river above the lock-gate. This was the largest and most expensive of all the experimental works undertaken by the squire, but though it cost a hundred thousand pounds to build and equip, and was superintended by French experts, it was doomed to failure after ten years' working. The villagers who worked at the distillery say that excessive duties killed the industry; whatever the cause of its demise there was no lack of energy on the part of the squire to make the concern profitable.

Nevertheless, in spite of his failures, the squire was a remarkable man. Whatever he attempted was on a grand scale, and if one scheme failed he immediately embraced another and was undaunted by difficulties, however great they might have been. The men on his estate worked nine hours a day and received fair wages. He staggered all the other farmers and landowners in the neighbourhood by reason of his profuseness, his unheard-of experiments, and his tremendous energies.

Beet was the material from which the spirit was extracted. A system of artificial irrigation was contrived to fertilise the hill ground; the water was pumped up from the river by the wheel. The squire manufactured his own manures for growing the beet, grinding up immense quantities of coprolite. Besides this he had quarries opened and lime-kilns built to produce lime for dressing the land. The hauling was done by steam-power. The whole countryside throbbed with life, and the earth quivered beneath the iron wheels of the heavy traction engines.

To cultivate his land he had several sets of steam-ploughing tackle of considerable dimensions. The engines were of thirty horse-power each, and each weighed thirty tons, that is, more than double the weight and three times the power of those ordinarily in use to-day. They ploughed night and day throughout the autumn and winter, until the whole of the land had been well broken up and cleaned ready to take the seed in the following spring. To enable the steam-ploughing to proceed by night a system of limelight was installed on the plant. If the ground was very wet the engines moved on timbers. The squire visited the field at all hours of the night, and provided relief gangs; he could brook no delays in getting forward with the work of cultivation. The squire's wife was as energetic as her husband. She was often to be seen striding through the fields with the tail of her skirt drawn through her knees and buckled to her waistband in front.

The first method of steam-ploughing differed from that followed in our own time, or even in Squire Campbell's early days. Then only one engine was employed. This was a portable machine, and was drawn out to the field by horses. If the field was of a moderate size the engine stood on one side, but if it was very large it was set in the middle. Near the engine was a heavy double windlass, with which the cables were wound, and which was driven by means of a belt from the engine. Situated at several points about the field were "porters," containing small pulley wheels through which the cables ran. These were attached to a large iron anchor which dug deeply into the earth as the engine was pulling from the windlass. When the plough reached the end of the field the cable was switched off on to another pulley and the implement went plunging back across the piece. The anchor was released from the earth and shifted with levers; several assistants, besides the engineman and steersman, were required to look after the tackle.

When the traction engine first made its appearance on the road it was provided with a set of shafts fixed in front and a horse, as it were, to draw the machine. This, curious as it may seem, was compulsory, in order not to frighten the horses attached to other vehicles on the highway.

A notable feature of the great house is its scheme of water-gardens. They are a series of fountains and their basins, constructed in terraces and connected by a tiny stream that flows down the centre. Lines of tall trees stand back from the arcade. Alongside the fountains are garden plots adorned with statues, sculptures, and massive carved Italian urns and pottery ware. Beautiful wax-like water-lilies float on the surface of the pools beneath the fountains; clumps of iris grow along the margin of the stones. In the open pools the goldfish sport and play and float with languid ease, or stand on their heads above the stone bottom. Big, lumbering carps wriggle about and hide beneath the lily leaves and among the gauze-like weeds, out of sight of the stranger.

At the end of the terrace garden is a curious arch made of the jawbone of a whale, and which is said to have been standing in its present position for more than a century. The length of the jaw is fifteen feet, by twelve feet wide at the base, and six feet near the nose — the swallowing capacity of the animal must have been enormous. In eastern maritime countries the ancient peoples, in building their houses, used fish-bones instead of timber, which must have been a valuable substitute. Although the arch has stood for a hundred years in rain, frost, and sunshine, it is practically unimpaired, and the bone is almost as hard as iron.

Besides the few carps kept in the fountains there are large numbers in the waters of the lake. They have their homes in the deep pools, and are seldom tempted to take the deceitful bait of the angler, though now and then one may lose its wariness and become fixed upon the sharp hook. Carps live to a great age, even for as long a time as a hundred, or a hundred and fifty years, as has been proved by trustworthy evidence. Carps will live longer out of their element than will any other fish. They have been kept alive out of water for a month and fed with bread and milk during that period.

Many small birds dwell in the wood under the protection of the keepers, who have charge of the lake and fish. Here also, in the lofty spruces and poplars, the herons rear their young close to the shallow waters of the lake, where they may be seen watching patiently beside the bank ready to stab their unsuspecting prey when it swims near. The nest of the heron is large and rather flat, resembling that of a pigeon, with this distinction, that it is provided with two deep holes, one on each side, for containing the legs of the bird when sitting upon the eggs. From this it is seen that the heron does not sit upon the nest with folded legs, as do other birds and wild-fowls, but while its body rests above the egg its legs are in the holes. Accordingly, when a heron rises from the nest its legs are seen to be suspended and are folded after-wards, while other birds rise with the aid of their wings, being cramped in the legs with long sitting.

The reservoir, into which the water for the farms is pumped by the wheel on the Thames, stands high above the lake. This is of twenty acres in extent, with an oval bed seventy-five feet deep in the middle. The digging of the reservoir was an expensive undertaking. This is looked upon, and justly so, as the most valuable work the squire did.

The reservoir on the hill is fringed with a growth of dark green bulrushes, standing in the water, and concealing the straight, artificially formed banks. Bulrushes, gathered not later than the beginning of September, are used for weaving baskets, seats of chairs, and mattresses. They are also used by the coopers, who lay a rush between the sections of wood to fill up the crevices and keep their barrels water-tight when the iron hoops are put round.

At the woodman's house many curios are to be seen. He is an enthusiastic student of birds, and, though unable to read or write, he has collected many rare specimens which he has stuffed and sold to naturalists. In addition to this he has been a breeder of moths and butterflies. These he hatched in thousands, by means of glass cases built against the walls of his cottage, and afterwards sold them to students and collectors. He has often taken the eggs of the kingfisher and reared the young, feeding them with minnows from the brook. The tiny birds eat from three to six minnows a day, though the old ones devour many more than this.

Of late years the woodman–naturalist has been afflicted with rheumatism and is prevented from following his vocation as taxidermist, but the cottage still contains a few specimens of rare birds, though they are not treasured as formerly. The splendid peregrine falcon, shot with a pigeon in its claws, is fixed upon a post in the garden to frighten the mischievous sparrows from the peas and cress, and the badger skins are nailed over the roof of the pigsty to prevent the wet from dropping on the swine beneath.

A narrow track branches off from the road and leads through a plantation of spruces and black firs. Within the plantation, half con-cealed with the dark boughs, is a notice-board containing the words, in large letters — To Eaton Weir. Farther down, in a small opening, is a pretty lodge and, below that, a tiny stream winds down to the calm-flowing river, half a mile distant. The old village of Eaton Hastings stood close to the river's bank. It has now disappeared, with the exception of the small church and several cottages, though its site is indicated by the enclosure called Town Meadow.

There is no lock alongside the weir, for the fall of water is no more than two feet. Consequently, small boats coming up or going down stream have to be drawn over the barrier on rollers, and large craft, such as steamers and barges, have to "shoot the weir." To enable them to do this the paddles on one side are taken out. The sinking of the water on the high side and the rising on the low side produce a level, and the boat passes through on its journey. Immediately the paddles are again fixed into the stout frame; the water is dammed back and flows over the top in a pellucid sheet.

The weir, officially named Eaton Weir, is called Hart's Weir by the local inhabitants. Thus, if you inquire of a rustic the way to Eaton Weir, he looks at you in silence for a moment and exclaims: "Eaton Wire, sir! You means Hart's Wire, don' 'e, sir?" This came about by reason of the inn upon the bank having been kept for several generations by a family named Hart. In time the name Hart's Weir was adopted as being shorter, and perhaps, because it afforded more ready and significant means of identification.

The innkeeper, according to the account of the villagers, was a notorious smuggler. He obtained his kegs of spirit from the bargemen who came up from London and concealed them in the bed of the river. To the kegs he attached ropes or chains; when he wanted one he took a long-handled iron rake and groped on the bottom till he struck the chain and so got it ashore. Whoever wanted whisky or brandy came down to the Weir after dark and was supplied by the innkeeper. The spot is lonely and difficult of access in the winter; there was little fear of being surprised by the Customs officers.

Over the wooden bridge above the weir a footpath runs through level fields intersected with a dike full of forget-me-not and loose-strife. On one side of the dike is a bank, three feet high, constructed to contain the water at high flood and save the country round about from being inundated.

So deep were the floods at Kelmscott before the construction of the bank that the cows swam over the tops of the walls bordering the road, and the inhabitants were compelled to live upstairs for six weeks at a stretch, where they were served with loaves handed up to them on pitch-forks by reliefmen in boats. During the greatest summer flood in the valley in modern times, the hay crops were totally destroyed, and the village youths amused themselves with diving above the hard road from the ancient market-cross standing before the inn.

St. John's Bridge at Lechlade is one of the most ancient on the Thames and has existed for seven centuries, though a more modern arch has been built upon the old foundations. Previous to the opening of the thirteenth century there appear to have been no stone bridges over the rivers in England. At that time the Thames was spanned by wooden structures. Huge rough piers and piles were fixed in the bed, with baulks of timber overlaid, and the road was conducted above them. The bridges were often destroyed or seriously damaged by the terrible floods that befell in the winter, which was a source of great inconvenience to travellers and expense to those upon whom devolved their upkeeping. At length deliberations were held and it was decided to build stone bridges over the rivers. The old wooden piles and piers were doomed; a new era was dawning. In the year 1209 London Bridge was built, and St. John's Bridge at Lechlade was soon afterwards constructed. King John encouraged the work and contributed twenty marks towards the cost of the Lechlade bridge. The old wooden structures disappeared and the bed of the river was cleaned and improved, though the devastating floods from time to time still swept the vale, washing away the crops and buildings and drowning the cattle alongside the banks.

A nunnery, and afterwards a Hospital or Priory, stood near the bridge in olden times. Nearly every town had its Hospital, at which the aged and sick were tended and poor travellers entertained and relieved in their journeyings from place to place. The Hospital of St. John seems to have been originally founded in order to shelter the workmen building the bridge, some of whom afterwards settled and remained there for the rest of their days. In course of time the Hospital or Priory undertook the care of the pile, and was endowed with lands and empowered to take tolls for that purpose.

The rules of the Priory were quaint and curious. It was imperative that the brethren should be dressed in russet-coloured garments, and that no one should possess anything of his own or have a locked chest. All clothing, food, and drink were held in common. The beds were in one dormitory, and the brethren were required to sleep in shirts and breeches. If a member of the community died the others were bound to say five hundred paternosters within thirty days, and one hundred paternosters were to be said for the brethren and benefactors of the hospital each week. After the dissolution of the Priory the building was turned into an inn and called St. John Baptist's Head. Now the Trout Inn occupies the site and is a favourite haunt of anglers that come to exercise the gentle craft and kill time and trout upon the banks of the beautiful river.

The Trout is first and foremost an inn for fishermen. The angling rights for some distance along the river go with the house, so that it is imperative to have the landlord's consent to take the fish. It is furthermore expedient, if you are a stranger, to have taken up your quarters at the inn; then you will be the better treated and admitted to the most likely spots for catching good trouts, perches, chubs, or barbels.

Chubs are very numerous in the deep pools of the river. They interfere with the sport and often disappoint the angler wanting to take better specimens. Accordingly, towards the close of every season, war is waged upon them and their numbers diminished. In order to do this special baitings are made at intervals of several days, after which the members of the local Angling Associations go out with their rods and take them by the hundred. As the chub is a coarse fish it is seldom cooked and eaten by any but the poorest people.

Poaching for trouts and eels with nightlines is common throughout the summer. The poachers set their lines about midnight and take them up before dawn; many of the finest fish are taken in this manner. Thames trout grow to a large size; they have been taken up to ten pounds in weight.

To-day the steeple town is full of bustle and excitement, for it is September Horse Fair. This is usually called "Flea Fair," or it should be "Harvest Bug Fair," because about this time harvest bugs disappear from the grass and stubble, and the farm hands and gleaners are no longer tormented with the troublesome insects.

The broad market-place in front of the inn and beneath the shade of the spire is packed with horses and people. Farmers and dealers, hands in pockets, stand in groups or saunter round the square, viewing the animals. Here a prospective purchaser opens the mouth of a well-groomed horse to examine its teeth; another lifts up a fore-foot and scrutinises that, or feels the fetlocks and knees. He is in want of a couple of good horses, for Poppet is getting a little ancient, and Colonel has a nasty limp on the near hind leg, and there is extra work to be done this autumn. But the bidding will be keen, and the farmer is considering whether or not he will be justified in making the outlay, though he knows something must be done.

There are several types of yeomen about the square and some individuals who have come from afar off, for the horse fair is attended by breeders and dealers from many of the Western Counties. There is the tall bronzed son of Somersetshire, with highly distinctive dialect; the bluff and hearty moonraker, dwelling near the breezy Wiltshire downs, spruce and clean shaven, or with stiff, bristling moustache and side-beard; the comfortable-looking Berkshire man; the thin-featured, gentlemanly Oxonian, and the short, sturdy, thick-set man of Gloucestershire, whose home is upon the strong-blowing Cotswolds. In addition to them are the loiterers and sightseers — the wooden-legged pensioner rigged in Sunday best; the town tailor, crippled in both feet; and, to be sure, the old blacksmith of ninety years, who has absented himself from the forge to-day in order to note the condition of the horses and the fashion in which they are shod.

Higher up the broad street are vans and vehicles with materials for constructing the merry-go-rounds, cocoa-nut shies, and stalls for gingerbreads and knick-knacks. They stand in lines, waiting for the horses to be sold, which will be by noon or soon after. When the dealers have finished they will occupy the square and the space before the inns, and the travellers will exhibit their wares for the young men, women, and children to buy. The afternoon and evening will be devoted to pleasure. Then the people will flock in from the villages round about and the streets will be full to overflowing.

A more important fair was held near the river on St. John the

Baptist's day. This was attended by a crowd of merchants, traders, and purchasers, who came, as to a universal mart, to supply their domestic wants for the following year. The merchants were classified according to the wares they had for disposal and streets bearing such names as "The Drapery," "The Pottery," "The Spicery," and so on, were formed in the meadow. The monks, nuns, and priests of the churches and priories, the Lords of the Manors and their tenants came to buy plate, pottery, armour, cutlery, wine, wax, spices, linens, woollens, provisions, and other necessaries. With the rise and increase of shops in the towns, the pedlars' and merchants' fairs decayed and soon ceased. Floods also interfered with the emporium in the meadow, and it was moreover said to interrupt the harvest work, for doubtless the rustics were not content to labour in the silent fields far from the noise and hubbub of the fair.

To supplement the fairs there were the regular weekly markets, held within the town from the beginning of the thirteenth century downwards. They began about noon on Sunday and were continued until the following Monday night. The market comprised local produce, such as fresh meats, fish fried or baked, pullets, geese, pigs, green cheeses, curds, cream, oaten cakes, and loaves of bean flour and bran — eaten by the labourers.

The Black Death and the Peasants' Revolt brought about a scarcity of agricultural labourers. Much land that had grown corn crops was consequently laid down and converted into sheep farms, and no part of the country was better adapted for this than were the stony Cotswolds, lying high and dry above the half-drained marshes and swamps of the Valley.

During the seventeenth century agriculture improved again and cheese and malt became the chief products of the country between the Thames and the Cotswolds. The channel of the Thames was cleaned out from Abingdon to Cricklade and weirs were made in order to allow the boats to pass freely upstream. Barges with a carrying capacity of eighty tons came alongside the Lechlade wharves, and no less than three thousand tons of prime cheese were brought into the town from the villages and farms annually in waggons and conveyed by water to Oxford and London.

Now all the horses are sold and led away from the market-place, with the halter of each one following fastened to the tail of the near one preceding. The proprietors of the merry-go-rounds and cocoa-nut shies make haste to occupy the square with their paraphernalia and get ready for the afternoon and evening sports. Several aged inhabitants of the town loiter in the locality of the inns, eager to talk of the fair, as it is, and as it used to be.

"What d'ye thenk an't to-day, Anngel?" inquires the old shepherd of the carter standing near.

"I sin better an' I sin wuss. 'Tis a very good lot o' ossen, takin' on 'em all together, but the faayer yent nothin' like so good as it used to be, an' Bampton comin' sa nigh 'andy this un 'tis oni the riff-raff yer to-day, like. Tha be a leetle smaller than I 'ev a knowed 'em, but, as I ses, I sin wuss. Tha be tarblish good, considerin' the dry saazon we've hed," the carter replies.

Now the busiest time of the fair is fast drawing on, for it is evening in the Thames Valley. A great crowd has gathered in the market-place and along the street in front of the inns. This is chiefly composed of Cotswold people, with a few from the Wiltshire and Berkshire side of the river. The cheerful shepherd from the downs, the carters and cowmen with their wives from the farms, the ploughboys with their sweethearts, and all the youth of the town are there. What matter now the long labours of the field in burning heat and rain, the dark hours of winter approaching, the hardships of everyday life? All are forgotten amid the noise of the street and the pleasure of meeting with acquaintances. And to-night all are cheerful. The harvest money has been paid; the pockets of all are jingling. Everyone is equipped with means to take his pleasure and to make purchases for personal use, or to adorn the walls of the cottage.

The strangest things are offered for sale by the Cheap Jacks, who dispose their goods on the ground and stand in the centre with smoky, flaring paraffin lamps. Here are gaudy-coloured pictures and painted ornaments, green and blue umbrellas large enough to cover a summer-rick, bright gay handkerchiefs, mufflers and ties, preposterous jewellery, with hundreds of alarm-clocks and cheap watches, all warranted to be the finest obtainable. It might be thought that no one would purchase these articles, but John and William, Jane and Mary, are out to buy, and will not go empty away from the fair.

The greatest changes that have taken place are in things pertaining to the river. The wharves are deserted; no barges, laden with produce, ever come to enter the old canal at the Round House and glide away to the Severn and Avon cities. During the severe frosts of the winter 1788–89 a festival was held on the river opposite the wharf. A fat ox was roasted upon the ice — protected with sods — and fifteen hundred people took part in the feast and games. At that time the bargemen carried firearms in order to be in a position to protect their cargoes, for thieves infested the countryside and lay in wait at night to steal corn, cheese, or coal from the boats.

The inns are full to-night, and more than the usual good feeling is evident among the ploughmen and farm hands, who beam at each other at the Red Lion, or engage in a long confidential chat on the year's happenings, the crops and harvest, lambs and foals, and draw comparisons between this and that time or season. Meanwhile Jonas and Dobbin, Shadrach and Angel seriously enumerate how many to their knowledge have met the Inglesham ghost, or tell of Betty the witch who lies buried on the roadside, three miles distant.

Old Betty was famed for many acts and was a sore trouble to the carters, cowmen, and shepherds round about, bringing the flocks and herds and pregnant mares under her powerful spell and working incalculable mischief upon all and sundry. At one time the lambs, calves, and foals were stillborn. The gates and doors would fall off the hinges; the pumps would not draw water and the cream would not set in the broad pans. The cobbler could not work his wax while she was near, and half the people of the countryside fell sick, while she danced in the streets at midnight and spat up hundreds of pins and young crows, as the villagers confidently believed.

Jonas, the ox-carter, had heard of a witch who had tampered with a neighbour's pig and caused it to go mad in the sty. The owner of the animal, a farm labourer, was distressed at the occurrence and uncertain what to do. At length it occurred to him to bleed the pig. Accordingly he took the scissors and snipped a piece out of its ear, causing it to bleed profusely, when, behold ! out of her house ran the old woman, grasping her fingers, which were streaming with blood. It appears that when the swine's ear was cut the witch, being in spirit within the pig, was also injured. The pig recovered, but the villagers left the old woman alone, and she soon bled to death.

A witch was in the habit of stopping every team that passed the road near her dwelling. This she did with her magic, simply by drawing a line across the road with her enchanted staff. One day, however, the carter, after stroking his horses and speaking kindly to them, cracked his whip loudly and fell upon the witch, striking her violently. Thereupon she ran and crept into a culvert and died there, and the teams were never afterwards molested.

Then Angel must relate what he had heard from his mother concerning a farm labourer who wedded a beautiful young woman, of whom he was very proud, and who proved to be a witch. Before they had long been married the husband discovered that his bride arose from bed at midnight and left him alone in the darkness. Not knowing how to account for her disappearance, he determined to say nothing but to watch her movements. Accordingly, when night came, he lay very still and pretended to be asleep. A little before midnight his wife arose and dressed, and was going downstairs. Then the husband sprang out of bed, seized her by the arm, and demanded an explanation of her conduct. As she insisted upon going out he announced his intention of accompanying her, to which she agreed, on condition that he should by no means utter a word, for if he did evil would certainly follow, said she. Then, without another syllable, she slipped through the keyhole of the door and drew her husband after her. Two milk-white calves were waiting outside. These they mounted and then flew off in the darkness, unimpeded by any obstacles. The husband thought it was an extraordinary adventure, but he said nothing till they came to the river, dimly seen in the starlight. Surely, thought he, the calves would not leap over that. They did so, however, with a mighty bound, and were just coming to earth on the other side when the bridegroom, who was a cowman, amazed at the feat, lost his self-possession and cried: "That's a good jump for a calf to make!" A moment afterwards the calf shot from under him and he found himself in water up to his waist and alone in the stillness, for the others had vanished. His wife, however, with loving kindness, called for him on her way back and took him out with her on the white calves many times afterwards, but he had the good sense to observe her injunctions and never to break the silence with any incautious remark.

Lechlade Bridge and Church

Chapter 4

THE COLN VALLEY, FAIRFORD AND A PLOUGHING MATCH

On coming up from Fairford to Northleach, I was saluted by no less than eighteen persons, chiefly carters and shepherds in company with their teams and flocks, either on the road or in the fields and farmyards adjoining the highway. This speaks for itself, and discovers the warm-heartedness and sociability of the Cotswold peasant folk. Theirs is a lonely life, and doubtless they love to see a fresh face now and then, and take comfort in exchanging a few words with a sympathetic stranger.

As I was leaning on the wall, chatting with a carter who was at plough in the field, a middle-aged woman, bearing a basket of goods bought in the town, came up the hill and, after a respectful nod to me, addressed the carter in a shrill, piping voice:

"'Ev you a-yerd from Car-rl?"

"No," replied he.

"We 'ev ed a letter," she continued. "'E yent agwain on at all well. A no business to a left Calcutt. A was barn ther' an' brought up ther', an' a'd never bin away afoore till a tuk this fit in is 'ed. But a wunt stop away long. A'll break 'is 'eart if a do. Poor Car-rl! A cried all the way ther', an' a bin that miserable ever since a don' know what to do wi' 'isself. A'll never finish the twelve months out."

"Poor Carl," as I learned, was a Cotswold carter who had been at one situation all his life and had only recently shifted to another village, with the result intimated in the good-wife's conversation.

But we are out to view the Downs, and to trace the valley of the little Coln that flows from the heart of the limestone region and, taking its final leap from the Cotswolds at Fairford, joins the Thames opposite the Round House at Inglesham.

The source of the Coln is near Charlton Abbots, about twelve miles to the north of Cirencester. From that point the river runs murmuring past the richly wooded slopes of Chedworth, a little below the famous

71

Roman Villa. Now it takes an easterly course, winding round through the old-fashioned villages of Coln St. Denis, Coln Rogers, and Winson, and presently reaches the picturesque hamlet of Ablington, with its grand old Manor House and the quiet beauty of its farms and cottages.

Bibury is the next village on the stream. Here the river is joined by a considerable spring that leaps out of the hillside, the waters of which scarcely vary, even after the driest summer. Near this is a commodious inn and a trout fishery, at which young fish for stocking the river are hatched and reared. Two large mills stand on the stream, and the ruins of a woollen factory are visible in a meadow not far from the banks.

The upper mill is silent now, but the one lower down, at Bibury, is still active and does a moderate amount of work, though only grist, and no wheaten flour. Twenty years ago the miller employed four assistants, whereas to-day he has but one, and he usually had fifteen hundred sacks of wheat shot out loose in the great loft waiting to run through to the stones that turned night and day, grinding the golden grain into flour for use about the near countryside. The walls of the mill are very strongly built. The beams within are as large as trees, which was necessary to enable them to carry such a great weight of corn and plant.

The large "under-shot" wheel that turns the stones is half of iron and half of wood. The beautiful water sings sweetly at its task, and the tame trouts come close up to the mill-head and thrust their noses against the iron grating, as though curious to see the wheel at work and to know what is going on within the cavern-like place.

The poet Morris considered Bibury the prettiest village in England. The scenery is Swiss in kind, though it has a softness and tenderness which are quite English. On one side of the small valley the road runs down gently for several hundred feet; on the other side the steep bank, clothed with beeches, elms, and spruces, rises almost perpendicularly, overtopping the Court, the church, the gabled farmhouses, and cottages. The tiny Coln, after running parallel with the street for a quarter of a mile, leaps down a cascade and curves round in the centre of the dale, showing like a band of silver between banks of sweet forget-me-not and willow-herb.

Presently Coln St. Aldwyns is reached — what a beautiful name! — and then, winding below the walls of Hatherop Castle, we come to Quenington, famed for its quaint Norman Church and Refectory, and, formerly, for its paper-mills, driven by the spouting river. From Quenington the Coln runs rippling in and out among the shadows of high elms, till, passing a green hill, it widens into a crescent-shaped lake, and then pauses, as though to gather strength, before it rushes down the cascade into the broad mill-pool behind the church at Fairford.

Nearly all interest in the tiny town of Fairford centres around the grand old church and its splendid windows, some of the most perfect specimens of Christian art extant. The church was built by John Tame, about the year 1500, and is considered to be a nearly perfect structure in Tudor Gothic. John Tame apparently bought the windows, or had them specially made, during his visits to the Netherlands. They were painted by a Flemish artist named Aaps, and despite the disturbances of the Puritan period, they were not materially damaged at that time, though a great tempest in 1703 severely shattered the most noble of all — that of the west front.

The cottage industries of spinning and weaving, wool-carding, and straw-plaiting, flourished in the town, and supplemented the earnings of those employed on the land. The woollens, when finished, were taken to the various centres for disposal, and the plaited straw was conveyed to London in the road-waggons and there sold to the manufacturers.

The men of Fairford were skilled in the use of the flails, and they travelled for many miles during the winter months, threshing out wheat and barley. When the machine threshers were invented the lively Coln was harnessed to the toil and threshed out the corn as well as grinding flour for the loaves. The Fairford horse-threshing teams also traversed the country around for a great distance. Four horses, attached to as many levers, supplied the power for the thresher. They were outside the barn, while the machine was set within. In the centre, from which the levers radiated, was a cage in which a boy stood to drive the animals; there he must stay in rain or snow, ofttimes drenched to the skin, and half-perished with the cold.

"Many's the time I squat in that owl' cage an' drev thaay 'osses round," the aged carter says.

"Warn thees jest about fancied thiself, dissent?" his wife replies, with a sly wink and a knowing nod of the head.

But there were hard times around Fairford and in the Cotswold villages during the "Hungry Forties," and the poor found it difficult to subsist even on the rudest fare. With wheaten flour at a prohibitive price and barley meal costing a guinea a bushel, what were the labouring classes to do? Yet live they must, and it is not to be wondered at if they took to poaching and stole a sheep now and then in order to satisfy the raging hunger within them. Hedgehogs were a common article of food. Badgers, also, were eagerly hunted and devoured, and the nimble squirrel was frequently trapped, cooked and eaten by the woodmen and labourers. The local squire was surprised at the carter's eating a squirrel. He thought the dish to be unclean, but the carter grinned broadly and replied: "Aa, zur, you don' know the vally of a squirrel. Tha be as dainty mate as ever you tasted, an' good anuff for the king to aat."

As to the eating of badgers, squirrels, and hedgehogs, that is not surprising to those acquainted with village conditions. One sometimes hears of the practice of eating fried mice and snails, and there is a labourer in the village in which I am writing who will eat live mice whole for, or without, a wager. Of the eating of rats I have not heard except when two young ploughmen cooked one in the brew-house, and, by a ruse, induced their mate to eat it. Having formed the plan they caught a fat rat, "cut 'is yed, paas an' tayul off, well weshed un, an' rawsted un an a stick a-vrunt o' the vire." When it was nicely cooked, and they heard Henry coming, they fell a-wrestling and quarrelling as to who should have the "bird," and while they were so engaged Henry quietly took the rat from the stick and ate it with a good relish, grinning at his supposed smartness. He felt sure it was a blackbird, and when his mates laughed at him and asked him how he liked "the rat," he still grinned and said it was "very good mate."

There is a story of two dealers who called at the inn on their way to fair, after an all-night ride, and found the house almost destitute of viands.

"Ane 'e got nar a bit o' mate, mother?" inquired one.

"Lar, no! Who'd a thawt o' seein' you?" replied she.

"Narn a mossel o' bacon, neether, ner it a egg?"

"No! But ther's that peggy-wiggy pie. I forgot that. You be welcome to a bit o' he. I oni made un the day afore yesterday."

"Fetch it along, mother, whatever 'tis, an' we'll pay ya for't," said they.

Accordingly the "peggy-wiggy" pie was brought out and the dealers liked it so well that they ate the whole of it, to learn of the old woman afterwards that it was made of the stillborn young of the long-eared white sow. She had made it for the children, who, she said, were very fond of it: she thought it would be "something for them to get down." Outrageous as this appears, it may have been true. It is certain that stillborn calves were sometimes eaten by the poorest labourers when other food was unobtainable, and the same kind of thing is done to-day, though people generally are not aware of it. More than one farmer, when his cow is delivered of a stillborn calf — provided it has not been too long dead — skins and dresses it, blows up the flesh with a pipe-stem, and hurries off with it to the nearest butcher to exchange it with him for a choice cut or a joint *from another beast*.

Gipsies swarmed about the Cotswolds during the fore part of the nineteenth century. They lived chiefly by poaching, stealing, and fortune-telling. In the summer and autumn they cut rushes and flags from the Coln and plaited them into baskets, or obtained withes and hazel-wood from the copses and wove them into wickerwork for chairs. To take the trouts they made "hoop-nets" and set them in the stream, and then stirred the weeds with light poles and drove the fish into them.

One cold day in January a dark-looking gipsy hailed the shepherd, who was attending to his flock near the wood.

"Hey! owld man, ood 'e like a basin o' sup?"

"Don' mind if 'e do. 'Tis a cowld blow this mornin'," the shepherd replied.

"Come on, then," answered the gipsy, and poured out a basin of liquor from the smoky pot.

After the shepherd had swallowed the broth, the gipsy addressed him:

"Do you know what you've had?"

"No, I don't. But 'twas uncommon good, whatever 'twas," replied he.

"That was house-rabbit, generally known as cat," the gipsy returned, walking away to the camp beneath the high oak-trees.

A gipsy funeral was an interesting event and attracted crowds of visitors to the grand old church. The gipsies often concealed a death in the camp. They buried the corpse in a wood or withy-bed, where the bones would not be disturbed, but when the Burial Laws came to be enforced they were compelled to inter their dead more decently. The last gipsy funeral at Fairford took place but a few years ago. There were about a hundred mourners, the majority of whom came clad in odd suits of black which they had begged, borrowed, or hired from the townspeople.

At the funeral of a true gipsy the corpse was dressed in its best clothes. Coins of copper and silver were placed in the coffin and bread and meat were set beside the dead person. It was the custom to have a hole bored in the lid of the coffin, in order to allow the spirit to have free access to its old abode. The next of kin to the dead person, carrying a bottle of wine, headed the procession. When the coffin had been lowered into the grave he poured the wine upon it and prayed in the Romany tongue. On returning to the camp the elders sat around the fire, muttering chants and incantations for the spirit of the departed, and continued so till midnight. For a week they repeated the ceremony; then they held a feast that ended in dancing and singing.

The toilers on the farms — not only on the Cotswolds but throughout the Thames Valley — had four feasts a year, namely, after sowing, shearing, haymaking, and harvest. The seed-feast — called "Sidcyek" (Seed-cake) — was kept at the end of April. This was held in the barn or brew-house, and was only attended by those who worked on the farm.

"Sherrin'" feast was on a somewhat different scale. A select body of shearers was chosen from a village. They took the farms around, one by one, and when they had finished all the flocks they were entertained at a public feast provided by the farmers collectively, who invited as many others as they thought fit. Games and songs followed the feast, and appropriate toasts were made by the shepherds and responded to by the farmers.

Harvest-home was the most important and the best-loved festival. The whole of the toilers — men, women, and children — attended this; the brewhouse and kitchen, too, were needed to hold the company. Besides the farm hands, the blacksmiths and wheelwrights came, invited by the farmer. The parson frequently attended, and the village constable managed to creep in and mingle with the rest. Both the farmer and his wife were well toasted, usually in the following rhymes, which were common throughout the Thames Valley:

"Then drink, boys, drink, and see you do not spill,
    For if you do, you shall drink two, it is our master's will,"

and

"Here's a health unto our master, our mistress shan't go free,
    For she's a good provider, provides as well as he."

The breezy carter — of fourscore and five years — has fond recollections of the old harvest-feast. "Ther' was maaster an' missis a-hippin' an't up in front an us, an' owl' Moll Fry a-skippatin' about wi' the cups. Presently all an us fell to. 'Lar'! faather, byent 'e gwain to saay graace,' missis ses. Then maaster stood up, shet 'is eyes, an' put 'is 'ands together an' said:

"'O Lard, make us able
    To aat all on the table.'"

'Oh, dad, you wicked fella!' cried missis, an' all the young uns baaled out 'Amen.' The paason purty nigh chokked 'isself wi' a lump o' bif an' 'ed to wesh it down wi' a cup o' ale, an' when tha sung 'Drenk, bwoys, drenk,' a sed 'twas no need to tell 'em that for tha could do that very well wi'out bein' telled. Tha allus reckoned to sip twice when tha toasted, but I chocked mine down at once an' maaster hollered out: 'Make haste an' put Willum out another, else a'll get all behind wi't.'"

Serious rioting took place in the riverside town during the disturbances of 1830. Threatened with the loss of their employment, and resenting the intrusion of the new-fangled machinery, a party of five hundred labourers, armed with scythes, hooks, axes, and sledge-hammers, marched through the town and proceeded to smash up the implements. The next day the military arrived and order was restored. This was effected not so much by a demonstration of force as by an accidental discovery made by the Captain of the Troop. He, on coming face to face with the mob, happened to glance down and perceive that one of his gaiters was only partly buttoned. Thereupon he turned to one of the rioters, formidably armed with a scythe fastened to a pole, and cried: "Hi, there! You fellow! Put that thing down and come and button up my gaiter, will you?" The rioter, taken by surprise, threw down his weapon and approached the Captain; he stretched out his leg and the gaiter was duly buttoned. The incident had a good effect on the crowd. There was no more fighting, and the rioters dispersed to their homes.

A story is told of a Cotswold labourer who stole a sheep and was strangled in the act of carrying it home. He had the sheep slung at his back and secured with a cord which he had put round his neck. On coming to a gate he attempted to climb over it but slipped, and as he fell, feet foremost, on one side of the gate the sheep, hanging by the rope round his neck, dropped back on the other and quickly strangled him. At another time, a hungry labourer stole a fat ewe, killed it, and carried it for six miles on his back and disposed of the carcass, but was arrested three months afterwards when he tried to sell the skin, that bore the private mark of the farmer.

"Then tha didn't kip 'e at Fairford along o' the wowardy," remarks grandfather Elijah, with a sly wink and an artful nod of the head. He is referring to the Retreat for feeble-minded, and by the "wowardy" he means the "waywardy." Even of this place the rustics tell a cheerful story. One evening, as a carpenter, with his basket of tools, was coming past the grounds of the Retreat, he saw an inmate climb down from the high fence and begin running towards him. He took to his heels, with the madman in hot pursuit and gaining ground every moment. Encumbered with his tools — there was a large sharp axe, a saw, and a bill-hook among them — he could not compete with the lunatic, and a deadly fear came upon him. At last, after running till he became exhausted, he threw down his basket and, with a groan, sank to the earth. Then the madman, with an exultant yell, dashed up to him, stooped down, touched him lightly on the shoulder and, happily playing the children's game, cried "Tig!"

There is furthermore the story of the Cotswold housewife who had never seen one wearing a veil. One day a young lady neighbour, who was dressed for a journey, came in to wish her good-bye. She, happening to be in her garden, was sent for to the house. Seeing the young woman wearing a spotted veil for the first time, she held up her hands in amazement and cried: "Lar', you! Whatever's the matter? Thees got a lot o' girt vlies craalin' all over thy vace."

For weeks past interest in the ploughing match has been steadily increasing for miles around the Thames Valley. In the field, in the stable, at home in the cottage, and in the snug little rooms at the Pig and Whistle, and the Red Lion, where the carters assemble at least every week-end, the talk has been of little else. The young men have been making mental lists of all the veterans and those famed for a straight, even furrow they can think of, and weighing their own chances. Similarly, the champions have taken a survey of the field and singled out their most dangerous rivals among the younger ploughmen, and made careful note of fresh-comers to the farms, gleaning whatever intelligence they could of their skill in guiding the plough and turning up the stubborn glebe. In addition to this, the ploughs have been overhauled and put into condition after lying idle during haycart and wheat harvest; the favourite and most easily manipulated implement has been singled out upon which to stake the prestige of the farm and its ploughing staff. The horses, too, have been chosen and are being well looked after. The harness has been cleaned and oiled, the brasses brightly polished, the ribbons, rosettes, and ear-caps produced from the carter's private chest or drawer, or new ones bought at the saddler's and harness-maker's shop.

And now the long and eagerly expected day is here. The clock in the stately tower has struck eight. Some of the teams and ploughs passed through the broad market-place nearly an hour ago, and others are still arriving. Those who were situated at the greatest distance came first, and those whose farms are near at hand will be the last to reach the field. But there is a reason for everything. Those horses that came from afar will need food and a rest before being harnessed to the plough, while the others, by reason of their nearness to the site, will come forth fresh and untired by a long journey on the road. The morning opened dull and close. A heavy thunder-shower fell early in the night, watering the fields. The land lies steaming in the sun that now and then peeps through the clouds.

"That drap o' raain couldn't a come at a better time. It jest mystened the ground fer the shers, an' 't ull 'elp the turmuts farrud. Our'n used to decler sich raain was wuth a pound a drap. 'Tis jest right fer ploughin'. That owl' clawver ood a turned up akkerd else if us 'adn' 'ad a drap," remarks the carter to his near mate.

There are two kinds of ploughing — with the double and single ploughs. The single ploughs are allocated to the clover-patch that has been carefully measured out into plots of half an acre. The double ploughs are given wheat stubble, as being easier to turn, for the clover has not been ploughed for two years, and has been well trodden down by the sheep and the haymakers. The competitors are of two classes — over and under twenty years of age. In several families father and son, too, are competing, the one in the senior and the other in the junior class. The youthful ploughmen have a portion of the field expressly allotted to them, but adjoining the other, so that they can exchange a few words with their fathers when they come to turn round in the middle of the field.

Jingle, jingle, jingle. Merrily the bells sound and brightly the brasses shine, as the horses, plump and sleek, with tails and manes plaited and interwoven with bright wheat straw and decorated with streaming ribbons and ear-caps, proudly enter the field, nodding their heads and neighing softly at the sight of so many of their kind. Surely they must all be here now, for it is past nine o'clock, and it is time a start was made. But no! There is one more team to come, from Aldsworth, four miles away, and it has been decided to wait for that.

At the same time there is no sign of impatience about the field. No one is in a hurry, for it is a holiday. The old carters walk up and down steadily, eyeing the youngsters' ploughs, and giving sundry words of advice. The young ploughman, with silver ring on his finger and surrounded by several mates who have come to witness the match and give encouragement to their comrade, calmly smokes a cigarette, and, with the touch and skill of a trained mechanic, screws up first one nut and then another, and takes careful note of the wheels, to have them secure when a start is made. The skim and coulter must be fitted after the signal is given. They are usually set with the aid of a new horse-nail, and the operation is performed with care, for it is of the utmost importance to have them correctly fixed. If the skim and coulter are not properly set a thin edge of green will show in the ploughing, and this will tell against the competitor. Most of the ploughmen carry an extra share, and some have a spare skim, too, fastened to the frame of the implement in case they should lose or break one. To do so would be a great misfortune, and would promptly settle their chances of winning a prize, and would moreover expose them to the laughter of all the rest on the field.

Here is a young ploughman singing by himself:

> "My owld 'oss died wi' the toothache,
> And left me here a-sorrowin'.
> Good-bye, Kit, and good-bye, Dan,
> I'm just goin' over the mountain.
> So I dug a hole and hit 'im in,
> Fare thee well, owld dar-ar-lin',
> Good-bye, Kit, and good-bye, Dan,
> I'm just goin' over the mountain."

Along comes a carter with critical eye.

"Yellocks!"

"What?"

"One trace is sharter than t'other, my bwoy."

"Which un?"

"That outside un yander."

"A yen much odds, is a?"

"A's a lenk difference. Let un go one. Tha's got un twisted, too, essent? Tha's better, locks!"

"Never tried mi luck afore. Can but try."

"Kip thi eye an the flag, and dwunt caddle thiself."

"If I caan't strik out a line straight away, I be done."

"Dwunt go too fast, ner it to slow. Dwunt get steam up too quick. Ther's a lot of stwuns in this piece. If tha dossent kip thi plough stiddy thaay'll uck un out an't."

"Now, Vylet! Stan' up, Vylet. Woa! Way! Tha's more at it. 'Tis no good to odds it when ya got it ready."

Here is a merry-looking little man, with pilot coat, small boxer hat, and stout ground-ash stick in his right hand, and an old blue umbrella with handle broken off under his left arm, nodding to everyone, and examining the horses and ploughs. Seeing the carter, he stops short; his eyes twinkle, and his face lights up, for he recognises an old acquaintance.

"Good marnin' to 'e, Robbut. 'Tis Robbut, yent it?"

"Yes. But I dwunt zim to call you to mind."

"Dwunt you know I?"

"Can't zim to recollect 'e."

"Why, you knows Quininton, dwunt 'e?"

"I was barned ther, awhever."

"To be sure! I know'd you as soon as I sid 'e. An' 'ow be 'e all this time?"

"Tarble well, e s'pose, considerin'. Caan't run awver very many."

"An' 'ow's yer missis?"

"A got the rheumatics. We byent so young as us used to be, narn an us."

"Aa! if 'tis thaay rheumatics, God bless 'e. I be yer for a day's pleasure, I be."

"Warn you jacked out work now?"

"Nat it. Still kips muddlin' on. I bin an one lot o' land fifty year, an' bin wi' our maester forty out on't. 'E's a good un, 'e is. All that time that I worked wi' our maester I never yerd 'e swer once — never!"

"Phe-e-e-ew!" There goes the secretary's whistle at last, calling the attention of the ploughmen and preluding the hoisting of the flag for the start. The Aldsworth team was so late in coming that special provision had to be made for it; to that has been accorded the privilege of beginning and finishing ten minutes later than the others.

At the sound of the whistle there is a general movement throughout the field. The young ploughman's mates fall back and stand clear of the implement, while he prepares to fix the skim and coulter as soon as the signal is given. The wise and cautious veteran, with great outward unconcern, gives a last glance round his traces and whipples. The spectators gather in groups and wait expectantly, and the horses, unmoved by the strangeness of the scene and the voices around, stand like statues, ready to go forward at the bidding of the ploughmen. The land no longer steams, for the surface of the field is dry. The mist has lifted from the woods, and the sun shines warm through the fleecy clouds rimmed with brightest silver.

Now the secretary, standing in mid-field, waves the flag and notes the time with his watch, held open in the other hand. In a jiffy, skim and coulter are set; the carters take the reins and shake them clear of the harness and, gripping the handles of the plough, point the share and speak to the horses, and the whole phalanx moves forward, some with a smart rush, some with a more dignified pace, and others creeping like snails. These are chiefly the veterans, who never make the mistake of starting off too quickly, but take things quietly at first, while the younger ploughmen, thinking speed to be the first essential, dash straight away and trust to luck rather than judgment to strike out a good furrow.

"You'll zee marks as straight as a arra, dareckly," the merry little carter exclaims.

Cleaning the plough-body, while ploughing in Berkshire

"Aa! an' as crucked as a anchor, too, from thase young uns," replies another.

One lean, middle-aged carter has met with an accident already, within a few seconds of the start. His skim, that was none too tight, has struck a stone and been wrenched out of place. In less than half a minute it is right again and on he goes, though somewhat behind the rest.

As soon as the teams have got well away a rush is made from point to point in order to see the first furrows. The bow-legged carter runs as fast as he can, stoops down and squints with one eye along each furrow and, with the other, winks at the bystanders. All sorts of remarks, accompanied with merry laughter and playful sarcasm, are passed by the youths and old men.

"Yellocks!"

"Ha! ha! ha!"

"'E got a smartish bend ther'."

"What did I tell 'e?"

"'E'll 'ef to pull towwerd a bit. 'E'll 'ev a job to get that out."

"That ull squer up bad, that ull."

"'E'll never get that out."

"'E got to show 'is rudge."

"Matey got a good mark ther', locks!"

"Thase be the two best furras."

"Well, done, Benjimun!"

"If 'e'd a got 'es chestnut along wi' that owl' brown un. Benjimun ood 'ev it."

"Aa! tha's cyapitaul ploughin'. Ther's a lot about everything, yent it?"

"That yunt deep anuf."

"Ther's plenty wuss than that."

"That wunt do. Tha's too much of a 'olla."

"Coom-e! Woa-utt! Wug-tt-a! Stand back, ther', an' let the 'osses turn round, ool 'e!"

"Thee bist nervous, owl' man."

"No, I byent."

"Yes, thee bist."

"It don' trouble I which way it goes."

"Tha bist main white about the gills."

"'Tis a pity Benjimun's turn-vurra dwunt shine a bit! A got a new plough an' fresh 'osses."

"That drap o' raayn jest tuk the polish off the rudge."

"'Tis too many stwuns in 't. It makes a difference wer 'tis sandy sile, er claayey, er brash. We ent a bin about all thase years fer nothin', ev us, Robbut?"

"Look at Willum yander! A got a mark like a rip-'ook."

"Dost thee want to get awver to Quininton? Tha bist gwain a long way round at it."

"I got the wrong 'oss. I wanted my owl' Jinny."

"Kip thi eye an that tree yander, an' get that cruk out, else tha't be zumwher' presently."

And so the ploughing proceeds amid the clatter of tongues, the laughter and jests of the young men, and the sage and witty observations of the elder carters. Here and there a youth accompanies his mate the length of the plot, walking alongside the plough to encourage him with his presence, though that will certainly not improve the furrow.

The old carter is very quiet and scarcely speaks to his horses, but they fully understand what is required of them and plod along at a steady rate, leaning slightly towards each other. As he turns round he half sits on the plough handles, halts a moment to tighten the skim and clean the turn-furrow with the paddle, and quietly resumes his way. The polished brasses and turn-furrows gleam brightly in the sunshine; the scene is one of great animation. The field is rapidly turning from fresh green to a rich brown; it is surprising how much land can be ploughed up in a short space by so many teams at once.

"Ther's one man as ull benefit bi the match, if nob'dy else dwunt. 'E'll get 'e's ground ploughed fer nothin', an' that ull save 'e's 'osses a main bit o' labour," a bystander remarks. The merry little carter and his friends continue to walk up and down, viewing the progress made by the teams and examining the furrows, giving a word of encouragement, or expressing sympathy where that is necessary.

"'E yander's 'aein' all the bad luck, simly. A lost one skim an' brawk t'other. The green shows along 'is rudge. That ull tell agyenst un."

"'E's a good ploughman else."

"Anybody can see that."

"Tha's a girt baffle to the man."

"'Tis no good. I shall be diskallified. Knows 'e shall!"

"Chent no use to caddle thiself about it now. Go into't."

"Tha's a good furra, that is."

"Aa! cyapitul."

"Ther's some good ploughin' yer."

"No mistake about that."

"'Tis as I ses. Ther's a purty deal belongs to everything, yent it? I was jest a tellin' Willum, ther' yent a bin a ploughin' match in Fayreferd fer sixty year. The last as was was in aishen tree ground. That was my fust, but 'e never gained nothin'. Was but a young un then, ya know."

"What! bist thee a minin'?"

"Minin', aa !"

"Tha't get down out of zight, 'osses an' all, dareckly. Tha dossent want to deg thi grave yer, dost?"

All the time there is a steady movement of the spectators, a continual coming and going, to and fro, and backwards and forwards, around the field. Some saunter this way and some that, these to watch the juniors and see how they are shaping, while those go through the gateway into the adjoining section to view the double ploughs. They are drawn by three horses, walking abreast, and as well as turning up double the space of ground they move much more quickly, for the stubble land is softer and more porous than the clover, and offers little resistance to the keen-edged share and coulter. The soil, as it is brought over the turn-furrow, breaks to pieces: it is useless to think of getting anything like an even, polished ridge here.

"'Ow be gettin' an wi't, Robbut?"

"Fairish, like,"

"Tha's got a good per o' ossen!"

"Thaay owl' stwuns keps ketchin' an in, an' jabbin' an in out on't."

"Wher's our Tom?"

"Up a t'other zide. Go up yander you can zin."

"What do you do now, then, sonny?"

"I be awver at Castle Aeton at it."

"An' 'ow's young Maester — ?"

"Aw! 'e's a larnin'. 'Evin a bit of a flash in the pan. 'E got a lot to larn yet."

"Aa! 'E got to find that out. You can farm fer the farm, er you can farm fer the pocket. 'E's faather was a good un. 'E looked round the outside an't, 'e did."

"Take that bit off thi turn-vurra, bwoy! Tha bist too wide an' too deep. The 'arra wunt shek the zid down. If the whate yent deep-rooted, the fust bit of a cowld nip ull cut it all to pieces. Tha essent got no rudge at all."

"This owl' man got a good furra. A's as straight as a gun-barrel."

"A couldn't a done't much better ef a'd a-tried at it, could a?"

"'E could shoot up 'e very well."

"'Tis the 'osses as doos it."

So the conversation is maintained as the spectators pass from point to point. All is bustle and animation. The ploughs glide along, and the toil proceeds.

More than half the ploughing is done now, for the match has been in progress above two hours. Some of the younger competitors have made great headway with their plots. A few of them will soon have finished, but then they were bound to hurry; no matter how hard they had tried, they could not have gone about it steadily. The old carters are more backward and have not done nearly as much, but they are aiming to win. At all events, they occupy the chief attention of the judges and are the only ones in the running in the senior class, excepting the Aldsworth man, who arrived last on the field. He is said to be shaping best of all, though he has not done much yet, for he is extraordinarily cautious and deliberate.

After two hours of hard ploughing in the hot sunshine — for the clouds have melted away and left a clear, delicious sky, such as October alone can give us — the horses foam and steam with the perspiration. Their nostrils are distended with hard breathing, and they require more words of exhortation or reproof from the man at the plough-tail. Some of the animals perspire much more freely than do the others. This may be the result of the day's feeling, of fitness or otherwise, though it usually depends upon what they have had for breakfast, and the kind of food they have been eating during the week previous.

"Tha's all accordin' to what ya gies 'em to aat. Ef thaay 'aes nothin' but graas, tha'll sweat like raayn. Put plenty o' wuts into the mannger. That'll mek ther ribs firmer," the carter says.

The colours of the autumn foliage in the noonday light are very brilliant. The long line of beeches shows in the distance like a blood-red flame. The brasses on the harness, the shares and turn-furrows gleam more brightly in the sunshine. Every particle of mist has disappeared above the woods and along the line of the White Horse Down, now radiant in the distance.

There is not much farther to go now. The clock in the church tower has chimed out the four quarters and the heavy bell has followed and struck one, which was plainly heard all over the field. Another half an hour and the contest will be over and the fates of the ploughmen decided. The prizes will have been won, and, with them, the title to the championship for the ensuing twelve months. One or two of the young men, as heedless now as when they began, are already on their last journey. Starting at a fast rate, they continued the pace right through the match and are finishing up at the same speed. Those whose furrows were out at the start and were not rectified by the time the middle of the plot was reached, find they will have to make one, or perhaps several half-turns in order to finish up. This leads them to think that the plot was not measured correctly and was consequently out of square, but the old carters soon tell them that the measurement was right.

"Ef thee'st a kipt thi eye an that owl' elm yander, same as I telled tha, thee'st a 'ed un right. 'Tis no good to caddle thiself about it now, an' blame the mizhurment. Jest tread that bit o' green in yander, an' kick thaay uts a one zide. Tha bist all up an' down like a dog's 'ind leg."

The older ploughmen are not as far advanced and have quite a wide strip to do yet. The nearer they get to the end the more slowly they proceed, ofttimes stopping half-way up the piece and taking a careful survey of the furrow, before and behind. When they come to the head-land they measure the remaining portion with the handle of the paddle, then re-set the wheels, skim, and coulter, to fit in with the reduced width of the strip.

"Ther's two as be a long waay a'ed o' t'othern, tha's the owl' man in the middle, an' 'e at the fer end yander. One o' thaay ull 'ae the fust," remarks the carter.

"The young uns ane't a done so bad, neether, considerin'. The ground's tarble akkerd fer thaay, wi' so many stwuns in't."

"Wher's Benjimun got to?"

"Essent thee purty nigh done thy bit, Benjimun? 'Ow much longer bist a-gwain to be at it?"

"One more go ull finish it."

"I should thenk so, too. Tha's bin long anuff about it."

"Yellacks! 'E's a-gwain to uck that all to pieces an' spile the lot an't."

"A might a bin commended else, if a'd a gone a bit stiddy, but you caan't tell the young uns nothin'. Tha got to find it out fer therselves."

By a quarter past one all have finished, with the exception of the Aldsworth man. He has several more journeys to make yet, and is exceedingly tardy; even with his additional ten minutes to go it seems that he will have enough to do to finish it in time. But he is cool and collected, and behaves as though he had all the afternoon in which to finish the piece. The other ploughmen have withdrawn their horses from the plots and stationed them alongside the hedge, where they stand cropping the leaves and twigs. The conversation, except for a steady stream of compliments, quietly expressed, on the Aldsworth man's work, has died down. There is little excitement or speculation as to the result, for everyone is agreed that his is by far the best piece of ploughing.

The committee men and judges, pocket-books in hand, take a final survey of the furrows and make notes by the way, then come and take a stand with the rest and patiently await the return of the plough, that has gone to the other end for the last time. Arrived there, the carter unhitches one of the horses and makes the return journey with but one animal. This gives him more room and a clearer view of the furrow; he can both see and manage the plough better with but one horse in front of him. Once or twice down the piece he stops to tread in a rough clod of earth, or to kick a stone aside, then resumes his way and, punctual to time, reaches the headland and draws his plough on to the green and coolly surveys his piece. Young and old view him with admiration and hasten to examine the plough, to ascertain its make, age, and general features, for all feel certain that this is the prize-winner.

"Why! this is a main owl' plough," remarks a committee man to the carter.

"Yes. 'E bin about a few years," the ploughman replies.

"How long 'ev you bin a-ploughin' wi' this un?"

"A bit over a twelvemonth. A led out in the ground a rustin' for dree er vower year till I fetched un out on't."

"Well! 'twas a good resurrection, at any rate," the committee man replies, and all the spectators show their agreement by various remarks and comments, while the carters stoop down and squint round the implement, feeling the skim, the coulter, the turn-furrow, and the whipples, and pat the horses on the neck or hip.

Now the carter boys come to relieve the ploughmen and take charge of the horses, and lead them back to the carts in the next field, where a supply of hay and corn is awaiting them. The spectators depart, and those who have taken part in the competition file off and make their way to the marquee in the park opposite, there to partake of a hearty meal and afterwards hear the speeches and the names of the winners announced. These will also be published in the local newspapers for the edification of all and sundry round about, while the prize-winners' certificates will be framed and hung upon the cottage walls, precious mementoes of victories honourably achieved and an example for the juniors, to stir them up to similar feats of skill and fine workmanship.

All the talk at the inns and elsewhere this weekend will be of the ploughing match and its result, the winners and those commended. The veterans will go steadily on with their accustomed toils, while the young men will pay greater attention to skim, share, and coulter, determined to be avenged for their defeat and to turn the tables at the very next contest that comes round.

A ford

Chapter 5

ON THE COLN, WHELFORD
AND KEMPSFORD

Now the match is over and the teams and ploughs and crowds of sight-seers are gone, the field seems strangely deserted. Never before had such a lively scene, with so much laughter and merry-making, been enacted there, and probably it never will be again. Next year the site of the match will be fixed elsewhere, perhaps many miles away, and so changed from place to place until the cycle of towns and villages in the area is completed. The carters and farmers, too, would complain if the match were confined to one locality; they count it a great compliment to any village to have the competition decided there.

Everyone was agreed that the prizes were fairly awarded, though one greybeard thought the Aldsworth man was fortunate in not being penalised for his late arrival. "If 'e'd a bin a-ploughin' along o' we in my time, an' 'ad come a minute aater the start, 'e'd a 'ad to a stood o' one zide. Tha'd a diskallified un, right anuff. Tha was moore perticler then than tha be now. But a's a cyapital ploughman, for all that, an' we dwun' know what pervented un on the road," said he.

The carter's cottage may be held as a fair type of the average home of the Cotswold labourer. The house is of moderate size, with two rooms downstairs and two above. One of the downstairs rooms is set aside as a summer apartment, for when the sun shines hot against the front of the house the temperature within is raised to an uncomfortable pitch. The other is the general living-room, constituting dining- and sitting-room and kitchen together. The furniture of the room consists of a large deal table, an ancient sofa covered with faded red cloth, a chest of drawers, and half a dozen chairs, including the arm-chair by the fire-side, in which no one else must presume to sit when the carter is at home. Standing within the door is an old-fashioned oak folding table, the envy of the dealers who pass by, who constantly make advances to the carter's wife and implore her to sell it, but to no purpose.

"Do you want to get rid o' that owl' table, mother?" the dealers ask.

"No. Shan't sell 'e. 'E's years an' years owld, 'e is, if anybody knowed the ins an' outs o' that owld table. Ther'd be jest about a 'ow d'e do if I was to get rid on in. 'E was left to mine bi 'e's grandmother, an' I knows 'e'll never pert wi'n," she replies.

As usual in a poor man's cottage, what is lacking in furniture is made up for in pictures and ornaments. There are no less than fifty ornaments on the mantelpiece. They are of all sorts and dimensions, but are chiefly old-fashioned stone figures and pieces of quaint chinaware, many of them interesting, and some highly valuable. Foremost among them are two fine old images of Tom King and Dick Turpin, the robbers, which the dealers have often tried in vain to buy; the modest sum of eleven shillings for the two was not enough to tempt the carter's wife to sell them.

As with ornaments, so with pictures and photographs; there are nearly a hundred hanging upon the walls of the living-room. Of these the most conspicuous are a reproduction of "The Stolen Duchess," in colours, and two old Scriptural prints — "The Finding of Moses" and "Moses in the Land of Midian." The mirror, before which the carter has his weekly shave, is marked with the name of a certain Embrocation, warranted "Good for Cattle," and the covering over the back of the good-wife's chair is a piece of hand-wrought embroidery depicting Joseph's flight with the infant Christ into Egypt. Hanging up are a hempen halter and a great horn lantern for use in the stables; upon the floor are a long brass-handled whip and a flag dinner basket.

The carter is a strong-made man, with broad shoulders, short, thick neck, massive head, and square face, and he has a loud, deep voice, just the kind to terrify the ploughboys when they have been guilty of any misdemeanour. His wife is a portly dame, honest and homely, whose chief pride is in keeping a clean house and having everything ready for her "man" when he comes home at meal-times and in the evening.

Their family is twelve in number — six sons and six daughters — though they are all grown up and away from home now. Of the sons one is a sailor, three are soldiers, and the others railwaymen. The daughters are either married or in situations, and do not come home very often. As neither the carter nor his wife can read or write there is little correspondence between them. The eldest son writes them a letter once a year — at Christmas; then they get one of the neighbours to come in and read it to them and write out a reply. Yet, in spite of many hardships suffered during a laborious life, the carter is bright and cheerful, and is able to tell a merry tale and recount several quaint customs of which he had heard his father speak, but which have been discontinued of late years.

One of these was that of "Chasing the Cock." It was the practice, on New Year's Day, for all the ploughmen to come home from the field at noon and stable their horses. Then the head carter, carrying the plough-spanner and a wooden wedge in his hand, and followed by the under ploughman and boys, proceeded to the kitchen, and laid them on the table before the mistress with the remark, "Now for the owl' cock, Missis!" or

"Rain or shine, the cock's mine."

After that the carter and his mates went outside and chased the cock round the farmyard for ten or fifteen minutes and then came into the kitchen and sat down to a substantial meal. There was no more ploughing that day. The afternoon was spent in the stables, cleaning the harness. On the morrow they went out, stronger and braver, to plough the regulation acre, provided the weather and land were favourable.

There is a conundrum many carters love to propose to you, if you are on friendly terms with them and have time to give to their simple requests. This is — "How much will it cost to shoe a horse, starting at a farthing a nail and doubling it each time to the end, counting seven nails to each shoe?" At first sight it seems that quite a modest sum would be sufficient to settle the bill, but those who care to work the matter out will find that a considerable figure will be needed to pay off the score.

At one place where the carter worked as a boy the old farmer was very eccentric. When harvest-home came round one year and the fires were burning brightly in the brewhouse and beneath the big copper boiler, he peeped through the shutters and was astonished to see the master throw an old pair of boots into the boiler among the meat and vegetables. Accordingly, when supper-time came and all the men were busy at table, he alone would not touch anything, but pretended to be sick, and lay on the ground during the meal. The next day he told the men what he had seen, and they gave him a good thrashing for not speaking about it earlier.

A rustic, notorious for his appetite, was accredited with eating a monstrous quantity of fat bacon; it was said that he could devour four pounds at a meal. To test the veracity of the report two farmers determined to put his appetite to the test. They arranged for him to go a journey of eight miles; at each end he was to be given four pounds of bacon with bread. It says something for his digestive ability that he ate the whole and then had a good tea on reaching the cottage.

At another time a teamster came home with a load of ashes the worse for liquor. Thereupon the farmer scolded him for his indulgence. Nettled by the master's remarks, the carter seized the bridle, led the horse quickly into the narrow barn, turned the waggon round sharply, and came out again.

"Yellock! Thee coussent do that," said he.

"No more coussent thee, if tha hassent bin drunk," the other replied.

Old Ambrose Archer, of Quenington, had three hoes which he used according to the price he was being paid for the job. One of these was for 2s. 6d. an acre, one for 3s., and the other for 5s. an acre.

"Good morning, David! Raw air this morning!" said the visitor to a rustic.

"Aa, 'tis, you! Dwun suppose a bin biled awhever," he replied.

And again: "Fine morning, John!"

"Marnin's all right ef thee't let un alone!"

So also with the farmer who addressed the labourer one cold winter's morning:

"Mornin', James! Fine mornin', James!"

"Fine marnin's no good wi' no bren cheese in the cubberd, maester," James answered.

A villager was going to the workhouse to obtain relief there, when someone addressed him:

"Good morning, Etherd!"

"Oy! Oy! I'm a-gwoin on yander. Some on 'em got girt sticks in ther faggots, but I got none in mine," replied he, meaning some people had meat in their broth, but he had none in his.

A few evenings ago John came in early from work and took off his boots, "to rest 'is vit," as he said. It is no wonder they were tired, for his boots weighed over twelve pounds. Asked what he had been doing, he said he had been on Fuzzy Hill ploughing with "one bull single."

The carter on the farm where John worked as a boy was "a very steern man," and the ploughboys were sure of a thrashing when they came late to the stables. Many a time John had stopped on the road and fought with his youthful mate to see which should "have it first" when they got to the farm.

One carter would never descend to the thrashing business, though the boys were never so late. Instead, he made them sit down till breakfast-time and then loaded them with the heaviest set of trace-harness he could find, and made them carry it to and fro in the stables during the meal-hour.

Another teamster was singular in never using a lantern in the stable, not even on the darkest night. When he went to "wrap his horses up" he felt his way about the stalls. As for his horses, he could recognise them anywhere simply by feeling their tails!

One day a travelling salt, on his way from Gloucester to London, was taking a short cut across Farmer B—'s field. When he was half-way over the farmer galloped up behind him and cried:

"'Owld on! Ther's no road yer acraas my land."

"Oh! Thy land, is it? And how comes it to be thy land?" said the salt.

"'Twas left to ma bi mi faather," the farmer answered.

"And how did he come by't?" the sailor inquired.

"'Ad it from 'es foorefaathers afoore 'e."

"And where did they get it?"

"Why! fowt for't, 'e s'pose," the farmer replied.

"Very good! If thee't get off that 'oss I'll fight thee for't, but I shan't go back for nobody," the salt answered.

Hearing the story told of the rustic who stole the butter and hid it in his hat and was then forced to sit in the chimney corner till it melted and ran down his head and face, the old carter grinned and said, "'A'd better bi 'aaf to a put it in 'is britches pocket."

The carter was seriously told by a waggish blacksmith that the foundations of Fairford Church were built of bricks made with stubble by the Israelites in King Pharaoh's time and brought from Egypt to England in the days of the Romans, which account he sincerely believes, notwithstanding the laughter of his wife and family.

From Fairford the crystal Coln, leaping merrily over the large stones that lie along the bed and shelter the wily trouts, flows down to Whelford, where it pauses a moment to turn the machinery of the mill and then hurries off beneath lines of graceful willows and aspens. At about every half a mile is a foot-bridge, made of stout planks thrown across the stream, with a small ash or withy pole affixed as a hand-rail. They are constructed chiefly for the convenience of anglers, in order to allow them to pass from side to side, though they are also used by the rustics to cut off a corner, or to attend to the hatches placed at intervals to flood the fields in the winter and spring of the year.

At the division of the fields a barrier is usually set to prevent the cattle from wading through and trespassing on the adjoining lands. Several of the barriers are made of parts of an old steam-plough cable, drawn across from side to side and fixed to posts at a height of about two feet above the face of the water. If the heifers standing in the river should place their heads beneath these and lift them up, they might easily enter the next field, but they never do so, preferring to stand with their heads held over and the wire pressing hard against the dewlap.

Water-meadows extend to a distance of a mile from the stream. The land lies low, while the river, supported by banks of earth and gravel, is conducted at an elevation, with the object of forming a bay and obtaining sufficient fall to drive the machinery of the mill half a mile farther down. Trouts — they may be of a good size — occasionally escape through the hatches and work their way to the extremity of the field in the winter, when the meads are flooded. This is their spawning-time and the close season: they would not be able to get through the gates at any other part of the year.

Every autumn, while the springs are low, the coarsest of the weeds are cut, the gravel flams dragged out of the river-bed, and the materials piled along the banks to strengthen them during the winter floods. In order to sever the weeds, scythe-blades are riveted together and a rope is affixed to each end. Two men, standing one on each side, manipulate these, drawing them backwards and forwards and proceeding steadily up-stream. Sometimes a trout, heedless of the commotion in the weeds, and slow of movement, is cut in two by the sharp blades and becomes the prey of the workmen, though this does not often happen.

Otters, though not uncommon in the Coln, are seldom taken with gin or trap upon the banks. Moving as they do for the most part in the night, and concealing themselves by day in hollow trees and inaccess-ible places, they easily escape the notice of passers-by.

Fishing in the River Coln, near Fairford, Gloucestershire

Otter-hounds come and beat up the Coln and Leach, and work round the small brooks three or four times a year, and usually kill a few animals. Occasionally, when the hounds are hard on the tracks of an otter, they start a hare out of the long grass or rushes and leave the otter to chase that through the fields. Though constantly diving in the sharp clear water and brushing through reeds, flags, and grasses, the otter is yet tormented with parasites; there are usually several large tics clinging to the back of its head and neck when it is captured by the dogs in the river.

Whelford lies a short way back from the Coln. The hamlet, never very lively — for the population is small and the situation is on a narrow by-road — seems more than usually quiet to-day. The teams are all afield, getting ahead with the tillage; the shepherd is busy with his flock among the sainfoin; and the cowmen are gone to milking. The good-wives are indoors, kindling the fire and preparing the evening meal against the return of the toilers, and the children are not yet come from school. Every few minutes the brilliant kingfisher darts across and disappears through a gap low down in the hedge. Only the sound of the blacksmith's hammer on the tinkling anvil, the hum of the mill machinery, and the musical rippling of water beneath the river-arch are heard.

The village smithy, though small, is not pokey within, as some rustic forges are. This is because of the blacksmith's sense of order, and his dislike of having things in a muddle. He likes to see everything in its proper place and neatly arranged, so that he can find his tools and uses on the shortest notice, and not be compelled to turn out several corners and rummage among heaps of rubbish in search of them. But it is remarkable what self-possession most blacksmiths have, and how patient they are under circumstances that would drive many people to distraction. No matter in what frenzied haste the farmer may be to have his horses shod, or the traces mended, he must abide the smith's own time and not attempt to hurry him. If he does, he will only hinder matters. The man with the hammer has one pace at which to work, and will not be hustled, but is calm and unmoved and master of the situation.

Conspicuous in one corner is a stock of old bicycle wheels, spindles, cranks, and brake levers, and a bunch of cones held on a wire suspended from the wall. These testify to the variety of work the country smith is called upon to do nowadays; he must be prepared for anything that comes his way. Sometimes the ploughing engines stop to have a chain welded and the gear set right. Perhaps the motor lorry is out of condition and wants seeing to, and, though the chauffeur of the rich man's motor is usually able to keep his own machinery in order, he is sometimes glad of the blacksmith's help to heave the car out of the deep ditch at the sharp corner just below the forge.

Another interesting collection is half a hundred keys, of all shapes and sizes, threaded upon a long wire and hung from a nail in the wall. These the blacksmith keeps in case of emergency; it sometimes happens that a cottager breaks or loses the key of his door and cannot get inside the house. Then he goes to the smith and searches among his stock of keys till he finds one that will fit his lock, and so saves himself further trouble and expense. To him the woodman brings his axe in order to have it tempered, and a new shaft fitted; the quarryman fetches his picks to have them pointed and hardened; the churns and milk-pails come from the farm to be soldered, and the cottager's fender, fire-irons, or bedstead are brought along to be welded or riveted.

Not all horses like being shod. Very often it proves both a difficult and a dangerous proceeding to supply a new set of irons to a mettlesome animal; but the smith is used to their behaviour and usually finds means to finish the task. A tripod stands beside the anvil; upon this the hind leg is set while the smith fits the shoe and drives in and clenches the nails. "If you treats the horses well they'll treat you well; but if you're rough wi' they an' knocks 'em about, you can be sure they will kick out an' land you one on the sly some day or other," says the smith.

Here the conversation is cut short by the arrival of one who has an urgent job for the smith to do, which is to come to his premises and ring a couple of young pigs. They are just beginning to throw the troughs about and are become otherwise troublesome with their snouts, and so much nasal activity must be checked; there is no other way of doing it but by presenting each with a ring.

Who would have thought the fire had gone out in such a short space of time? But it is a small matter to light it; a bit of newspaper and half a match-box will kindle it again. Accordingly the smith rakes away the dead coals from the nose of the bellows, lights the paper, and covers the whole with half-burnt cinders. Now he grasps the handle of the bellows — and puffs away: in a moment he has a bright fire burning. To make the rings he takes two new horse-nails, heats them, flattens the heads on the anvil and makes them concave. Then he rounds off the stems and files them smooth, holding them in the vice and making the tips nice and sharp to accelerate their passage through the gristly snout. In less than ten minutes the rings are ready, and the smith, after damping the fire with a mop, takes a stout rope provided with a slip to hold the pig by the mouth, and departs with the cottager. In the evening after tea, he will come back and hammer out a few new shoes by fire-light, or do a little soldering, not that the job is urgent, but because he is happy in doing it, for he is his own master, and independent.

The mill is of ancient foundation, dating from before the time of the Domesday survey. In years past a monastery stood at one end and was inhabited by the friars, who had charge of the grinding: monks and mills seem to have been very closely associated during the Middle Ages. Four hatches bay back the stream. Behind are four conduits, fitted with iron gratings, which are raised by day and lowered by night. They serve to catch the slippery eels that sometimes come down the stream and swim over the hatches. Once over the doors and on to the grating there is no chance of escape for them: down they slide clear of the water and fall wriggling into the trap, to be taken out by the miller in the morning.

To-day the trouts are very busy in the shallows, where the water is not more than several inches deep now that the stream is low. They are preparing to spawn, and are leaping and wriggling about, with their backs and tails out of water, lying first on one side and then on the other, and making such a merry splashing noise as to astonish the pert-looking blackbird that has come on to the flam yonder to pick up a few sweet mouthfuls. The redbreast and wagtail keep him company on the flam and gather up the insects; there is no lack of food for them at any time of the year.

The mill has been in the occupation of the same family for more than two centuries, and is one of the busiest in the locality of the Upper Thames. When every other mill-wheel for miles around was stopped at the end of a hot, dry summer, those on the Coln could still go merrily round, so inexhaustible is the supply of water that leaps from the heart of the stony Cotswolds.

Old Elijah's cottage at Inglesham commands a pleasing view of the Vale above the Coln, looking west to Kempsford four miles distant. The scene is one of considerable charm, calmly and quietly beautiful. The winding river bordered with hawthorn clumps and the water showing in silvery patches, the broad meadows beyond, and the stately tower of Kempsford Church rising above the tree-tops in the distance form a delightfully harmonious landscape.

Gramp, though admiring the outlook as well as any, has his appreciation of it marred by the remembrance of something that happened when he was a boy. "I allus thenks o' the jackdaas when I ketches zight o' that owl' tower," says he. Then he goes on to relate how two farm boys climbed to the top of Kempsford tower in search of young jackdaws. When they reached the top — a hundred feet high — they looked over and discovered a nest in one of the gargoyles. Being unable to reach it by leaning over, one boy took the other's hand and supported him while he got through the battlement and stepped down to the nest, which contained six young birds. Then, in that perilous position, they began to argue over the division of the spoils.

"'Aaf an 'em be mine. I shall have 'aaf an 'em," said the one above.

"I knows tha ootn't have 'aaf an 'em, neether," the other replied.

"If I don' have 'aaf an 'em I'll let tha down," said the first.

"Let ma down, then, if thas likes, but tha ootn't have 'aaf an 'em," answered the other, and his crazy mate, not realising his crime, loosed his hand and he fell and was dashed to pieces on the hard stones beneath.

A bridge spans the river at Hannington Wick. Up to this point the stream is both wide and deep, but beyond the depth varies from ten feet to as many inches, and in the summer time "the bruk," as it is now called, is nearly dry in places. Formerly there were weirs at intervals up to Cricklade, but when the traffic in butter and cheese came to an end they were removed. The farmers said they kept the land wet and injured the pasture, and there was no very real need of them after the railways were made and the local trade in dairy produce ceased.

The farmhouses at Hannington Wick are old and picturesque buildings. They lie off the road and are surrounded with pools and dikes that do not become dry in the hottest summer. The deep ditches yield a heavy growth of reeds and rushes which are cut every autumn and used for thatching the ricks, and as litter for the cattle.

The little house martins delight to dwell beneath the eaves of the buildings; last year I counted no less than fifty nests packed as tightly as could be along the front wall of one of the sheds.

Moorhens, ducks, and dabchicks breed among the rushes and flags of the dikes. Here their nests are concealed, and they are free from disturbance by anglers and others who pass up and down the riverbanks and would interfere with the eggs and young. During the winter the birds repair in flocks to the Thames and are unmolested, except by an occasional visit from the farmer. Nearly every little pond has its pair of moorhens that hatch out two broods each year, and yet the birds do not appear to increase in number. A great many of the young fall victims to rats, pikes, eels, and otters that work up the ditches by night, which accounts for their disappearance.

During the floods widgeons, shelducks, golden-eye ducks and divers visit the meadows near the bridge. Not long ago a local farmer killed seven wild fowls at one shot as they were crowded on the shallow water. Shortly afterwards he was witness of an exciting combat between an otter and four herons, which was waged for the possession of a fish. The birds followed the otter for half a mile along the river, repeatedly beating it with their wings and striking at it with their long, sharp bills.

Kempsford church is a noble structure and is the pride of the villagers from the vicar, squire, and farmer to the cowman, shepherd, and ploughboys that tend their teams in the stables immediately fronting the walls. The building dates from the Norman period and contains, in addition to portions of the original walls and doorways, many specimens of choice workmanship in the carvings and chevron work, the ornamental columns and arches, the lofty panelled oak roof, the lantern of the tower, and the splayed windows.

The amazing tower is of fourteenth-century work, with corner buttresses reaching to the top and terminating in pinnacles ten feet above the leaden roof. It is supported by pillars and arches, and the lantern is richly decorated with the arms of the Earls of Gloucester and Lancaster, and bosses and frescoes, unusual in a village church, and more frequently found adorning the interior of some stately cathedral.

Dr. Woodford, afterwards Bishop of Ely, was for some time Vicar of

Kempsford. He was remarkable for his absent-mindedness. It is related of him that soon after coming to Kempsford, being in conversation with a farmer, he heard the word "ewe" articulated for the first time. "I am so glad to know how to pronounce that word. I have always read the passage 'e-wee lamb,' " said he.

Being in need of a horse he timidly approached a churchwarden and asked him to buy one — "A horse quiet to ride and drive and, I think, about fourteen or fifteen feet high," explained he.

The village of Kempsford is poor in appearance. A single street runs from end to end of the place, and the cottages, many of them little, old dilapidated buildings, stand ranged in rows and groups, with doors opening on to the road. Half-way down the street is the village green, and in the centre of this stands a large elm, called by the inhabitants "stocks tree," and "crass tree," because it was there that the ancient market cross and stocks were formerly situated.

The canal, that cuts across from Inglesham to Kempsford, almost touches the river beyond the church and then continues away to Cricklade. There are several locks of great depth between Inglesham and Kempsford, and others occur at intervals to beyond the Thames Head. They bear witness to the constant rise towards the river's source; it is far greater then you would guess by merely following the channel of the stream. The stones that compose the bases of the bridges are ready to tumble into the shallow water; the wharves are ruined, the towpaths deserted, and the bed is choked with vegetation.

"The closin' o' this canal was like takin' a link out o' the middle of a chain," says the old bargeman as he sits and calmly smokes his pipe, while his wife stitches away at a new shirt for her grandson, and looks over the top of her spectacles to note the effect of her good-man's words. For more than half a century they had lived in the barges. Backwards and forwards, year after year, they travelled with their burdens of corn, cheese, coal, stone, and timber, at one time frozen in for weeks at a stretch, at another aground for days in the dark tunnel, and again washed out into the mouth of the Severn by the boisterous tide. Yet, though they suffered hardships, they were fond of the life and were never so happy as when gliding through the beautiful meadows, or halting for the night in some secluded spot above the lock, where the spouting water gushes out musically of a warm summer's evening. Both the bargeman and his wife are stout and robust. "It don' look as if it 'urted arn an us, do it?" inquires the dame, with a broad smile, again looking up over the rims of her spectacles.

The most alarming accident that the old bargeman had experienced occurred at Bristol Docks. There he had his barge alongside a steamer that was taking on board sacks of corn, when one of the sacks, raised to a great height by the crane, slipped from the chain and, striking him upon the breast, threw him into the water and carried him to the bottom of the dock, twenty-five feet deep. On reaching the bottom he got free, however, and in less than half a minute from the time of falling he was on top again and was hoisted into the boat.

"Be 'e gwain to Cricklut, mother?" inquired the bargeman, Adam Twine, of the stout old dame who, with basket on arm, took the towpath at Marston bridge on her way to the town one afternoon.

"Aa, I be," she replied.

"If you likes to jump in you can ride. We be off directly," said he.

"Oh Lar'! I never bin aboord ship but I'll come wi' thee. 'Tool rest mi vit an' legs a bit," answered the old woman.

Accordingly she got in and went below and sat in the cabin, and the two conversed on various subjects. Meanwhile the boat had started noiselessly and without a tremor. The boy was at the rudder and the conversation was maintained. By and by mother became fidgety.

"'Ow much longer bist agwain to be afoore thas starts?" she inquired at length.

"Afoore 'e starts!" exclaimed old Adam.

"Aa! cos I be tired o' waitin' yer. 'E could a got 'aaf-way ther' bi this time," she continued.

"We shall stop in two or dree minutes, mother," said the boatman.

"Stop another two or dree minutes! Why essent a telled ma as tha wassent agwain to start afoore, nat kip anybody yer an' make a fool an ma. I could a got ther' bi now if I 'edna looked aater thee," cried she, burning with indignation.

Just then the boat gave a bump — they had come alongside the wharf.

"Yer us be, mother. You can get out now, an' mind not fall in an' be drownded," said Adam.

"Lark a massey! What! be we at Cricklut, then? An' I didn' know as we'd a started," exclaimed she, stepping out of the boat in amazement.

Although the greater part of the country adjoining the Thames is pasture there is yet upon the slopes and levels a considerable quantity of arable land that produces heavy crops of wheat and barley. At the same time, it is common knowledge that milk is the more profitable investment in this country today, though many farmers make the admission regretfully, and think it is a pity it should be so. One old farmer, in order to prove that a good loaf of bread may be made from unadulterated English flour, baked large loaves of flour ground from his wheat, took them to market and set them in the open mouths of the corn-sacks, which were soon surrounded by a crowd.

"What d'ye call this thing here?" inquired one.

"Well! This is a real English home-made loaf, if you want to know," the farmer answered.

"Why didn't 'e bring some cheese?" another drily inquired.

"You can allus tell wh'er a man's a good maaster er nat bi 'ow 'is work-vawk stops wi'n er le-affs un," says old Shadrach, who lives in a roomy cottage at the far end of the village. Though this may be accepted as a general axiom there are exceptions to the rule. Many farm labourers have a natural inclination to rove from place to place, and cannot be cured of the propensity. The old system of fairs encouraged this tendency; the habit of going to be hired became ingrained in the men and youths. As the time came round they began to grow restless, as do birds at the season of migration; they were bound to obey the innate prompting and look about for new quarters.

An almost infallible plan of getting to know whether the men intended to stop at the farm or not was carefully to watch their gardens. If they were kept clean and well-stocked with cabbages and winter greens the farmer was persuaded that Bob or Jack intended to stay with him; but if none of these were planted and the plots were allowed to become untidy, that was a sure sign that the men would be on the move at Michaelmas.

Very often, too, the men would stop at a place but their wives will not consent to it; they have the same inclination as the husbands to change their quarters and experience "fresh fields and pastures new." One day, a little before dinner-time, a cowman came to the kitchen door and asked to see master.

"Can I 'ev 'aaf a day off, maaster?" inquired he.

"Oh aa! Thee cast 'ev 'aaf a day, Bob, if thas wants one. Anything the matter?" said the farmer, guessing his intentions.

"No! Don' know as 'tis, maaster."

"Anything I can do for tha?"

"Nat as I knows on."

"Anything wrong wi' thi mates, or the cows? Dost want more money, or what is it? Bist dissatisfied at all?"

"No! Nat I byent, but the missis is. A dwun' like the 'owse," he admitted hesitatingly.

"Dwun' like the 'owse? But 'tis a good 'owse."

"The rooms be too big bi 'aaf. 'Er dwun' like un."

"Well! I tell tha what I'll do. I'll come over an' 'ev a look round, and put some pertitions up an' make the missis comfortable, an' gie tha another shillin' a wik an' ten shillin's extra at Michaelmas. Think it over an' see 'ow tha's like that."

Thereupon Bob went away, apparently satisfied, and for a week said nothing more about leaving. Then he came to master again and told him it was no good, he did not feel settled, he thought he should go to fair and get another place. The story of his wife's dissatisfaction with the cottage was invention. The roving fit was upon him; he could not resist the impulse to leave and find a new master.

The shorthorn herdsman is a clever little man, with fine features, soft, smooth voice, and merry sparkling eyes. He is quick of perception, is not backward nor yet too forward, with a ready supply of words, possessed of much useful knowledge of birds and animals, rustic work, life and lore, and abounding in fun and gentle humour. In stature he is but just over five feet. His shoulders are slightly bent with age, and he limps a little with one leg, the result of having a contracted muscle caused by an accident when he was a young boy. Naturally sharp and intelligent, his position as caretaker of the prize cattle, which brought him into contact with other people, helped to develop those qualities. Many strangers came to see the beasts, and the long journeys by road and rail taught him much that he would not have learned by staying in the village.

As well as being superintendent of the prize stock, he acted as commander-in-chief of the ox-teams when they were used for ploughing up the fields alongside the winding river.

"Thaay owl' oxen went as well as any 'ossen in the world, an' thaay was as deedy an' knowin' as ever you or I be. When I 'ed my owl' Champion an' Lion I didn't keer for the best 'ossen you could put up o' zide an 'em," says he.

Besides the oxen, Champion and Lion, there was the famous old bull Britain, that weighed a ton, and was equal in strength to a team of horses. When the engine and thresher were to be set, or an extra heavy load of hay or corn brought in from the field Britain's aid was invoked. Though all the others failed, if he was harnessed to the shafts the heavy weight was soon shifted. "Gee up, Britain! Come agyen, Britain!" shouted the herdsman, and the patient beast, bowing its neck to the yoke, pressed steadily forward and overcame the difficult task.

The herdsman's cottage stands at the bottom of the street, close beside the tiny inn. Its dull grey walls and roof of thatch, blackened with age, give it a dingy appearance from the outside, but the interior is bright and cheerful, thanks to the good-wife's cleanliness and care, and her desire to have the "old man" comfortable. There are four fair-sized rooms — two upstairs and two down — to the cottage. The furniture and ornaments are above the average for a labourer to possess, and the whole go to make up an interesting lot, though nothing is held in higher esteem than a certificate for rick-building, formerly gained in the local competition. As soon as the herdsman reached home with this he took it to show "missis" and "our young miss," and she declared it must have a suitable frame and paid for one out of her own pocket. A flitch of bacon, wrapped in a newspaper, hangs on one side of the great old-fashioned chimney mellowing in the heat of the wood fire that smoulders beneath.

Many curious odds and ends are poked away in the side-board and in the old oak drawers — quaint ornaments, photographs, and other things treasured for memory's sake, and last, the cottage stock of medicines, everything prepared of the mandrake, or bryony root, and purchased at the very last cattle show, at which the dealer — a specialist in uses of the root — has a stall every year. Here are boxes of pills and ointment, embrocation to be rubbed in for sprains, rheumatism, and stiffness, tonics for indigestion, a bottle of smelling "salts," and powders for headache and toothache, warranted to cure in a moment.

"Ther' yent no headache stuff ther', is it?" inquires the good-wife, looking up from her newspaper, that she is reading by the aid of two candles.

"Yes 'tis, fer 'edache an' all an't," the herdsman replies, rummaging amongst the papers in the drawer.

"Oh Lar'! I wish I'd a know'd that this marnin', then, for I was purty night crazy wi't," says she.

"Then thee oostn't a tuk it," the cowman answers while the mistress smiles benignly and continues reading the newspaper.

Presently the herdsman, after expatiating on the subject of flocks and herds, breaks into rhyme, and delivers the following verses, of his own composition, upon the features and qualities of a perfect Shorthorn beast, *The Prize Shorthorn:*

> "He's broad in the rib, and long in the rump,
> With a straight and flat back, and never a hump,
> Deep in the chest, and thick in the thighs,
> Clear in the nose, and mild in the eyes;
> Full in the flank, and well up in the chine,
> Straight in his joints, before and behind,
> With a long silky coat, and thick in the skin,
> He's a grazer without, and a butcher within."

This rhyme was composed, without pen or paper, as the herdsman went about his work in the yards and stalls, or as he lay a-bed at night, and was first of all communicated to old Shadrach and the shepherd, sitting in the small room at the little Axe and Compass Inn, at which they delight to meet now and then and talk over the day's experience, and see which can tell the quaintest item of news, jest, or story. By far the greatest part of the talking is done by the herdsman, however, while little Shadrach, with white corduroy suit, clean-shaven lips, and thin fringe of grey beard, sits smiling across the narrow table, proud to be in the others' company and to listen to their "oondermenting," as he calls it.

"'Tis instinct as doos it wi' tha beyassten, else 'ow ood thaay know?" says the herdsman, discussing the characteristics of the animals under his charge in the stalls. "Ther's thaay caaves! I can gie thaay the vly in the middle o' winter wi'out ever touchin' an 'em."

"Gie 'em the vly in the winter? Never yerd tell o' that afoore," says Shadrach.

"Tha's yezzi enuff," answers the herdsman. "I goes out in the paddick an' carrs 'em a bit o' 'aay in one 'and. When I gets to 'em, I jest begins buzzin' like a beg vly — 'Z-z-z-z-z,' an' drives 'em silly. As I ses, it must be instinct, cos we all knows as there's no vlies about in the winter."

One day the herdsman is sent for in a great hurry to go down to a neighbouring farm, where a strange accident has happened. A milking cow, in trying to leap a gate, has got half-way over and is hung on the top spar, with all four feet off the ground, and no efforts of the farmer or his men can avail to get her clear of the gate. But it is an easy task for the herdsman. He goes to the cow, puts one shoulder under her belly and gives a good grunt and a heave, and she, straining in sympathy with it, leaps over the gate.

One here relates the Cotswold jest of the town youth who had come to learn dairy work. He, being provided with a stool and appointed to milk a nice quiet cow, went into the yard as directed. By and by the farmer at the top end of the yard heard a scuffling noise and went to see what was the matter. Arrived on the scene he found the youth struggling violently with the beast.

"What b'e got at wi' 'er? Why don' 'e let the cow bide?" said he.

"I can't get the old hussey to sit down, sir," replied the youth.

"Now get ready to yer a good lie, if you never yerd one afore," says the herdsman, with an artful smile, whereupon little Shadrach pricks up his ears and the shepherd pays stricter attention, gripping his staff firmly with both hands and leaning his chin hard upon it.

"Is this a true lie, or a damn lie?" inquires Shadrach, with a wink at the shepherd.

"'Tis true as I yerd un, but I can't vouch far'n no further than that," replies the herdsman.

> "As I was going to Romford, 'twas on a market day,
> I saw the finest ram, sir, that ever was fed with hay,
> The wool upon his back, sir, reached up into the sky,
> And in it was a crow's nest, for I heard the young ones cry.
>
> 'Twas there I bought a flock of sheep, the finest ewes and wethers,
> Sometimes they bring me wool, sir, and sometimes they bring feathers,
> And I swear, by good St. Oswald, at every change of the moon
> They bring me a pair of lambs, sir, each one of them full soon.
>
> And there I bought me a little bull, nine yards round or more,
> Such a pretty little bull, sir, you never saw before,
> But when I drove him up the street he set up such a sound
> That all the walls of London came tumbling to the ground."

"'E was beggar than thy owl' Brittin, then," says Shadrach, while the shepherd, tickled with the notion of the fine ram and ewes and the wonderful fleece thick enough to conceal a crow's nest, laughs immoderately and thumps on the table with his fist to summon the landlord with a full cup, at the same time crying loudly: "Thaay was Cotswuls! Thaay was Cotswuls! Ther's nothin' like the Cotswuls fer big jints an' fleeces."

Chapter 6

CASTLE EATON, THAMES HEAD, CRICKLADE AND BLUNSDON

John Archer, of Lushill, was the best known of all the worthies of the Upper Thames Valley. Men of stronger individuality than he possessed there certainly were. Squire Campbell, of Buscot Park, was a vigorous and indefatigable farmer and experimentalist. His chief qualities, however, had a commercial bent. He was essentially a man of business and was lacking in the picturesque. Lord Radnor, of Coleshill, though a well-known figure, was a stern and trenchant politician, and was never on terms of real intimacy with the farmers and villagers who were his neighbours alongside the Cole. Squires Calley and Akerman, of Blunsdon, were of a different order. They quarrelled, pulled up each other's fences and caused the cattle to stray, and strove to see which could squander most money and gain the greater reputation for liberality, but their estates and influence were small, and their fame never travelled far beyond the actual village.

Squire John, however — the people invariably called him "Jacky," which name he acknowledged good-humouredly and often applied it to himself — combined most of the qualities usually found in the sporting lord of the manor. He was courteous and amiable to farmers and labourers alike, was possessed of artistic tastes, and a *naïveté* which was refreshing and amusing, and which counterbalanced the few faults he had and at the same time endeared him to the villagers. John Archer was, in fact, a real old-fashioned squire, a little feudal lord, if you like, the father of his workpeople, and the pride of the neighbourhood. Whether at home in the circle of his intimate friends, in the field a-hunting, at market in the town, or about the farmyard, he was the centre of all attention — what John Archer said and what he did was, rightly or wrongly, looked upon as of very special importance.

Squire John sprang from an ancient stock. His ancestors were a hardy race, noted for the excellence of their farming and their passionate devotion to fox-hunting. For four centuries they had occupied lands round about the river, and had successively reaped the harvests of the bounteous old earth and steadily prospered.

John kept between forty and fifty teams of oxen for ploughing and general work on the land, and he paid £3500 in wages every year. He employed nearly the whole population of two villages, besides a small army of casual labourers, or "strappers." Whatever the weather, he desired to have everyone employed at some task or other. When it rained he supplied waterproof coats for the men out of doors, and he used to say in such circumstances: "I wants 'e all to stop at work if 'e can, and remember, if you can stand the weather I can stand the pocket." Farm wages were low at that period, and Squire John paid no more and no less than was the custom in the locality. When his labourers had become too old to work he pensioned them off; he would no more have thought of sending his favourite hound to a dog's home. The system was crude and economically unsound, but it was about the best of its kind at the time.

Squire John was a little, wizened old man, with a clear complexion, merry, inquisitive eyes, and strong white hair — in appearance he was about as shaggy as a terrier. He hunted three and four days a week, riding gaily off on his brown nag dressed in his well-worn familiar pink jacket and velvet cap, both of which, according to local tradition, had served him for forty years. On every other day of the week he rode about his farms mounted on a shambling pony with the reins hanging loosely over its neck, or, wearing the shabbiest of coats and hats, drove a pony and cart through the fields and lanes. He discovered his present mood to the workpeople by the position of his headgear — hat on forehead meant good humour; hat on poll meant ill humour. Though normally of a genial disposition he was "a okkard man to plaaze when a body 'ad 'uffed un," but he was easily reconciled, and it is admitted by the majority of the old labourers that "Jacky Archer was the best man as ever trod in Cassul Aeton." In the evening, after a day's hunting or a ride over his farms, he dressed for dinner in front of a fire of logs in the dining-room, and when the meal was over he propped himself up on the sofa and perused the *Times*, while his daughters played to him on the harp. He kissed all the young girls and pretty women openly and publicly. This he considered to be his prerogative, and he exercised it without taking into account the lady's social rank and position.

Standing on top of the hill the squire could see the hay being gathered, the ripe corn felled by the reapers, and the teams of mottled oxen at plough, and could send out instructions to this or that group of toilers, as a general, posted on an eminence, overlooks his troops and marshals them for battle on the plain. A certain amount of country house state was maintained, and Squire John received many visitors. Among them was the worthy Dr. Woodward, of Kempsford, who frequently crossed the river in his boat and wended his way to Lushill to take dinner and discuss theology with the farmer squire. John, who was a staunch follower of Keble, was often assailed in the field and the town by local leaders and exponents of evangelicism, but he replied to them boldly and answered all arguments with quotations from a Bible which he carried in his pocket so as to be equipped for any emergency.

The squire had a keen instinct for farming, which was not at all blunted but rather sharpened by his devotion to fox-hunting: he used to declare that he earned fifteen shillings every time he went out with the hounds simply by looking round other people's farms and studying their methods. "To be a good farmer you must look round the outside of things and try to keep your workpeople satisfied. I pay twenty pound a week for no return, and it's no good for any man to think of getting on without putting his hand deep into his pocket," he would say. He sometimes complained to the blacksmith about the expenses of the farms and the difficulty of making both ends meet, but the man of the forge answered him boldly, and told him he had so much wealth he was unable to calculate it.

Although John was a peaceable subject and a loyal churchman he nevertheless had a long-standing quarrel with the Vicar of Castle Eaton. This was concerning a piece of glebe alongside the river, to which the squire laid claim, but the parson, fortified with documents, stoutly opposed him. By and by the parson took his revenge. In the middle of haymaking rain set in, and the river, overflowing its banks, washed a field of hay from John's side over to the parson's glebe where it lodged, and the vicar, when the water subsided, hired labourers to dry it and had it carted home to make into ricks for his own horses. That ended the dispute of the glebe. The parson had scored a point, and John was content to let the matter drop.

When the squire got old and feeble he grew sad at heart, and felt concern for the welfare of his farms and workpeople. With his companions of the hunting-field long departed this life, the conditions governing agriculture rapidly changing, and machinery displacing hand labour on the land — though he clung to the old methods when all others around him had cast them aside — he became melancholy and despondent. "I'm above the age of man, and when I'm gone I've got nobody to see to it as I like to have it done. No man will carry on my business successfully and keep things together when I'm gone," said he, which remark, though it might have seemed impertinent at the time, was justified by subsequent events. "Give my love to my people," were the squire's last words as he sank breathless upon the pillow. His mortal remains were borne from Lushill to Down Ampney, by roads which he had travelled for upwards of eighty years, and the bells that rang at his wedding, sixty years before, sounded a muffled peal as he was laid with his forefathers of ten generations.

Castle Eaton is about a mile and a half below Lushill. It is a small but ancient place, very compact, and it lies high and dry of the river. In winter, when the country around is buried deep beneath the floods, the inhabitants of the village are themselves secure, though they were often isolated from the rest of the world. In early times the site of the village

Harvesting

was an island, as is indicated by the name of the place. Formerly this was Eiton, or Ettone, made up of the Saxon words "ey" an island, and "ton," a dwelling or village. The old castle has long since been demolished and its site eradicated. No trace of the ruins exists in the meadows: there the fritillaries and purple orchis thrive and bloom, and the cattle graze quietly amid the rich pastures.

The village, viewed from the Thames' side, shows grey and hoary. The cottages, built of local stone, stand in little streets and squares, and the gardens slope down to the river's brink. The wells beside the doors are shallow, and are commonly surrounded with a low, dry stone wall, the appearance of which is suggestive of the Biblical East.

The church is Norman in design. A mixed choir of men and women — toilers on the land — sang in the church and accompanied the rude orchestra. The duties of clerk devolved upon the hoary carter, who stood in the small gallery and announced the hymns and psalms in choice vernacular: "Let us zeng to the praaze an' glary o' Gaad the 'underd an' vartieth Zaam," or whatever it might have been. A buxom young farm woman, who carted manure and picked stones the workaday part of the week, was the leading treble.

In a big hollow withy tree, below the church, an otter has had her litter of four; they were several times seen by the cowman as he went after his herd in the early morning hours. Growing along the river-banks are loose-strife, hemp-nettle, and yellow cress. About the mead bloom bed-straw and milk-vetch; the purple heads of the great burnet show conspicuous alongside the cream and rose of the dropwort.

Above the bridge the prospect is more open. Although comparatively near to the river's head there is no diminution in the breadth of the stream: it is almost as wide here as at Buscot, fourteen miles lower down, though the bed is shallower, and the current more swift. At every few dozen paces is a flam of sand and gravel that was washed up by the turbulent waters during the winter. These are cleared out and the tangled masses of weeds and vegetation — water-hemlock, cresses, and brooklime — cut and removed in July, so as to have the course clear and unobstructed against the advent of the floods.

Out from the farmyard in the village, a mile distant, the sound of the thresher is borne. For a week the men have been busy with the tackle in the farmyard. Rick after rick was attacked by the sturdy labourers, who first of all cut the tarcord and pulled out the sprays that held the thatch and uncovered the stack: the machine had been set alongside and coupled up with the engine, about ten paces to the rear. The sheaves thrown quickly down from such a height, fall on the deck of the thresher with a loud flap, and sometimes strike the feeder on the legs or shoulder, but he takes no notice and proceeds to cut the bond and pass the sheaf into the drum, distributing it as evenly as possible in the short space of time allowed for the operation. The conical top of the rick is soon removed and the height diminished; in two hours, with good luck, it will be reduced nearly to the level of the machine. An ordinary sized rick provides one day's work for the tackle and yields from sixty to eighty sacks of wheat, though John Archer's ricks yielded as many as a hundred and ten sacks. The size of the straw rick afterwards is much greater than that which contained the sheaves, for they were stacked in compactly and were well compressed together, whereas the straws, after passing through the drum of the machine, are crumpled and loose and take up much more room. If the wheat is in good condition a sack of grain will be run out in about four and a half minutes; if the ears are small and inferior the time required to fill the sack will be correspondingly longer. Yesterday the men threshed out seventy sacks of wheat in five and a half hours. This they considered good work; but the sheaves were unusually heavy, and the yield worked out at fifteen sacks to the acre.

The thresher is a prize model, made with the latest improvements of drum, fans, and screens — a simple yet beautiful piece of mechanism, running smoothly and easily under the power of the engine that is transmitted by means of the long heavy belt. A father and son are in charge of the machinery. They take the engine and thresher in turns, each alternately feeding the sheaves into the drum and seeing to the engine fire and boiler. The old man is very proud of the tackle, and tends it with a parental affection; the son is of a different temperament and looks upon it in the most matter-of-fact light, thereby marking the progress of a generation. The farmer frequently comes and stands before the sacks and catches the beautiful grain as it rattles down from the screen, and the workmen continually wheel away the full bags and stack them in the crowded barn near by.

In a cottage opposite the farmyard dwell old Thomas and Jane — the Darby and Joan of the Thames' side — who, though both within one year of a century, retain an active and intelligent interest in the life and work of the village, and especially in the threshing, which they can view sitting before their cottage window. Very different indeed are things now from what they were when these two were first wed. They have seen generations come and go and have outlived their own time, till they have become very strangers to the village in which they were born and to the scenes amid which they have so long dwelt.

Ninety-three years is a long time for a mortal to remember a thing, yet old Thomas's memory extends back so far. When he was six years of age he used to run into the farmyard to watch the men at work with the oxen and horses. One day, in the presence of old farmer Archer, the men were trying to yoke a big bull to a manure cart, but, try as they might, the animal would not back into the desired position. At last young Tom became impatient and, to the amazement of the men and the delight of the farmer, cried: "Let I 'ev a try, an' see if I can wutt un in." The farmer smiled at the youngster and exclaimed: "Go on! Let the child try."

Accordingly, young Tom, who was so tiny that a good snort of the beast might have knocked him down, took the halter, cried "Wutt back!" to the bull, and backed it into the shafts very simply and easily. Then old Archer laughed heartily at the youngster and told him to come into the stalls, and thereupon appointed him master of the bull and gave him three shillings a week in wages, which was double the amount received by the other boys who were older than he.

After that he took the oxen to plough, learned to sow, reap, and thresh, and performed the hundred and one duties of the farm. His wife's father was a maker of baskets and sieves for winnowing the corn in the barn after hand-threshing, and her mother was a lace-maker at a time when the cottage industries had not entirely disappeared from the region of the Thames Valley. A family of twelve followed their marriage; they have between two and three hundred grandchildren and great-grandchildren, and several sons who are in receipt of the Old Age Pension.

Of the two, granny is the more active and energetic. Clad in an old faded gown, with woollen vest, a pair of knitted stockings, with feet cut off, drawn up the arms, and quaint little cap on the head, she hops to and fro with surprising agility, cleans the grate, sweeps up the floor, dusts the ornaments and pictures, and sees to her housework generally, while the old man grips his fork or spade and toils in the garden among the potatoes and cauliflowers. "I got a goodish spirit an' tha's what kips I up," says granny, while Thomas smiles approvingly, reaches his pipe, half burnt away, from the mantelpiece, fills it with tobacco, and lights it with a spill from the hob.

"I got to master'n now, same as 'e allus 'ed," granny says, with a triumphant little laugh and a knowing wag of the head, at the same time giving her husband a playful cuff. Gramp wears an old pair of trousers with patches half a yard long over each knee, a thick woollen overall, and a little brown felt hat, which he keeps on his head indoors and out.

Their daily mode of living and general routine are as follows: Rise at 7 a.m., breakfast at 8 ; dinner — a little meat, broth, bread, and potatoes — at noon; tea at 3.30 ; supper at 6, and retire at 7 p.m. Granny's breakfast consists of a basin of bread and water sops with a lump of butter and a little salt and pepper added. This she prepares every afternoon ready to heat in the saucepan the following morning. For supper she takes a cup of warm beer with bread; to this habit she attributes her long life and good health. Years ago they lived principally on butter, milk, and "skim dick," *i.e.* cheese made of skimmed milk, which form of diet may have been the cause of their attaining to such a great age. Old Thomas says they never felt the need of butcher's meat — it made them sick to eat it.

Every Saturday the big living-room in the cottage is subjected to an extra special turn out. The tables and chairs are moved aside, and granny, provided with pail, brush, and house-cloth, scrubs the stone floor and then whitens it with freestone, rubbing it round and round and describing many curious and fantastical figures that resemble a child's first exercise in caligraphy. This is performed early in the morning, before breakfast; then grandfather has to lie in bed an hour later so as not to obstruct the most important operation of all the week.

"Afore I married 'e," says granny, "I used to help missis in the dairy. I can remember 't as well as ef 'twas but isterdi. Maaster used to go to church every wik, an' one Sunday marnin', when us was all set at dinner, a turned to I an' sed: 'Byen you well to-day, Jane?'

"'Yes, I be all right,' I sed.

"'Cos thaay bin talkin' about you in church.'

"'An' a good job too! I don' keer what tha doos,' I sed to 'n."

This was when the banns were published. Afterwards master and mistress subscribed and bought her a wedding gown, and made them a present of a side of bacon and a cheese that the cunning little mice had nibbled slightly with their pretty teeth.

Their wedding took place about the time of Queen Victoria's Coronation, which was celebrated in the little Thames' side village, and when several droll compositions were recited and committed to memory by the rustics.

"I say! Mrs. Fairplay, what do you think of our young Queen? I'm told she's going to do wonders in favour of the women. My old man told me he heard a man say another man had told him he heard one read it in a newspaper. There's going to be a Parliament of women. Mother Bounce is to be Prime Minister, Mrs. Grieveling Secretary for War, and Mother Chat-all is going to be Lady Chancellor. Can't make a Lord of her, you know. Every man that beats his wife has got to be locked up in an empty garret till he begs her pardon."

"Won't that be nice!"

"Yes! And that's not all. Every woman in England, Scotland, Ireland, and Wales is to have a gallon of gin to drink the Queen's health — when she can get it. For if the sea was all ink, the fishes of the sea all writers, the trees all pens, and the earth all parchment, it would not be enough to describe the good qualities of the women.

"So maidens, wives, and widows all merrily sing: 'Long life to the petticoats and Heaven bless the Queen.' "

Though the highest Thames spring is at Coates, the potential Thames head is at Kemble. The local inhabitants claim that the river really begins to rise in the neighbourhood of Culkerton, five miles to the west of its acknowledged head, and that it is conducted by a subterranean course to Kemble. Culkerton represents one of the highest summits of the western Cotswolds and is the starting-point of two rivers. On the eastern side the waters of the Thames springs are gathered, and on the west smaller springs originate to supply the Bristol Avon. The highest mill on the Thames banks stood a mile and a half from the head. The old house, called Mill Farm, still remains, though the wheel and machinery have been demolished for over a hundred years.

Half a mile below its source the spring was forded by a road, and foot passengers crossed on stepping-stones. By daylight the journey was safe, but at night it was attended with risks, especially when the springs were high. Then most people waded and ignored the stones. Will Darby, the short-sighted old tile-digger, found them by instinct and could usually cross in safety, though once, at least, he came to grief. That day he had been to Ciceter Mop and was returning in a state of mental elevation. "I shall go into the bruk to-night, as sure as the day," he repeated to himself on the road. When he came to the stones he put the wrong foot forward, missed at the second step, and went floundering into the stream.

Around the source of the Thames is clustered a group of ancient villages and hamlets containing many imposing farmhouses and cottages, and rich in historical traditions. From earliest times the wooded hills that guard the birthplace of the river were inhabited. To the south-west is the town of Malmesbury — one of the earliest homes of English learning and art ; Cirencester, the ancient *Corinium* of the Romans, and but little less famous, lies three miles away to the north.

The abolition of the local inn has metamorphosed the life of the place, and sports and games have disappeared, though there were many amusements formerly. In addition to the annual festival of Jackiman's Club a village Wake was held at which there was morris-dancing for ribbons, back-swording, and wrestling. Agriculture and stone-digging comprised the principal out-of-doors work; wool-spinning was carried on in the cottages. Wassailing was the favourite sport at Christmas-time, and the jovial custom was observed in all the villages upon the banks of the Thames streamlet. The wassailers rigged themselves out in fancy dress and carried a bowl decorated with ribbons and holly round to the farmhouses, where they sang their merry song and received money and ale. The effigy of an ox preceded the company as they journeyed from house to house. The effigy was formed of the skin of an ox set on a skeleton frame, with the head and foreparts stuffed with straw, and with two bottles for eyes. Two sturdy wassailers crept inside and bore it along, imitating the motions of the beast, to the delight of the rustics.

The last inn at Kemble was kept by one "Damper" Adams, who was a maker of wooden ploughs. He sold such notoriously bad ale that a gang of men set upon the house, rolled out the casks, smashed in the heads, and sent the beer tumbling down the hill into the river.

Both Ewen and Poole Keynes together would now make no more than a good-sized hamlet, though Poole has been a famous place. Few country mansions surpassed in stateliness the grand old fourteenth-century house — the home of the Barons Plat — that covered an acre of ground. This was almost totally destroyed by fire early in the seventeenth century. All that remains is one splendid room — said to have been part of the coach-house and now used as a kitchen for the farm that has been built on to it — a fine octagonal stone chimney, and the gruesome attic in which the last of the Plats hung himself in grief for the destruction of his property.

The High Street in Cricklade, Wiltshire, about 1883

Ewen — pronounced "Yeowin" by the rustics — possessed neither church nor stately mansion, but it has many picturesque farms and cottages and it is backed with magnificent timber. No spot on the Thames is more beautiful, and certainly none is more healthy, to judge from the great age and appetites of its inhabitants. Centenarians were almost as much the rule as the exception, and for a hearty appetite who could excel the redoubtable Cornelius Uzzle that, in the presence of living witnesses, unostentatiously devoured twelve pounds of bacon — six pounds raw and six pounds parboiled — at one meal for a wager at the old Wild Duck inn? The thatched cottage by the roadside yonder has had but two tenants in a hundred and fifty years. The aged occupant's memory extends back through his father for nearly two centuries.

Three mills stand on the Thames near Somerford Keynes. They date from the earliest times and were founded by the Saxons, who built a beautiful church and adorned it with sculptures and frescoes, some of which are still preserved. Agriculture is the staple industry of the village. "Plenty o' 'ard graft an' nat much bezide at Zummerverd," says the rustic, leaning on the stone wall in front of his house. North of the village is the forgotten hamlet of Shorncote with its quaint little Norman church; two miles lower down, we come to Ashton Keynes, the largest village on the Thames above Cricklade.

It is possible that Ashton Keynes is older than Cricklade and that it was looked upon in prehistoric times as the highest point on the Thames for general navigation. When the Romans came to the island and founded Bath and *Corinium,* and, with characteristic energy, surveyed the country and projected the great road from Cirencester to Speen, they decided to cross the Thames at Cricklade, and, by so doing, definitely established that as the starting-point of the river's commerce. Whether there was a ford or not previously mattered little to them. If there were no means of crossing they soon made them, for the Romans seldom deviated in order to avoid a difficulty but overcame it boldly and scientifically.

Whether Ashton was before Cricklade or Cricklade before Ashton may be open to question, but it is impossible not to be impressed with the charm of the place. The little Thames, flowing in several parts, unites in the centre of the village and runs rippling beside the broad street, passing through several stone arches and leaping down a pretty cascade, washing the foundations of the manor-house before it hurries off beneath a line of drooping beeches. The cottages, built on the opposite bank, are reached by foot-bridges. Along the stones of the walls creeps the pretty toadflax; here and there the golden mimulus blooms. This is rare, however; I have never seen it anywhere else on the Thames bank.

Glove-making was for several centuries an important industry on the banks of the Thames brook between Cricklade and Kemble. There were local tanyards for preparing the skins, and workshops for cutting out the leather. This was distributed throughout the villages and the gloves were sewed in the cottages by the women and girls, who earned from five shillings to seven shillings a week at the work.

Cricklade is about half-way between Ashton Keynes and Castle Eaton, astride the famouse Roman road of Ermin Street.

What the early election riots and fights at Cricklade were like can only be imagined at this time. Doubtless they were serious risings, attended with bloodshed, plundering, and devastation, for Crickladians had the reputation far and near of being a most boisterous and pugnacious people. When a stranger was located the cry went up: "Put un in the bruk," and the suggestion was usually no sooner made than carried into execution.

The "funnel trick" was frequently the cause of fighting at the inns. When a stranger came on the scene the novelty was introduced to him, and it usually ended in an uproar. The trick was played as follows: First a funnel was thrust into the stranger's garments about the waist. Then he was required to hold back his head, lay a coin on the middle of his forehead and, by repeated movements of the brows, to wriggle it down his nose and so let it fall into the funnel. The offence committed against the stranger is obvious. While he, with his head held back, was wriggling the coin someone dashed a potful of ale into the funnel, and the trouble began.

In former times the Cricklade elections lasted for eight days, which were spent by the townspeople in feasting and drinking. Then "open house" was kept at the inns. All voters, and any others who might be able to influence a vote, paid frequent visits to the inns, ate here and drank there, and seldom declared for their candidate till the date of the poll. Canvassing had been on for six months before this. It was usual for the candidates to visit the homes of the poor voters and attempt to buy something or other, offering a fabulous price for it in order to secure the householder's vote. "I'll give you ten pounds for that picture," or "I'll pay five pounds for that canary," the candidate would say, and the bargain was made.

Another practice at the Cricklade elections was for the candidate to lend money to probable supporters without the precaution of a security. The amount of money required in anticipation of the vote was signified by the number of bars in a gridiron which the voter roughly chalked on the outside of his door. The ordinary gridiron possessed ten bars, and a corresponding number of sovereigns was accordingly tendered as a loan to the householder. There is on record but one case in which the borrowed money was repaid: the voter, after receiving the money, was stricken with such remorse that he drowned himself in the river, whereupon his widow refunded the amount with interest.

The following bill for "open house" and general expenses connected with the Wootton Bassett election in 1774 proves the costliness and suggests the depravity of the system. There were four candidates to bear the outlay.

										£	s.	d.
(For food and drink at the inns.)												
Star ..	..	..	..	..	..	..	..	..	..	52	4	7
King of Prussia ..	..	..	..	..	..	..	..	..		90	10	0
Shoulder of Mutton	..	..	..	..	..	..	..	..		56	10	0
Horse and Jockey ..	..	..	..	..	..	..	..	..		107	4	0
Wm. Henley's	..	..	..	..	..	..	..	..		35	0	0
Waggon and Horses	..	..	..	..	..	..	..	..		78	11	0
Oak ..	..	..	..	..	..	..	..	..	..	336	0	0
Three Tuns	..	..	..	..	..	..	..	..		54	0	0
Three Goats' Herds	..	..	..	..	..	..	..	..		47	0	0
Cross Keys	..	..	..	..	..	..	..	..		90	0	0
Hay and Corn	..	..	..	..	..	..	..	..		3	16	0
King's Head	..	..	..	..	..	..	..	..		76	17	1
For Cockades	..	..	..	..	..	..	..	..		77	13	0
First Canvass ..	..	..	..	..	..	..	..	..		152	0	0
Money paid for various expenses		..	..	..	..	..	..			11	11	0
Total of votes, then computed at 135, 30 guineas each ..					..	..	..			4252	10	0
Money to men deserted or dead ..		..	..	..	..	..	..			441	1	1
										£5962	7	9
Item	..	..	..	..	..	..	..	..	..	11	0	0
										£5973	7	9

The price of 30 guineas for a vote was above the average: 20 guineas was the sum ordinarily paid. Occasionally, however, the cost of a vote was considerably increased, and in the year 1807 the local price rose to 45 guineas. The sum of £77, 13s. for cockades is a big item, though the ribbon bill was invariably high. It is said that at one election in North Wilts a candidate was pressed to sell fifty acres of good pasture land in order to pay for ribbons worn by his friends and supporters.

Squire Archer, of Lushill, was to the fore at election times. He stood in the market-place and made speeches in support of his candidate, while the crowd surged round yelling "Jacky," "Jacky," and jeering at his oratorical efforts. Elections proved both troublesome and dangerous to the squire. He would have been well advised to refrain from active participation in them, and especially from speech-making, but he boldly faced the multitude and took all interruptions, and even personal assaults, in good part. Though his politics were distasteful to the bulk of his workpeople they bore him no particular ill-will on that account, though he was often taunted about the low wages he paid to the men on the farms. Thus, when the disturbance on polling-day was at its height and "Jacky" was in the midst of the scrimmage, a witty labourer at the rear cried out lustily: "Dossent go to 'it the owl' man. Dwun' go to 'urt un, cos a'll allus find us plenty to do if a wunt gie us nothin' far't." On one polling day he lost no fewer than three top-hats, and he was finally chased home across the fields wearing the rim of one of them round his neck.

Many highwaymen resorted to the neighbourhood of Cricklade and committed deeds of plunder and murder in the Bradon Forest. The last outrage of the kind was perpetrated by one Watkins in the year 1819. He waylaid and shot a salt dealer named Rodway, who had been trading at the farms. Watkins attempted to fix the guilt upon another, but he failed, and was hanged at Purton Stoke. When the body was cut down from the gallows a farm labourer named Matthews ran forward with scissors and cut off the dead man's ear to keep in memory of the event. The labourer was subsequently known as "Crop" Matthews, and his deed was mentioned in a song composed upon the crime and execution of Watkins.

> "This barbarous man, who chanced to be there,
> What a barbarous fellow! he cut off his ear,
> When the rope it was severed and down he did drop,
> And for this same reason we all call him 'Crop.'"

It was while Zechariah Giles was constable that the mail van was attacked and robbed near the borough town. Old Zechariah showed his bravery on this occasion by climbing up a high elm-tree, but the robber was taken, tried, and gibbeted near at hand.

All the old sports characteristic of Wessex — bull-baiting, back-swording, boxing, wrestling, and cock-fighting — were carried on at Cricklade until the fairs were abolished. For those of a more gentle turn of mind there were other amusements, such as morris-dancing, skittling, bowling, fiddling, and flute-playing. At Christmas-time the mummers went about playing *Robin Hood* or *St. George*, or, with a collection of old and new songs, perambulated the town and paid visits to the villages and remote farmhouses, where they were well received and entertained.

It was usual for those engaged at the tanyards to observe a festival at the end of "bark harvest," which fell about the beginning of June. After the bark had been dried, stacked, and thatched, the proprietors of the tanneries gave a supper to their employees. This resembled the harvest-home of the farmers. Food and ale were supplied, and the hours till midnight were spent in mirth and merriment.

Following a discussion at one of the inns concerning the weight of a bushel of corn, one Will Simpson made a wager for a guinea that he would wheel a sack of wheat from Cricklade to Gloucester — about twenty-five miles — within twelve hours. This feat he straightway performed, though the time of year was midwinter, and he had to traverse many miles of unrolled stones upon the roads.

It is said that the parson of a village church near the borough town was famed for boxing and pig-killing. He boxed with the villagers —

farmers and labourers, too — and killed the poor people's pigs, gratis, with skill and despatch.

It is not many years since Betty Hall, a maiden lady, held the farm at Water Eaton, and, with the help of a horse and a bull, ploughed her fields and afterwards sowed the seed, reaped and threshed the corn, mowed her meadow, milked her cow, and managed her affairs without the assistance of a male. At another farm near the town dwell several ladies, nearly four-score years in age, who have never seen a railway, though for thirty years one has been laid not a mile from their door.

The ancient manor-house was once inhabited by a large family among whom were several maids who, for want of space, were forced to sleep in the attic. The roof, which was of thatch, happening to be in a bad condition, the squire made arrangements for the necessary repairs. The workman arrived early in the morning and mounted the ladder. Before he had been long engaged a portion of the decayed thatch fell through upon the maids. They, in ignorance of what was being done, began to scream and call for help. "It's all right, missis," cried the thatcher, peering down upon them, "I'm only lookin' through the rafters."

One day, three-quarters of a century ago, as Farmer Smith and his neighbour Mundy were riding down the hill on their nags to Cricklade market, they saw the poor folks at work enclosing the ground and building cottages. Then Mundy cried: "This won't do, Smith. We must see an' put a stop to this. We must get that hedge shifted back an' knock they walls down. If us don't do summat we shan't be able to get neether up ner down."

"Damme, let 'em bide, an' dwunt interfere wi' 'em. Ther's room enough for thee an' I," answered Smith.

The other, however, attempted to stop the operations, but was unsuccessful. By and by Mundy fell into misfortune, and was reduced to the necessity of working on the roads for a livelihood. Then old Paul Hancock, who lived down the hill, ran out from the cottage and gloated over his downfall, and shouted: "Hello! Hello! Is a wide enough now far tha? A's wide enough now, I'll lay a penny."

"Pray, my good friend, can you tell me how far it is to Cricklade?" inquired the traveller on horseback of a tall, raw-boned youth digging potatoes by the roadside half-way down the hill.

"Dursay I can, gaffer," replied he, with a grin. "It used to be reckoned vower mile, but now tha cut the 'ood away the zun shrivelled the road up an' chent about dree. The vust 'owse as you comes to is a barn, and the zecund is a 'aay rick. Owl' Shammel Giles's 'owse is a good way yon' that. Tha plagues our maester moore ner a bit, thaay do. 'Is zhip yets our turmuts and 'is gels gets into the orcut (orchard). Gaffer zets the dog aater the zhip an' I aater the wenches, an' between us we makes the 'ool an' the petticwuts vlee."

"Ah! and how is it that one of your legs is longer than the other?" inquired the traveller.

"Well! I never 'lows nob'dy to meddle wi' my grass-stranglers, gaffer, but since 'tis you I don' mind tellin' you I was born so at my perticler request, so as when I 'owlds plough I can walk wi' one vut in the vurra an' t'other on the land, zo's nat to lop awver, d'e zee," the youth replied.

Christopher, the carter, had been and married a wife upon the Downs and was bringing her home to Cricklade with the horse and waggon, lent for the occasion. On reaching the brow of the hill Christopher drugged the wheels and mounted the waggon. Then he shut his eyes and addressed his bride.

"Everything that I can see now's mine," said he.

"What! all that yander?" exclaimed his wife.

"Everything," he repeated.

Near the bottom of the hill, for several centuries, stood an inn with a large signboard, upon each side of which was painted a red lion, and a rude rhyme as follows:

(On the lower side.)
"Before this hill you do go up,
Look in and take a jovial cup."

(On the upper side.)
"Safe down this hill, all danger past,
Call in and drink a jovial glass."

The surprising roughness and disproportion of the walls of many of the old cottages owned by labourers along the roadside is accounted for by their having been for the most part built at night. There was a custom — respected till towards the middle of the nineteenth century — which, under certain conditions, allowed a man to enclose a piece of ground on the roadside and claim it as his rightful possession. If he could manage to start his walls, build the fireplace and boil a gammon of bacon over the hearth he had made himself secure, and no one could deprive him of the holding. Half the old cottages down Blunsdon Hill were built in this manner. At a later time efforts to take the cottages were made by farmers and landlords, especially where the old owners had died and the claim put forward by the new person was doubtful. But if it could be proved that the house had stood for twenty-one years the property could not be interfered with.

As well as being indispensable, the local blacksmith was otherwise important, and he used to give a supper to the carters and ploughmen every year at his own expense. The custom was also observed by the village carpenter; it was held common throughout the Upper Thames Valley while the wooden ploughs remained in use. The blacksmith gave his supper as having to do with the ironwork of the ploughs, shoeing, and keeping the traces in order; the carpenter because he supplied the woodwork — the whipples, and so on. The ploughshares were of wrought iron and they often wanted a new edge welded on. For this the blacksmith charged 10d., and 1d. for every new link or broken trace repaired.

In the autumn came the church festival, known in the locality as Blunsdon Slan Feast. At that time it was usual for the villagers to gather ripe slans or sloes to make a pudding. The festivities were kept up at the inns and cottages for a week, and while the local gamesters had a bout at back-swording, Bob Kempster and Dick Hornblow, with their followers, stole off to cock-fighting. Gipsy Smith played so merrily and well that the floor at the inn gave way and let grandfather Eggleton, who was dancing, fall through into the next room upon the head of old Moll Phillips, just as she was in the act of drinking a health to her neighbour, Joe the Marine, in a glass of home-brewed liquor.

Not many places possessed such a number of inhabitants noted for sturdy, quaint, or eccentric qualities as did the village of Broad Blunsdon, though it was commonly known and spoken of as "a roughish place," by the people round about. There were Squire Akerman and old Moses Akerman the farmer, Squire Calley, Farmer Snook of Bury Town, Dick Ockwell and "Leather Breeches" Ockwell, "Ratcatcher Joe," "Joe the Marine," Tom Call the burglar, and Betty his wife, Tom Hancock and his mother Moll, Poll Packer, and, greatest of all, old Bet Hyde, the most famous witch that ever dwelled in these parts.

Squire Akerman was son to Moses the farmer. His birth was marked by a mighty brew of ale at the farmhouse, and casks containing a couple of hogsheads were stored up to remain till his coming of age. When he came to be twenty-one the people on the farms were feasted and the strong ale was served out at the rate of a pint for each individual. When a third of the strong beer had been consumed other ale was poured in, and so the cask was replenished.

The squire, according to the account of "Crazy Dick," was "as tall as a Yankee herrin'," and "not worth a cold fourpence." This description may not be entirely reliable, however, since it was the squire who put Dick's grandfather, "Ratcatcher Joe," in the stocks and kept him there all one Sabbath till the folks went to church in the evening. Squire Akerman was both magistrate and constable at the time, and "Ratcatcher Joe" was overfond of the liquor, and was moreover very disorderly when he had imbibed too much. Whether it was the fact of Joe's having recently come into some property or that he had secured an extraordinary haul of rats in the farmyard is uncertain, but without doubt he was very drunk or the squire would not have taken the trouble to confine him. But Joseph proved to be a greater nuisance in the stocks than if he had been at liberty, for he did nothing but sing and shout and speak rudely to all who passed that way. In the evening, when the people were going to church, and the squire's wife and daughters were passing, he made more noise than before and shocked them with his rude and irreverent expressions. Then the squire, for very shame, set him free, and no one was afterwards put in the stocks there.

This is one of "Ratcatcher Joe's" feats. First he drank a pint of shoe-oil. Next he ate one pound of tallow candles, two pounds of boiled fat bacon, hot, and a large cow cabbage cooked with it that when cut would not go into a peck measure. Then he swallowed the greasy pot liquor, and afterwards drank a quart of beer, completing the whole within half an hour.

Joe's property was of the kind described as keyhold — that is, he was master of it who happened to be holding the key. Joseph took possession of the cottage by the singular rite of striking an axe into the trunk of a large plum tree standing in front of the house. The tree, though it had never previously borne fruit, was scarcely known to fail afterwards. "Ratcatcher Joe" did not long remain in possession of the property, for a lawyer found means to make him drunk and then induced him to sign away his rights for a song.

In sharp, cold weather Joe used to wrap the newly caught rats around his body, next the skin, in order to keep himself warm.

The squire was noted for many artful devices. He was moreover inordinately fond of his money, but he met his match one day in Jack Sanders, the ditcher. Jack had cut and laid a mound and cleaned out the ditch that twirled and wriggled like a serpent, and came to the squire to settle up the account.

"The mound's two chain long," said he.

"Daal! He's more than that, gaffer," replied Jack.

"Knows a yent! I mizhured un this ten year," returned the squire.

"I wants un mizhured a–new, then," said Jack again.

"Very well! Please thiself. Who'll drag the chain?" said the squire.

"Thee cast drag un," cried Jack.

The squire accordingly took the chain and struck a bee-line to the bottom.

"Yer! That wunt do, gaffer! The ditch is crucked," said Jack.

"I told tha a was but two chain," the squire cried.

"Damme! Ther's odds between the ditch an' thy chayn. Thee let I 'ae'n," said Jack.

When he had correctly measured the ditch it proved to be nearly as long again as was shown by the previous measurement, and the squire had to own to it and pay the extra money.

When the squire got old he used to play with his money, and he died with a good round sum in gold under his pillow, which circumstance caused the rustics to remark that he had placed it there in readiness to pay his passage down to the lower regions.

Old Moses Akerman, the squire's father, was of a different type. Plain and homely in his dress, manner, and speech, he was nevertheless a fine farmer, was generous to his workpeople and kind to strangers. About the farm he rode a shaggy black pony; when he went to market it was in the old-fashioned gig drawn by one of the plough horses. And what a merry time was had at the harvest-home! There was not another such a feast in all Blunsdon. Old Moses did the carving and the ale was so strong that the very smell of it overcame Moll Hancock and made her intoxicated. Dick Hornblow sang of the Fly and the Grasshopper:

> "Said the fly unto the grasshopper —
> 'Thee bist a hopping dog,
> And let thy mother be what she will
> Thy father sprang from a frog.'"

and Joe Packer followed with an ancient and ridiculous ditty:

> (Solo)   "A fly stood on the steeple-top, the steeple-top, the steeple-top,
>   A fly stood on the steeple-top —"
> (All)   "Yellacks a is now!"

Several times old Moses Akerman's sheep got through the fence into Squire Calley's field until the squire lost his patience and quarrelled with him about it.

"God love the fella! I s'pose thees thinks nobody got money but thee. I'll tell tha what I'll do. I'll show money wi' thee an' buy tha up," cried Moses.

"Ah! Akerman. You can load a jackass with money till he breaks down to the ground, but you'll never make a gentleman of him," Calley replied.

In the end Moses left the farm that his family had rented for a hundred years, because the landlord would not build him a new cowshed, though he afterwards declared that if he had known what he was worth he could have bought the place and put a gold fence round it.

It is said of Farmer Snook and his wife, of Lower Bury Town, that they had twenty-one children twice. This at first appears incredible, but it is explained in the following manner: Their twenty-first child died, afterwards another baby was born, which a second time brought up the number to twenty-one.

The old man possessed several peculiar characteristics. The work-people called him "Dandy" Snook, because, as he rode about the fields on horseback, at every few paces he stopped, took off his sleeve hat, brushed it, and, with the aid of a small pocket mirror, carefully combed his hair.

He rented three farms situated at a triangle and each about a mile apart, and he shouted his orders for all three from the top of Castle Hill. One morning, as the boy was bushing the field, nearly two miles away, he heard the master shout to someone: "Tell Eggleton to leave the bushing and go to Stanton Mill for some grist."

Without waiting for the messenger the boy unhitched and left the field, and presently met the bailiff on horseback.

"Where are you going?" inquired he.

"I be off to Stanton Mill," the boy replied.

"Who told you to go there?"

"Maester zed 'e was to go."

"You young liar! I'm only just come to tell you now."

"You needn't fret yerself. I yerd what maester zed, plain enough," answered Eggleton.

Notwithstanding the farmer's wonderful vocal ability, and his energy in other directions, he failed in business and soon afterwards died, and it is said that his corpse was arrested for debt in the street at Highworth on the way to burial at the church, and was only released upon one of the mourners undertaking to pay a proportion of the amount due.

Was there ever one more crafty than Dick Ockwell, who performed the duties of cowman, hen-minder, and egg-collector? It is said of him that he could pick out eggs for a sitting so cunningly that every chicken hatched should be a cock. This he often did for a wager, according to the account of the villagers, whose belief in his powers is unshakable. They say that he was able to do it merely be examination of the eggs — by holding them up to the light.

A cunning old fox caused Richard much trouble and anxiety. Time after time he had tried to take it with a trap, but had always failed. At last, one morning, on going to the pen he found reynard, that had broken in and devoured several hens and could not squeeze through the hole to safety. Upon looking a second time the warden of the roost perceived that the fox was stretched out stiff on the ground, as though it were dead. He accordingly turned to open the door more widely and shed light on the matter, when up sprang reynard, leapt upon his shoulders, and, darting through the door, was gone in a jiffy.

"Leather Breeches" was kinsman to the hen-minder and was an odd man about the village. The buckskin breeches he wore, according to a carefully preserved tradition, had been in the family for a hundred years, and as well as being wrinkled and withered with age they were filthy with grease. People said that all he had to eat with his barley bread was fat from his breeches obtained by frizzling them before the fire.

Then there was "Joe the Marine," Tom Call, and Betty his wife. The first-named of these was a tinker, while the other two were of no certified occupation, but were known for a precious pair of house-breaking thieves and rogues. The husband was a notorious purloiner of corn, which he stole by getting beneath the floors of granaries and boring holes in the woodwork.

Betty's forte was egg-stealing, and she used to keep a hen of her own indoors so as to be in a position to account for any eggs she might have in her possession. But one day a dozen turkey's eggs were missing, and on a search being made they were discovered at Betty's house.

"Where did you get these from?" inquired the constable.

"Bin an' becas me little 'en led 'em," Betty replied.

About the same time Tom Call was caught in the act of house-breaking, and was transported, and Betty was forced to enter the workhouse, where she ended her days with the paupers.

"Joe the Marine" was a hero of Waterloo, and could testify to the straight shooting of the French soldiers. Five minutes after the battle began he was shot through the calf, and in less than three minutes more another bullet tore through his top lip and carried half that away. Then he was taken to hospital, but when he arrived there, though the fight had only just begun, he was refused admittance, for there were hundreds of wounded men. When he returned to Blunsdon his mates laughed at him and told him it was no wonder he was hit in the head, for that was of such a size that no one could possibly miss it, and as for the other wound, that was entirely his own fault — he should have put his calves out to grass at Bury Town and not have taken them over there to Waterloo. Then Joe grinned and cursed Bonaparte, and said he'd learn tinkering, which he did of Mark the Gipsy who camped in Golden Rose Lane, and came to be a maker and mender of pots and kettles, and constructed a "dandy horse" with which he used to ride up and down the streets of the village. As he grew older he lived like a hermit and was called a "wise man" and a "dreamer," and when the farmers lost anything they would go to him for advice and he told them where to find the missing property. He was also said to have commerce with Satan, who was frequently seen in the shape of a crow perched on the back of his chair in the firelight. A good many deny this tale, however, and say it was Bet Hyde, who lived below Cold Harbour, that Satan used to visit under the guise of a crow.

Moll Wilkins was not so well known at Blunsdon, since she had removed to Cirencester, ten miles off, and there were other witches without going all that distance. But Tom Hancock, "journeyman farmer," of Blunsdon Hill, having need of the services of a wise woman, and distrusting the two local ones — he really owed each of them money, one for information as to the weather when he wanted to gather up his haycocks, and the other for a consultation about his white sow that was soon to farrow — made a special visit to Cicester and proved the infallible skill of the witch. He had lost a white fustian coat from the clothes-line in the garden, where he had hung it to dry after having been out in the rain ferreting rabbits. Accordingly he put a new fourpenny bit, to pay old Moll, in his pocket, and tramped off to Cirencester. When he arrived there and came to the house, she took him into a little room that was now pitch dark and now brightly lit, as though someone were continually switching on and off an electric light, though such a thing as an electric lamp was unknown then.

"Canst thee see this picture?" asked Moll at last, opening a little black box and taking out the portrait of a man.

"Yes," said Tom.

"Dost know who 'tis?"

"No."

Then she showed him another.

"Dost know who this is?"

"No."

"Well! wait a bit. Now," said she, producing a third card, "Hast ever seen this fella?"

"Yes," replied Tom.

"Well! Tha's the man as got thy coat. Thee go to Ashton Keynes an' ther' thee't see'n werrin' they jacket."

So Tom gave her the fourpenny bit and went to Ashton Keynes, and the first person he saw was a drover wearing his fustian coat with the big pearl buttons, just as old Moll had shown him in the picture at Cirencester.

Tom Hancock was a "love child," and was born in what was called the "Bastard House" at Blunsdon. Many towns and large villages had one of these houses in which unfortunate young women were detained. When the child was born and the mother had recovered she was taken before the magistrates and committed to prison. Poor labourers could not afford to keep their children in distress. The "Bastard House" was administered under the Poor Law, and the term of imprisonment was a punishment for those who had been forced to accept relief, and a warning to them not to transgress further. When Moll Hancock appeared before the magistrates to answer for her fault she took the opportunity of passing scathing remarks on the practice of sending young girls to prison for such an offence. "And now, gentlemen," she concluded, "you can send me to prison for as long as you like, but I'll have another child when I come out, as sure as you're sitting there."

Poll Packer was an inferior kind of witch, though she was greatly dreaded by the carters and cowmen, whose horses and herds she tampered with, stopping the teams on the road and causing the cows to get loose in the night and jump over the highest gates and fences. She was able to bewitch plates and saucers, knives, forks, and spoons, and even the very innocent slices of bread and butter, and to make them dance upon the tea-table. Her greatest feat was to make a waggon-line stand straight up in the air in the hayfield and so tease the farmer half out of his wits, who wanted to bind the hay on the wain and get it down to the rickyard before the rain came on. But poor Poll was often blamed for what she knew nothing about, and she suffered many a curse and execration that should rather have been levelled at her powerful rival and neighbour, Bet Hyde, who lived in a tiny thatched cottage below Cold Harbour.

Even titled lords and ladies came in their carriages to see old Bet, to ask her advice, and to hear her prognostications. When the crusty old Baron was about to begin a lawsuit against the indomitable Squire Q, who would not have the great grandfather elm-trees lopped, nor yet give up to his Lordship the little field in which he turned loose his favourite hunting nag — to which the Baron laid some sort of claim, though in reality the meadow should have belonged to one of the Hancocks — he thought it best secretly to visit the witch to hear what she had to say about the issue of the suit. Then old Bet, sitting on her low stool by the fireside, after hearing his account of the matter, spat up the chimney back and cried in a squeaking tone of voice:

> "Cuss'd be the hand
>   That strikes at the tree,
> And cusséd the meadow
>   If it channgéd be;
> For the grass shall wither,
>   And the tree shall fall,
> And the Spirit shall fetch
>   Squire, Baron, and all."

It is furthermore said that Satan, in the shape of a crow, came hopping out from beneath the table and perched on the old hag's shoulder, croaking loudly. That was all the witch spoke in reply to the Baron, who hurried off and allowed the suit to fall through and did not further molest the Squire. The big branches — some of them ten tons in weight — have nearly all fallen off the elms, and the trunks are rotten and hollow. The little field has been ploughed up and is now used for the production of potatoes, peas, and cabbages.

Ladies came to see old Bet for various reasons. If one was in love and had a troublesome rival she came to learn the best means of overcoming her. If another wanted to know her neighbour's secrets she came and bribed the old woman to discover them. If this one wanted to get rid of warts, freckles, or sunburn she came to have them charmed away. All things lost, stolen, or strayed were sought for — and that successfully, it is said — at Betty's house.

"I wonder if the old bitch is at home," said Mary Ann to Emm the cook, as they were going to see Bet one Sunday afternoon to have their fortunes told. When they came to the cottage the old woman was standing in the doorway.

"Yes, the old bitch is at home. Walk in, my dears. My pretty black bird told me you were coming," said she, pointing to the crow, that was perched upon the clothes-horse, looking very wicked and cunning. Then she went on:

"You've got a mole on your right shoulder and a strawberry mark under your left breast, and you've got a bad leg that'll never be well. You had a bundle of clothes, a letter, and a purse to take to the house-keeper, but you hid the clothes in the box bush coming down the lane, looked in the purse, and read the letter. There's a new place waiting for you, but the gentleman will die. You will marry the second cowman, and he will run away from you the Sunday after Michaelmas. You will both be widows and cripples in your old age because you despised old Betty and her pretty black bird.

> "For the devil shall pinch them and scratch out their eyes,
> Plague them with grasshoppers, beetles, and flies.
> Strip them and rip them and on their heads ride,
> That mock at the wisdom of old Bet Hyde."

Chapter 7

STANTON FITZWARREN, HANNINGTON AND OLD ELIJAH'S CHRISTMAS EVE

When Farmer Snook lived at Bury Town — the same who shouted his orders from Castle Hill, and whose corpse was arrested for debt in Highworth Street — he made many discoveries of old forgotten things on his farm, but, like a true barbarian, he demolished them all and so deprived those coming after him of the pleasure of their investigation. In the meadow called Town Close he employed William Gleed, the quarryman, at digging stones for over two years to make a road through the fields to his farm. There he unearthed numerous interesting relics, such as arms, tools, and implements, a coat of mail, coins impressed with the figures of the most august Roman Emperors, rings, trinkets, and cartloads of mosaic stones and "panches," or pottery ware. One day, as they were removing some large slabs of stone the iron bar slipped through and disappeared, and made a noise like thunder when it struck the bottom, which caused the quarryman to quake with fear, and he ran off and would not return to work any more that day. When Squire Akerman came to hear of it he had the stones set in place again and forbade further disturbance of the ground, and no one living now could say where the spot is.

The church feast at Stanton Fitzwarren, formerly held in honour of Saint Leonard, has now died out. The killing of a man at the backsword games was the prime cause of its abandonment. I have heard, when a boy, from my old grandmother — that, following a quarrel, a murder was committed near the village, and the culprit was tried, gibbeted, and buried on the roadside, and a sharp stake driven into the earth through his body. The news of the gibbeting travelled far and wide and attracted a big crowd. One venerable dame, whose boast it was that she had witnessed every public execution in the locality for three-quarters of a century, tramped a distance of twenty-four miles to see it, and made the forward and return journey each last two days, coming equipped with money and food to supply her on the way.

It was related to me by an aged person at Cricklade that when two young men, brothers, were hung from an oak tree outside the town, and the bodies were left suspended for the customary three days, the mother of the culprits took her sewing and sat beneath their bodies, apparently unconcerned.

A moderate-sized mansion and a farmhouse, several centuries old, occupy the site of the manor of Fulk Fitz-Warrene, the famous opponent of King John. A singular feature of the farmhouse is its fireplaces. They are provided with a thin iron wheel, an inch and a half in diameter, fixed behind the chimney-piece; this was intended to revolve and so draw the smoke up the chimney. Another device adopted for the prevention of smoky chimneys was the hanging a brass globe, filled with water and provided with a small aperture, in the chimney at a height a little above the point reached by the greatest flame. As the water became hot it evaporated, and the steam was supposed to draw up the smoke that otherwise would loiter in the chimney.

In common with almost everything else the chimney was called upon to support a tax, the proceeds of which were called "chimney-money" and "hearth-money." By a statute of Charles II it was decreed that the fire-hearth and stove of every dwelling or other house in England and Wales, except such as paid not to church and poor, should be chargeable with two shillings per annum payable at Michaelmas and Lady Day. The tax proved unpopular. The people declared it to be an oppression, and it was accordingly abolished, or, rather, exchanged for the impost on windows.

The lake below the House has been made for a hundred years, and is replenished by the clear spring that flows in at the upper end. The tall rushes and reeds, growing in the shallow parts, get stronger every year and push out, taking possession of new territory, to the satisfaction of the moorhens, coots, and dab-chicks. In addition there are the thousands of white water-lilies that, with their large oval leaves, float on the surface in matchless beauty through the summer, and sink to the bottom, lashed and beaten by the vicious waves, when the stormy south-west winds blow. The water-lilies multiply with great rapidity. Fifty years ago the first two bulbs were planted in the lake, and they have now increased to such an extent as to cover over an acre of its bed. At the same time — the woodman, with mathematical nicety, informs you — there were but seven rushes growing on the banks; now they might be gathered by the waggon-load.

Numerous pike inhabit the lake and grow to an enormous size among the reeds and lily leaves. As the water is private they are not molested, and there are shoals of small roach for them to feed upon, with many a sleek fat rat and frog, young water-fowl, or snake, that finds its way into the jaws of the monster as it swims across from yonder bank.

Snakes eat minnows and small roach, which accounts for their frequent presence in water. In the aviary at Stanton House there was kept a choice collection of canaries that one by one mysteriously disappeared. At last the owner one morning discovered the cause. Inside the lattice a snake was imprisoned by reason of its having swallowed a large bird. Being late, and not having time to digest the meal, it could not squeeze through the meshes to freedom.

Numbers of squirrels haunt the plantations, and a few badgers have their home about the banks and slopes. The marten, or martlet, survived in Stanton woods and park down to the early part of the eighteenth century, though it is now quite extinct in the region of the Upper Thames. The marten was of the size of a cat, though with longer body, shorter legs, and claws less sharp. It was of a deep golden colour, with white throat and bushy tail, and it had its haunt and gave birth to its young in the tops and hollows of trees. It is said to have played great havoc with poultry and game, and on this account it was hunted like the fox, though the hounds were not permitted to eat its flesh by reason of its unwholesomeness.

In a corner of the wood opposite a large cherry-tree, the top of which was broken off by the tempest, simple daffodils grow, blooming around a shallow well approached by means of several stone steps overgrown with moss, ferns, and violet. Many years ago a stone cottage stood on the spot, out of sight amid the trees and boughs, far from the high road and the village. In the cottage dwelt an old woman named Mary Taws, who might easily have been termed of evil repute, of the class of Bet Hyde and Moll Wilkins, but nothing is related of her by the villagers except that she loved the little old cottage, the well of sparkling water, the beautiful cherry-trees and the pretty "daffy-down-dillies." These she planted around the well and out beyond the garden fence, and in time they spread to and fro and filled that part of the wood with a sweeter beauty, inducing the boys and girls to come and pluck them with the primroses, violets, and bluebells. Every vestige of the cottage is gone now except the stones of the well, though the old woman's memory survives in the name given to that part of the wood, which is known to the villagers as "Moll Taw's Corner."

Poaching in the woods was common, and several kinds of gins and traps were set in the thickets to ensnare the depredators. Most dreaded of all were the man-traps. They were great iron gins having strong jaws fitted with sharp steel teeth that flew up and clutched a man about the calves and from which he could not extricate himself without assistance. Somewhat similar to them were the leg-traps. They were of steel and were so contrived that when they closed up they gripped a man firmly by the leg and locked automatically, and none but the keepers had keys to undo them. Spring guns were set among the low bushes and briars, and were provided with lines stretched across the paths at the height of a foot. Immediately the poacher's leg struck the line the straining of that both pointed the gun and fired it at the trespasser.

Another plan was to fix dummy pheasants to the branches of trees, and then to lie in wait for the poachers. When they fired at the dummies their whereabouts were discovered, and the keeper and his men promptly ran out after them. One Bob Lewis, the village sweep and a notorious poacher, when chased to his cottage by the keepers contrived invariably to disappear. In the wall, half-way up the chimney, he had built a secret recess. When he was hard pressed of a night he ran indoors, leapt up the chimney and descended into this, completely baffling his pursuers.

The timber of Stanton Woods is of a first-rate quality. This value results from the properties of the soil in the bed of the hollow, and from its swampy nature. The waters of the lake frequently overflow making the floor of the wood "goggy" and "patey," as the villagers say. The trees thrive on the moisture and the timber becomes extraordinarily tough.

Every species of tree — according to the woodman — is divided into two classes, the "he" and the "she"; and there is a corresponding difference discernible in the timber, whether it be of oak, elm, ash, beech, poplar, maple, or even the old stumpy hawthorn that grows in mid-field or by the roadside. The timber of the "he" tree — to follow the wood-cutter — is always harder and tougher than the other; that of the "she" is soft and mellow, as befits the feminine nature. The "sexes" of the trees may easily be ascertained in the spring-time when the buds are opening. The female tree, bush, or bough, always shoots first. Those loitering, as though unwilling to put forth their velvety leaves and drink in the fresh air and sunshine, are invariably the males.

Every spring some part of a wood is cut and the timber sold on the spot by auction. The heaviest ash poles, intended for the wheelwrights, are trimmed and placed in separate piles. The lighter poles for fencing are similarly set by themselves and the small wood for faggots and pea-sticks is arranged in drifts. The usual crowd invariably attends, this one to make purchases, that one to look on: there are those who have not missed the event for over half a century.

The wood sale possesses an irresistible attraction for the aged road-mender, who walks forth to meet old friends and make a few purchases of poles, pea-sticks, or faggots, and is hailed by acquaintances whom he has not seen for a year.

"Hello! Jacky! Bistn't thee dead yet?"

"No. More bistn't thee. But tha's ought to be."

"Oh! 'Ow's that?"

"Never done no good to nobody."

"I'm goin' to live as long as I can purpose to eggrivate everybody."

Here now is the auctioneer.

"Hello! Bridges. You're got over here, then!"

"Yes, sir. I brought a gentleman to do a bit o' business wi' ya."

"All right, Bridges. You know your way about."

"I don't know so much about that."

Presently a move is made, and the crowd, headed by the auctioneer, comes and stands by a pile of timber.

"Now, Bridges! Come on! How much for this lot? A pound? Twenty-five shillings, or what?"

"I'll gie two shillin's."

"What! You're getting generous, aren't you, Bridges? Two shillings I'm offered. Who says a pound?"

"Five shillings."

"Eight."

"Ten."

"Fourteen."

"Go on! There's plenty of room yet."

"Now, sir, Jacky's goin' to gie ya one more shillin', and only one. Fifteen. Now go on."

"All done at fifteen? All done, I say? Mind you, they're worth double. Once more; have you all done? Right! There you are, Bridges! Take 'em along. That's the cheapest lost that's been sold in the wood. Two tons of good ash poles for fifteen shillings, you artful old cove!"

Yonder cottages huddled on the hillside have sheltered a hardy stock, though their former occupants are extinct. There you may learn half the history of the village: of good Aunt Betsy, mortally afraid of a concertina, but who lived to a great age and became so childish that she set the bed on fire and was nearly roasted alive; of old Moll Garrett, "Kit" Rimes, and Patty Jones, who reaped and sowed, milked, thatched, and quarried stones as well as any man in the village. And you will hear of Mildenhall, the miller, so hearty and strong that he could pick up two sacks of flour — one under each arm — and race about with them, and, with a half-hundred-weight hung on his thumb, reach up and write his name on the ceiling of the mill; of "Nobber" Kibblewhite, the thresher, who lay in the barn with the rats and owls and the mysterious White Lady; of "Stivvy" Legg, who sat on the great sarsen-stone all night waiting for it to turn round at cockcrow; and, not the least famous, Tom Fowler, the carter, noted for an extraordinary feat of strength which he often performed for the entertainment of the villagers. Of him it is related that he would lie on his back beneath a farm waggon, place his feet against the hind axle-tree, lift up the waggon with the strength of his legs and back, and turn the two wheels round simultaneously with his hands.

The following is a record of Father Fowler's mowing, preserved since the summer of 1836:

Stanton Mead.	Brick Field.
Wyld's Ground.	Call's Piece.
Bean Lands.	Ram's Close.

Number of acres, 45 0 10 perch. Sum per acres, 3s. Amount to receive, £6. 15s. 4d.

One day the young shepherd went out mowing with the old man,

A mower walking to work, with his scythe over his shoulder, about 1881

though he could make but little progress. "Tackle wants graacin'," said he, darkly.

"You! What did the owl' fella mean bi saayin' as my tackle wanted graacin'?" inquired the shepherd of his mate at night.

"Thee take an' gie'n a good piece o' bacon an' 'e'll put the zithe right far tha. Tha essent a got un zet right, locks!" answered he.

Old Farmer Hunter knew everyone's footprints but his own: so, when the boy Fowler borrowed his master's boots to go plum-stealing, he was at a loss to trace the thieves and he put it down to strangers.

From its abundance in Wiltshire the common elm has been called the "Wiltshire Weed." So prolific is it that it has been claimed that if the scythe and cattle were kept out of the fields for twenty years the valley would be covered with a forest as dense as it was in prehistoric days.

The wych-elm is propagated by seed, and the common elm by suckers, since the fruit of the last-named rarely ripens in Britain. In former times the young wood of the wych-elm was used for making bows and was considered not much inferior to yew. Many villagers, in cases of cold or sore throat, strip off the inner bark of the young wands and chew it raw, or boil it and drink the liquor. This, when cold, settles into a brown jelly that is not unpleasant to the taste. I have often taken it as a boy, preparing it according to the directions given me by my old grandmother, who was skilled in the use of herbs and in the making of ointments from "Jack-by-the-Hedge" — garlic mustard — young primrose leaves, and other plants and flowers.

The village of Hannington lies beyond the avenues. At one time it was larger than it is now. When the land was laid down for pasture fewer hands were required. Little by little the population decreased. The houses were demolished and no more were built to replace them. During the last fifty years many cottages have been destroyed and not above half a dozen new ones erected. The two old inns — the Cat and Mouse and the Dog — have also disappeared, though a small farmhouse in the hollow was converted into an hostelry, and the sign of the Jolly Tar was hoisted above the door. An incident that occurred during the building of the inn did not tend to make the house popular, and it may be that it reflected the feelings of the villagers at the time. It is said that the local carpenter, after hanging the new sign of the Jolly Tar, went home and hung himself.

The two inns, the Cat and the Dog, played an important part in the life of the village, and though some of the proceedings carried on within them might have shocked those imbued with modern ideas of civil refinement, they were a proof of the hardihood of the population. The sports of bull-baiting, cock-fighting, wrestling, and boxing were regularly indulged in, and were witnessed and countenanced by the local squire and the parson, who admired the Greek nature of the games, and saw no harm in them, even though they might be attended with a little rough play towards the close, as in the fate of Harry

Waterman, the gamester of Highworth. For several years in succession he had come down to the feast and had made himself objectionable to all and sundry. At length, the villagers, headed by one Giles Draper, set upon him furiously, tore the clothes from his back, and chased him home naked across the fields to Highworth, in spite of efforts of the constable, who shouted loudly for help "in the Queen's name," and tried hard to arrest the ringleaders.

The constable was a big burly man and was noted for several feats of strength. It is said that he could lift a heavy farm waggon from the ground on his back, so it was comparatively an easy matter for him to carry off refractory villagers to the Blind House, or to set them in the stocks that stood opposite the old Cat and Mouse Inn. It chanced that the last man to be imprisoned in the stocks, by name Davy Garrett, had a wooden leg. His offence was that of being drunk and unable to walk. He pleaded hard with the constable and begged that only his wooden leg might be infixed in the instrument, but the man of the law was inexorable and compelled him to sit there from sunrise to sunset during the next day, which was the Sabbath.

Giles Draper, who led the villagers against Harry Waterman, disturber of the feast, was an old soldier and a famous mower. He was able to cut two acres of grass in a day and to keep up the effort for a week at a stretch. Such extraordinary exertions naturally made him very hungry and thirsty, and it is not to be wondered at that he discovered an enormous appetite, though it is difficult to believe that he really ate a quartern loaf and two pounds of bacon and drank a gallon of fresh beer at a meal. As he advanced in age the hard toil of the fields told upon him. His joints became stiff and feeble, and he thought of his earlier years. "I shall hae to do all that mowin' over agyen," said he to Dick Willis, the ox-man, who was puzzled at the time to know what he meant, though he understood it afterwards.

There was a long list of Hannington worthies while the ancient village stood. First was Squire Montgomery, who lived at the Hall. Next was Humphrey Baden — as good a farmer as ever brewed ale; Mary Rowlands, Moll Higgins, Sarah George, and Martha Hedges — haymakers, reapers, cheese-makers, and dairy women; Jack Woolford, cowman, Finch the woodman, Daniel Yeates, the ancient miller, Joe Jarvis, blacksmith, and Bob Hewitt, cobbler, bell-ringer, church clerk, and gravedigger. Old Hewitt had earned renown as a cobbler and gravedigger, though he was deficient in his duties as clerk, which was probably a result of his too frequent attendance at the Dog Inn, which was a favourite resort of his. Almost every Sunday, during service at the church, he fell asleep in his pew beneath the high gallery, and as soon as he awoke, without waiting to see at which point the parson had arrived, he loudly shouted out: "Aaff-menn." Fixed to a beam in the ceiling at the Dog was a stout iron hook. From this the shoemaker clerk, when he felt so inclined, would hang with his left hand and continue chatting with one and the other till he had drunk a gallon of strong beer.

"By gad, Finch, this will never do," cried the new squire to the old woodman, meeting him one night on the way home with a large faggot, provided with two forks and a "stand up" at his back. "You'll ruin me, man."

"Baggin' yer pardon, sir, 'tis nothin' onusual," answered he.

"Nothing unusual!" exclaimed the squire. "What do you want with those two forks besides the faggot, there?"

"Them's the bear-aways, sir," replied the woodman.

"The bear-aways, eh! And what's the one hanging down behind you?"

"That's the teal-away, sir."

"Oh! the teal-away, is it? Well! for the future you shall neither bear away nor teal away my wood in this fashion, but be satisfied with a small faggot and one fork, and see you bring that back with you every morning."

Humphrey Baden courted one of two sisters, both of whom "wanted" him for a husband. The young lady of his choice being poor, that circumstance gave the other — who had money — an opportunity of pressing her suit. She accordingly met Humphrey in the lane one night and boldly addressed him. "If I was in your place I should look after somebody different to my sister, for her got nothing," said she. Thereupon Humphrey took the hint and proposed to her on the spot, and they were soon afterwards married.

Humphrey's fame as a good farmer and cultivator and a kind master had spread around the Vale, and was only eclipsed by that of John Archer, of Lushill. When the steam-ploughs came on the scene and other farmers got rid of their oxen, he kept his and went on as before. "Ya owl' fool!" said a neighbour to him at length, "Why dossent zill the beyast an' 'ae the steam uns?"

"I can work oxen an' aaterwerds fat em an' zell em, locks! but neether thee ner I, ner nobody else, can fat a ploughin' ingine," Humphrey replied.

Strong and hardy, blunt and outspoken, but honest and straight forward were the women who toiled in old Humphrey's fields hay-making and harvesting throughout the summer and autumn. Sarah Geoge, the carter's wife, was the recognised leader of the feminine element, and Moll Higgins was respected as her lieutenant. Without doubt a little scandal was sometimes discussed among the haycocks and wheat sheaves, but Sarah spoke her mind with perfect candour and answered a squeamish remark with: "Aa, damn tha! Some fawks channges mutton for mutton, dwun em?"

"Sally! What sart of a tree do you call this un?" inquired Jack Woolford, the cowman, of Sarah one day, pointing to an exotic shrub opposite the Hall.

"Why! a ooden un to be sure, ya fool!" replied she, passing quickly on her way.

After Moll Higgins' husband Tom died and the men took to chaffing her about marrying again she declared that she "wouldn't hev the brightest man as ever wore a head," though she finally succumbed to the charms of Dick Willis, widower. Then one of the daymen said to her: "Mary, I thought you said you oodn't hev the brightest man as ever werred a head, an' now yer be you agwain to marry Richat Willis, as ardinary a man as ever lived in Anninton."

"Ya fool! I 'edn't 'ed the chance to 'ev t'other un, 'ed I," answered she.

The old blacksmith, "Whistling Joe," what time he was not engaged shaping horseshoes and forging new shares and coulters on the anvil, made nails of scrap iron and sold them at 4d. a pound. He served his apprenticeship at Buscot and had to attend the neighbouring village of Kelmscott every morning in order to do the shoeing. When the Thames was in flood, he crossed the river at Buscot Lock, took off his clothes, tied them in a bundle, placed them on his head with his nail-box, hammer, and pincers, and walked naked for a mile through the flooded meadows, often with the water to his breast.

> "I walked by myself, I said to myself, self said unto me —
> 'Beware of thyself, take care of thyself, for nobody will take care of thee,'"

is a favourite rhyme of the smith's. This he learned of his old master, the Buscot blacksmith; he often quotes it at the age of fourscore and five.

Those were the days of tinder-boxes, lye-droppers, rush-lights, home-made candles, and potato starch. Tinder-boxes have long disappeared from the cottages, and the old-fashioned lye-dropper has also become a thing of the past. The lye-dropper was used for the softening of water for the wash-tub before soda became cheap and common about the countryside. It was in the form of a box, eighteen inches or two feet square at the top, a foot and a half in depth, and about twelve inches square at the bottom, the board of which was perforated with a nail-passer. A quantity of charcoal was placed in the lye-dropper. That was then set over a pan or tub, and the hard water was poured upon the charcoal and allowed to filter through into the vessel beneath. The water, after passing through the charcoal, was called the "lyes" — lees — and so the vessel was called the "lye-dropper." The process of water-softening was a rather tedious one and it was usual for the house-wife to be engaged for several days at the "lye-dropping."

Potato starch was made by grating the potatoes into a pot or pan and adding a sufficient quantity of boiling water. All night, before Highworth Fair, Fanny Beckett toiled hard to have her new dress ready for the occasion, and only realised at three o'clock in the morning that there was no starch in the house to finish it.

"Oh, mother! whatever shall I do? I shan't be able to wear my new frock, for we got no starch," cried she.

A blacksmith at work, Bradfield, Berkshire, early twentieth century

"Run out in the garden an' uck up a few taters," her good mother answered. So she ran and got the potatoes and made the starch, and between them they finished the dress, and Fanny looked very pretty in it and danced merrily in the booth with the young carters and shepherds.

The majority of the cottagers made their own rush-lights and, at a later date, their candles, using for the purpose tallow, or mutton fat. Old Elijah, of Inglesham, was highly expert in the making of both rush-lights and candles. To make the first-named he obtained rushes from the lowlands by the Thames, removed the green skin — all but one strip — from the pith, and when that was dry dipped it in the hot fat and allowed it to set.

The common way of making candles at home was to obtain a supply of dry teasel "gixes" from the hedgerows, cut them into convenient lengths, draw a small string or thread through the middle, and then to fill them with hot fat. When the fat had set the dry gix was cut away and the candle was ready for use.

The meal for making "barley-dodkins," "barley-scawters," "barley-bangers," or "pot-cakes" was usually shaken through a piece of coarse muslin. When Sarah George and Moll Higgins were preparing their weekly batch, however, they sifted the meal through their Sunday bonnets.

Old Betty Ockwell's favourite dish — and one she provided for her children — was nicknamed "bang-belly." This consisted of milk, well stiffened with wheaten flour.

Frog-water was drunk in the place of tea when that was too expensive for poor people to buy. First a frog was placed in the teapot and boiling water poured upon it. After standing for a few minutes — or it might be boiled — the liquor was fit for use. The "frog" was the thick crust cut from the bottom of a loaf and blackened in the oven or before the fire.

"Plaaze to gie ma a bit o' 'ood to do mi bakin'," said Davy Garrett to "Lord" Withers, of The Nell, meeting him one day down Golden Rose Lane.

"Man! Man! Man! I got no 'ood. All's I got to bake mi own loaves wi' is a bit o' green eldern, an' missis slips it into the o-ven an' ther' 'tis a 'oppin' an' poppin', spettin' an' 'issin', jumpin' an' crackin', an' when the bread bin in a hour an' moore chent narn a damn bit the doneder," returned he.

The omnivorous gipsies that encamped in Hannington Lane would dig up a pig that had been buried for three or four days and devour it, turning it into a savoury meal. They considered that any kind of flesh was good for food provided it would "take salt."

Four local farmers courted a beautiful dark-eyed gipsy girl, the daughter of Mark the Gipsy, who, though he practised the trade of a tinker, had twelve good horses and was said to own land "from London to Bristol." He had three daughters, and he caused it to be known that he was prepared to give a dowry of £1000 with each of them.

Not only gipsies but others have made use of swine that had died and been buried. Jack Hughes and Tom Bailey, hearing that the road-mender's sow had died in farrowing, and coming to know where it was buried, went to a spot at night, dug it up, plunged it into a large tub of hot water, dressed it, and then carried it off and sold it as prime pork in the town.

Farmer Hunter, having forty sacks of potatoes for sale, and having received an offer from a dealer at Chippenham, put them on rail, but took the precaution of getting in the waggon under the sheet and travelling down with them and demanded cash at the other end.

"Thenk ee ver a veow zwedes, maester," said Geb Zillard to old Pete Smith.

"Wants thaay for my ship," said he, striding by.

"Aw right, maester," said Geb quietly.

Presently the farmer turned round and strode back.

"Aa, Geb, thee cast hae some swedes," said he. "Thee cast go an' pull one, two, dree, vower, vive, zix, zeven, aaight, nine, ten, 'leven, twelve, up to twenty, an' when thaay be gone tha cast hev another lot, if thas likes to."

Hannington Feast, Marston Feast, and Wroughton Feast all fell on the same day, which chanced to be about the middle of haymaking. Jack Kibblewhite, having a chum at Wroughton, and wanting to see the backswording for which that place was famed, going there on the Sunday was induced to stop the week and was brought before the magistrates for being absent from mowing.

"I only went to Wroughton Feast, sir," said he to the Chairman, in extenuation of his offence.

Then David Archer, brother of the Squire of Lushill, gravely returned: "Ah! young man, we're all well aware of that, for it is a sure thing that if you hadn't gone to Wroughton Feast, Wroughton Feast would never have come to you."

Previous to that three men — one a cousin to Jack — had been sheep-stealing, and would have got clear if one of them had not turned Queen's evidence. When the other two were brought up, to every question addressed to them they soberly answered: "I was there," and uttered not a word besides. They failed materially to impress the squire, however, who merely remarked: "I quite believe you," and committed them to prison for a certain term.

One Jeremiah Ewer lived at Crouch at that time. He was noted for acrobatic feats and was clever at somersaults, and particularly at standing and "walking" on his head, though he was so idle that he would not even put the rudge chain over the horse's back for the carter. He placed the boy Jack in charge of the women in the fields and called him his "bailey," and asked his advice on all matters pertaining to the cattle and crops. Jack was so sluggish that he would lie down anywhere and sleep for hours, but Jeremiah only laughed at him and called him a "lazy scamp" and a "wosbird," and "a purty fine fella to be a bailey." As Jeremiah advanced in years he became reserved and eccentric. He clapped on his knee with his hand so frequently that he wore a new smock into a hole in a week. At length he retired into the attic and stayed there for sixteen years without once coming down, not even when his aged father and mother died in the same house and were carried off for burial.

What is a "Journeyman Farmer"? He is not really a farmer at all, but a labourer, a "Jack of all trades," that can turn his hand to ploughing, sowing, hoeing, reaping, mowing, threshing, shepherding, sheep-shearing, cartering, milking, hedge-cutting, ditching, draining, tree-felling, thatching, hurdle-making, faggoting, and anything else that may be needed of him, as well as being able to help the master with particular advice concerning the exact times for sowing and the quantities of seed required according to the soil and season, cutting and carrying crops, complaints in cattle, and being a reliable weather prophet into the bargain. Such were old Elijah Iles of Inglesham, "Wassail" Harvey of Cricklade, Tom Hancock of Blunsdon Hill, and Gabriel Zillard of Hannington.

> "When the moon lays on his back,
> Then he holds wet in his lap."

and

> "If it rains on Easter Day,
> Plenty of grass but not much hay,"

say the villagers. If the ducks and geese quack and cackle clamorously and come running home from the pool, or the cocks and hens rub themselves in the dust, or the old sow runs squealing to and fro grubbing with her snout; or if the bees remain in the hives, or the spiders run up and down the walls at night, or the water boils away swiftly in the pot, or the mischievous moles cast up the earth with more than their usual energy, rain is sure soon to follow. But if the cows lie down, or the bull follows the herd to pasture, or the swallows mount high, or the pretty pimpernel, wood-sorrel, and dandelion open their petals in the early morning, that is a sure sign of fine weather.

Grandfather Elijah of Inglesham had been promised a special visit, one that should last a whole night without interruption, and he was eagerly looking forward to it. The fact is, grandfather Elijah had several old songs he wanted to sing, and one or two quaint rhymes to repeat, and he was furthermore very anxious to recite to us the play of *Robin Hood and Little John*, as acted by the mummers when he was a boy. Christmas Eve was the date of the proposed meeting at old Elijah's house.

A little before four o'clock the sun set, dropping down behind

Lushill, and soon afterwards the station lamps at Highworth were lit, showing afar off like the lights of a ship at sea. The interior of Gramp's cottage was warm and bright. A fire of logs blazed up the chimney-back and a large lamp stood in the centre of the table beneath a rather low ceiling. Numerous pictures and photographs hung on the walls around. Above them were set sprigs of holly and mistletoe, or little boughs of ivy. On each side of the chimney was a recess fitted with cupboards and shelves containing dishes and chinaware, mugs, and tumblers, gleaming in the merry firelight. The small clock on the mantelpiece was twenty minutes ahead of time. This is not an uncommon thing to find in the cottages, for the villagers love to be deceived in the matter of moments, and to feel that the hour is not really as far advanced as is indicated by the hands of the instrument. Inside the door was a thin partition to protect the fireplace from draught. Behind this old Elijah always sat, and never thought of shifting his position out of consideration for any.

Each of the visitors to the cottage had brought Gramp a small present. Clothes he needed not, nor yet a new pair of boots, for he seldom wore anything but slippers, either indoors or out. Books and newspapers were useless to him, for he could not see to read, and he had a sufficient stock of knowledge crammed into his old head to last him for the rest of his days. This his children and grandchildren knew, and so did not trouble to buy him anything that would be of no use. Instead they brought him a few good things to eat — cakes and oranges, a piece of beef for Christmas dinner, several ounces of tobacco, and a little flask of whisky. With all these Gramp was greatly pleased, though it was easy to see that he most preferred the tobacco and the small flask of barley juice, which, after all, was quite natural for one of his years. His delight in the tobacco was unbounded. "Ho! ho! ho! H'm! h'm! h'm!" chuckled he, taking up the packages and holding them in his mouth one after another, and tossing his head the while, before he stowed them away on the shelf beside his pipe and spills, and sat down in the arm-chair with a triumphant expression upon his countenance.

Gramp was the hero of the hour. This he knew, though he tried to be natural and to conceal his joy at having the company present. His daughter called him "a regular owl' toff" and teased him about wanting a "hair-cut." The grandchildren laughed and chattered like magpies, but old Elijah smiled the smile of one who is master of the situation and sat quietly and comfortably in his chair, smoking, and awaiting a convenient time for beginning the entertainment. He was dressed in corduroy trousers, with woollen waistcoat and cardigan jacket, and he had on a new felt hat such as is worn in the fields at haymaking. His wooden pipe was laid aside for a new clay with a long stem. His long snow-white hair fell gracefully over his shoulders and gave dignity to his form; he was really a grand old man, whose worth could not be over-estimated.

When the table had been cleared of the tea-things there came a lull in the conversation. Then Mrs. Lawrence, Gramp's daughter, gave the fire a vigorous rout, brought more coals and set on the kettle again. Suddenly, without warning, Gramp burst into song with a clear, ringing voice, and we knew the time for festivity had arrived. He only sang one verse of the ditty. This was concerning two farmers who took refuge in the church porch during a heavy thunder-shower.

> "Says Mark O to Peter O — 'This is very funny weather.
> This will make the little seeds to grow and all things spring up together.'
>
> "Says Peter O to Mark O — 'I'll trudge along, in spite of the weather,
> For three wives buried have I got snug in this churchyard together.'"

Then he went on: "I was jest a thenkin' now 'e be got yer 'e med as well do zummat, 'cos Time's on the wing an' waits for no man, an' 'tis a very good thing to do the same as Farmer Bernard when he went to zee owl' Yalla-britches, the laayer, an' never put off till to-morra what you can do to-day. What be us to hae fust? A bit of a zong or a tale, or what? We'd better lave owl' *Robin 'Ood* till last, 'cos ther's a longish piece o' 'e. 'Tool take two or dree hours to spake 'e off, all an in."

"Wha's that about owl' Yalla-britches?" inquired Mrs. Lawrence.

"'Bout owl' Yalla-britches? Why, Farmer Bernard an' 'e."

"Well, what is it?"

"Farmer Bernard was at a loss what to do wi' 'isself, an' bolts off to market. Ther' a met wi' other farmers. Walks an' strakes about the market. Couldn't zee nothin' to 'tract 'is attention. Goes by owl' Yalla-britches' office.

"'Le's go in an' zee owl' Yalla-britches, an' yer what 'e got to talk about.'"

"Knocks at the door. Out comes Yalla-britches.

"'Oh, good morning.'

"'Good morning.'

"'What's the business?'

"'I come for a little o' your advice to know 'ow to get on in the world.'

"Yalla-britches stood an' considered a bit. Goes to 'is desk, lays olt of a bit o' paper, pen an' ink — all at 'and. Writes on paper — 'Never put off till tomorrow what ought to be done to-day.'

"Wraps it up, gies it to Bernard. Bernard takes it.

"'What's the fee?'

"'Zix an' aaight pence.'

"Farmer Bernard thought he was foolish to gie zix and aaight pence for what he know'd afore. Anyhow, he got 'is owl' nag in the trap an' went off early, an' 'is missis congratulated un for bein' home early. 'Ad 'is tea an' telled the missis about owl' Yalla-britches. Rap comes at the door.

"'Maaster come home?'

"'Yes.'

"'Wants to zi'n.'

"Bernard goes to the door.

"'What's the matter, carter?'

"'Nothing the matter, maaster, but ther's that bit o' whate. We be anxious to get it in. If you be agreeable we'll ae't in 'fore us gies out.'

"Well! tha went on an' got it done. All comes in to zupper. Off home to bed. Latish. In the night a thunder-storm comes on. Farmer Bernard opens window.

"'It rains cats an' dogs, missis. A double zix an' aaight-pence the fust night.' Jumps into bed. Everybody else's whate washed away but his'n."

> "Oh, bad luck it can't be prevented,
> Fortune she smiles and frowns,
> That man's best off that's contented,
> And mixes the ups wi' the downs."

Several suggestions were made as to songs. One asked to hear "The Jolly Tinker, or Preaching for Bacon," others preferred "Lord Bateman," "On the Banks of Sweet Dundee," "Butter and Cheese and All," "The Carrion Crow and the Tailor," or "The Oyster Girl," all which Gramp knew. Finally the matter was left for himself to decide.

Then Gramp said: "Zeein' as we got a goodish company I thenks we ought to hae healths fust an' drenk to one another."

A jug of ale was accordingly brought and the tumblers were reached down from the shelf. A little weak whisky and water, with sugar, was made for old Elijah. Then the glasses were clinked, and the young people stood up to drink.

"Now, then! What is it to be?" inquired Gramp of the first.

Then the granddaughter replied:

> "Here's a health to the world, as round as a wheel,
> Death is a thing we all shall feel ;
> If life were a thing that money could buy
> The rich would live, and the poor would die."

"Aa! Tha's a very good un. Go on wi' t'other," said Elijah. Here the grandson spoke:

> "Here's success to the plough, the fleece, and the flail,
> May the landlord ever flourish and the tenant never fail."

"Aa! Tha's a owld un, that is. I've yerd my grandfather saay 'e many a time when I was a bwoy. Wha's the next un?"

Elijah's son spoke next:

"Here's a health to that as 'll do that good when the body and soul is taken from it!"

"H'm, h'm, h'm. Tha's a teert un. Don' know the meanin' o' 'e —
No."

"Yes you do know, too. What is it as does a ooman good when 'er
baby's born? You knows as my mother allus used to gie a cup o' hot
beer to the ooman as soon as the child was born when 'er went a
nursin'."

"Ah! ah! ah! To be sure. I forgot that. Tha's as much as to say: 'Yer's
a health to the cup o' beer as doos the ooman good when 'er baby's
barn.' Go on wi't."

> "Here's to the man with a ragged coat,
> And with no means to mend it,
> And here's to the man with plenty of cash,
> And who doesn't know how to spend it."

"H'm! h'm! 'E dwun' live at our 'ouse, nat the last un, awhever.
Ther's one more to come."

> "Happy have we met,
> Merry have we been,
> Happy may we part,
> And merry meet again."

"Ah! ah! An' there's one very similar — what I med zaay — agrees
wi' that un very well.

> "Let them be merry merry there,
> And we'll be merry merry here,
> But — who can tell wher' we shall be
> *To be merry another year?*"

'Ev 'e all done? Spose 'tis my time now then?" said grandfather, rising
from the chair and taking up his glass from the table, while all eyed him
eagerly. Holding the glass on high and inclining his head a little to one
side, old Elijah delivered his toast:

> "Here's to the inside of a loaf and the outside of a gaol,
> A good beefsteak and a quart of good ale,"

cried he, and drank off the contents of the glass amid much laughter.

"But you got neether beefsteak nor yet ale, for you drunk whisky an'
water," cried Mrs. Lawrence.

There was no holding Gramp after that. His old face wore an
ineffable expression, and he shook with frequent laughter. First he sang
"Paddle your own Canoe, my Boys," then ran into "The Four and
Nine," and ended with "Blow the Candle out." Afterwards followed a
short bit of patter, then came "Parson Jingle-Jaw's Adventure" and the
song of "Sweet Peggy O," newly remembered after sixty years.

Just then a galloping of horses, accompanied by a loud, rumbling sound, was heard outside.

"There goes the mailman from Lechlade! 'E's late to-night," cried Mrs Lawrence, looking up at the clock on the mantelpiece.

"You'd better begin *Robin Hood* else you won't get through 'n to-night," cried his daughter.

"Aa! Better 'ae owl' *Robin 'Ood*, cos Time's on the wing, an' if 'e dwun 'ae'n to-night 'e mightn't 'ae the chance aaterwerds. You'll be zumwher' else to-morra," Gramp replied.

Thereupon Mrs. Lawrence made Gramp a small tumblerful of weak whisky and water, while he filled his pipe, lit it with a spill taken from the shelf beside the mantelpiece, and sat down in his arm-chair again. When he had half finished the tobacco he extinguished it with the top of his thumb, replaced the pipe on the shelf, emptied his glass — wishing good luck to everybody — gripped a stout stick standing in the corner holding it between his legs with both hands, and sat rigid in the chair with his felt hat pulled down tight on his head, and his bushy eyebrows lowered. Then, after a few words as to the number of players, the manner in which they were dressed, and so on, he proceeded with the piece: *Robin Hood and Little John.*

Gramp spoke all the parts with great relish: the Tanner, Robin Hood, Little John, the Doctor and Jack Vinney, the clown. The play took little time to recite, and soon Gramp was singing Jack Vinney's song with its refrain:

"It's rolling in the dew makes the milkmaid so fair."

After finishing the song old Elijah sat back in the chair, replaced the stick in the corner, and took up his pipe, by which we knew the play of *Robin Hood* was ended. Then one of the young people exclaimed disappointedly:

"Is that all?"

"Whatty?" returned Gramp.

"Is that the lot of *Robin Hood* ?"

"Aw, eece! Tha's all o' *Robin 'Ood.*"

"But you said 't 'ood take two or three hours!"

"Ah! so 't 'ood, probably, if you was playin an't, cos you could make it last as long as you liked, but we spoke un off quick. 'Tis a purtyish zong at the ind an in. What! be 'e off a'ready, then? Thought 'e was gwain to stop a bit," continued Elijah, as one of the company prepared to leave.

"Another half an hour and it will be Christmas morning," replied he.

"Well! good-bye to 'e, if 'e *must* go. Look out for the owl' black dog o' Engleshum," said Gramp, and the visitor, after wishing every one "Goodnight," and "A Merry Christmas," opened the door and left the cottage.

The night was calm and clear. Above Coleshill Wood the yellow half-moon was rising, topsy-turvy; the stars glittered brightly overhead in the frosty sky. Down below the sound of the Cole leaping through the hatches could faintly be heard, otherwise there was perfect silence. The street lights were out in the town on the hill, but the old church tower stood black against the sky and was visible several miles off. As I passed beneath the dark trees a black dog came running by, and I thought of Gramp's parting words at the cottage, in which he referred to the Inglesham Ghost, though that was probably one let loose from the neighbouring farmyard.

Old Elijah became so merry after my departure that he stayed up till after two o'clock, and it was feared that he would not be got to bed at all. Even after he was put there he kept singing, and only fell asleep an hour before daybreak, to wake again with a song when the postman's rat-tat came at the door signifying the arrival of the Christmas letters and parcels.

Junction of the Thames, the Coln and the Canal

Chapter 8

TADPOLE, NEWBRIDGE AND LONGWORTH

At the end of the lane is a forked turning, one branch of which leads by a bridle track through the fields to Tadpole, and the other approaches the ford, where a crossing is made to the Oxfordshire side of the river. The passage is upon the old channel, in the middle of a sharp southward loop, where the stream, turning at right-angles, zig-zags towards the ridge and is opposed by a steep bank that diverts the current northward. To obviate the tediousness and inconvenience of the loop a cut was made across the neck some years ago, and a new lock and weir were established. This both assisted in the dispersal of flood-water and rendered navigation much simpler and easier. At the best of times the loop was an awkward and even a dangerous stretch for bargemen to traverse; and when the river was high it was next to impossible to distinguish the exact position of the shore at the curves and angles. An ancient weir stood below the ford; by means of this the depth of water was regulated, whether to permit traffic to cross to the opposite shore or enable bargemen to pass the shallow with their heavily-laden craft.

No easy matter it was in former days to navigate the upper reaches of the river and convey full burdens of corn, coal, stone, timber, bacon and cheese from Cricklade to Oxford, passing on to Reading and London: the skipper of a coasting steamer, or the captain of a large liner that ploughs the open ocean, occupies a post in many ways more leisured and desirable. Tempest he may fear, fierce winds and tumultuous seas; but the rocks were never so numerous nor so difficult to avoid as the sharp shelving shores, the points and peaks, the rising flams and broad shallows of the river. And though a thousand fathoms may be a fearful depth in which to sink, in case of a wreck, many a waterman wished he might glide upon the surface of such a pool on finding his stout barque, with its fifty ton load, fast upon a bank, and no prospect of obtaining a sufficient flow of water to enable him to re-float before the lapse of days, or even weeks, if it were the golden summer-time.

Watermen had their grievances and sometimes objected to the tolls of the weirkeepers; as long ago as the time of Henry VIII it was deemed advisable to appoint Commissioners "to prevent exactions of occupiers of locks and weirs on the Thames from London to Cricklade, in the County of Wilts, and for ascertaining the rates of watermen on the river." Grain was carried loose in the boats and was liable to be pilfered by dishonest bargemen. A favourite method was to obtain sticks of elder, and, after removing the pith and perforating them, to thrust them into the grain and allow water to trickle through them. This caused the corn to swell; and since the grain was measured out at the end of the voyage, anything in excess was claimed and retained by the boatmen. Other sources of revenue were open to all who made use of the waterway: such as fishing and fowling with nets and snares, and the conveyance of illicit liquors, which were readily received by the inn-keepers who dwelt upon the banks of the river.

Although the Evenlode has the larger watershed and gives the greater discharge during flood-time, the Windrush is more constant and perennial, and is, therefore, the most considerable tributary of the Isis. Rising afar in the heart of the Cotswolds, it winds for many a mile, singing above its gravelly bed and turning the wheels of numerous mills before it mingles its waters with those of the silent river.

There is no other structure on the upper river so sturdy, massive and typically English as Newbridge, where the junction with the Windrush takes place. Swinford Bridge is handsome and stately, but its graceful length and ornamental form belong to a later age, and exhibit features and characteristics different from those of Newbridge. As I walk in the meadows and look upon the series of arches from a distance, or stand upon the structure itself and examine in detail the piers and parapet, I am struck with the strength and rugged grandeur, the apparent indestructibility of the work. An iron-like purpose was in the heart of the architect who planned, and the workmen who shaped and fitted those stones, which for centuries have stood secure against the mighty mass of waters that, sweeping round yonder curve and moving forward above the broad pool, rush headlong upon the solid piers and masonry, impregnable against the heavy attack.

Although the building of the bridge was excellently carried out, an economy was effected on the lower side. Here extension of the piers was not considered necessary, so that the whole wall is flat from end to end. On the upper side, to break the force of the waters in flood-time, are the usual wedge-shaped buttresses, and these are continued to the parapet, where they form a series of recesses, in which one might be safe from the press of traffic, or be sheltered in a defence of the bridge against any attack of besiegers. Another peculiarity of the bridge is that the scheme and height of the six pointed arches is not progressively regular, the fourth arch on the left being slightly the highest, where we should have expected the third and fourth to be equal. That this corresponded with the design of the architect is not to be doubted; but though the formal order was interrupted the feature added to the originality and distinctiveness of the work, so that we may justly say there is no bridge to be compared with ours on this or any other river. Radcot Bridge is of similar design, but much smaller; both date from the time of Henry III. Two inns stand upon the banks, one at each end of the bridge. If the river was crossed previously by a ford at the spot it might well have been a dangerous undertaking in the winter. The rapid Windrush, entering immediately above, would sweep away pedestrians; and pack-horses with their burdens would not be able to withstand the current.

The ruined house known as Thames Side Farm, opposite "Poplar Island," was properly on the banks of the old river, according to local tradition. The line the stream formerly took is indicated by a depression, and two lines of willows; but if this were ever the true course then the way was narrow, judging by present appearances. But centuries of mud, the wreckage of trees, grasses and reeds, and the filling in by generations of husbandmen, once the new course were adopted, would account for its narrowness at this time. Local people say the current is swifter below Duxford than anywhere else upon the upper river; but I do not know that the claim is strictly accurate.

An old road, now a green way, leads up from Thames Side past Harrow Down to the village on the ridge.

Gorse covers one side of the down — that towards the ridge and the village. This in winter gives to the hill a dark and sombre appearance; but what is able to surpass the rich golden tint of the massed blooms in early summer? To the farmer, however, its presence denotes poor ground, generally useless for tillage without the expenditure of much labour, and the cleansing and enriching of the soil with manures and fertilisers.

Many of the hedgerows and boundaries were made of gorse raised from seeds: but as the bushes tended to become naked at the base, and let the sheep through, they were abandoned for white- and black-thorns. Poor people used to cut the gorse from commons and wastes for fuel to heat their ovens; it was also useful for the drying of malt. I have heard that horses and cattle were fed with the young shoots of the plant, which was cultivated from seeds. Farmers passed the foliage through a rude mill, which crushed the shoots and the spines; it was eaten with chaff, or chopped straw of oats or barley. I have thought that where gorse is plentiful the seeds might be harvested and put to some useful purpose, since they are easily separated from the pods in autumn.

Blackbirds and thrushes, though they do not entirely avoid the gorse for nesting purposes, prefer thorn, box, or the thick mass of the bramble, where it is to be had. Here on the hill, at the base, are both brambles and hawthorns; the gorse is accordingly abandoned to the linnet that revels in the almost impenetrable bushes.

Boys of the village used to take young linnets at four days old to train for singing, and feed them with bread and boiled rape-seed. If they wished the birds to imitate a goldfinch, or a canary, they hung the cage containing the fledglings beneath the one whose song they wished them to acquire. I was told of one who taught a linnet to speak; its tongue, it is said, was split with a threepenny-bit. I have seen the siskin at Harrow Down and at several other points of the Vale. As a visitor it is not common; but it might easily pass unnoticed among the linnets and greefinches.

Badgers periodically take up their quarters upon the down, where they entrench themselves and speedily multiply and form a colony, till war is waged upon them in the interests of local huntsmen and they are dug out and destroyed. In spite of the unremitting persecution, however, individuals contrive to escape; or others, scenting the earth from a distance — for few animals have a better sense of smell than the badger — travelling under cover of darkness, arrive and secrete themselves in the deep buries.

Local tradition credits the badger with exceeding longevity; it is said that individuals will live to be a hundred years old. Gamekeepers tell me thay have taken badgers that had lost all their teeth through age; but a hundred years is a long time for such an animal to survive. I have heard of a badger being grey with age; but this may have been a freak, something like a "black" fox. One also occasionally hears of a "silver" badger, and this might be explained in the same manner. It is by nature a rude and shaggy beast, which gave rise to the proverb "As rough as a badger."

There is a variety of opinions and beliefs concerning the badger in the Thames district, and farmers, gamekeepers and earth-stoppers differ much in their accounts of the animal and its habits. A popular theory is that it hibernates for twelve or sixteen weeks; but individuals are certainly on the move during that time. The heaviest badger of which I have heard was one shot by the old gamekeeper of Besselsleigh; it turned the scale at fifty pounds. The fat of badgers is still accounted of high value for swellings and sciatica. The hindquarters were cured and eaten, being considered equal to the finest bacon hams; the long hairs were used for artists' pencils.

The simplest method of ascertaining whether a badger occupies a bury is to place a little clean straw outside the entrance at evening; if one is within it will be sure to draw the straw inside for its bed before morning. If a terrier is sent in to turn it out the badger will contrive to cast a barrier between itself and the dog and repeat this a number of times. If it is being dug out of sandy soil it will bury itself almost as fast as the men can operate with the spade; but it has no chance of final escape. In fighting a dog it lies on its back and makes use of both teeth and claws; woe to the luckless cur in whose flesh the teeth of the badger become firmly fixed!

Rustics say that a badger has the power of inflating its skin so that the bite of a dog or beating with sticks will not harm it; but a smart blow on the nose will usually prove fatal. If it is desired merely to destroy one without the risk of being bitten, a well-soaped noose is set at the entrance to an earth, and the badger, if it gets its head inside, is fairly certain to strangle itself. It was always held, by the rules of good sportsmanship, that, like the fox, the badger might be hunted, but not deprived of the sanctuary of its earth when dogs failed to dislodge it; and none could justify breaking the soil and digging it out, as is too frequently done at present. Fortunately, there would seem to be no danger of the badger's disappearance by extermination. Many exist throughout the ridge from Wytham to Cricklade, and along the slopes of the chalk downs stretching past the White Horse into Wiltshire.

Longworth is a straggling village, scattered over a wide area, with miles of roads and lanes, and groups of rose-covered cottages. The country is open and slopes southward towards the distant downs, that, with Oriental features, lie basking in the summer sunshine. The soil is light, deep and fertile — warm and "kind," as we say; so that it is an ideal district for gardening and fruit culture. Cherries and apples thrive and yield heavy crops of fruit, and currants are prosperous and prolific. Fields of early spring cauliflowers, untouched by the winter frost, testify to the geniality of the atmosphere on the ridge; whereas in the lower regions of the Vale, where clay predominates, every green herb and plant was blasted and withered by the severe frost and chilling breezes. Ground damp is the principal cause of this, which is abundant above clay and stiff loams; on the gravel lands, even at the river's level, such destructive frost is seldom experienced. Worst of all happens in the small valleys and pockets. There the cold vapours become confined, and though the air, several hundreds of feet above them, may be quite warm on a night in May, chilling frost often occurs beneath and destroys the tender buds and blooms, with all the fair promise of spring-time.

The village church, with lead-covered roof, small tower and enclosure crowded with ivy-covered tombs, stands on the edge of the hill where the road led down to cross the river by the ancient ford. Near by is the manor house and farmstead that stood amid noble elms, whose years were numbered by centuries. A large pool lies between, fringed with fennel, willow-herb and plants of the golden iris. Twittering swallows skim the surface of the lake, darting beneath the branches of the trees.

Briars thrive well in the deep soil of the village; it is by reason of this that the Longworth roses are unsurpassed by those of any other nursery in the country; year after year the gold cup and championship are secured by the local growers. The culture extends to one hundred acres, and these support annually 100,000 roses, which are sold off and the ground cleared and afterwards planted with wheat, which restores the soil to a condition suitable for propagating new plants. Australia, France, America and India order roses from the shores of Isis: what souvenir could be more acceptable to lonely dwellers in far-off countries? I remember the roses of Cawnpore, at their best about Christmas-time, and kept alive during the subsequent terrific heat by flooding the beds with water from the Ganges. The plants were supplied from England; but the means by which they were kept alive in transit is to me a mystery.

The stocks for dwarf roses are propagated on the ground; but the briars for standards have to be sought elsewhere. Gipsies and labourers obtain these from the lanes and hedgerows about the riverside and bring them in bundles to the village, receiving payment at the rate of £5 per hundred. Young, healthy briars are necessary, of from four to six feet in height; and they need to be cut with care, having a small portion of the root stock, but not more than several inches in length. They readily strike when planted in the fertilised soil of the sandy field, and few losses or failures are reported.

The establishment of a hop-garden is more of a speculation than filling a field with roses. The preparation of the ground and setting the plants may not prove necessarily expensive; but the cost of poles and the labour of training the runners are considerable items. A cold, backward spring, a season of drought, or much wet and rough wind might prove injurious, if not disastrous, to the crops; where nothing else is grown the farmer needs to be assured that his labours are not destined to end in total failure.

New land was considered more suitable for hops, sand or light loam above stone being especially preferred. On stiff clay, or wet spongy soil, the plants will not thrive; it would be a waste of time and money to engage in such an experiment. Maple poles for training are often used; but ash are the more durable. Poles of chestnut are more desirable still; but where none of these are to be obtained resort may be had to willows. The young hop-tops from the hedgerows are boiled and eaten in spring, and are held to be excellent for the blood. The housewives of the village have yet much faith in a pillow made of hops to induce sleep in cases of fever or nervous breakdown.

The old Waggon and Horses Inn, on the highroad opposite Longworth, is one of the best-known houses in the Vale. As its name implies it owed its popularity to the fact of its being a convenient halting-place for travellers and teamsters in pre-railway days. One John Kent, waggoner, occupied the inn a century ago; he was noted for a famous turn-out consisting of a large covered wagon and eight horses, which was known far and wide as "John Kent's Team," and "The Longworth Team." His route lay between London, Abingdon and Gloucester, and he crossed the Thames by St. John's Bridge at Lechlade. Farmers and dealers prepared their carcases of meat and waited his arrival at certain stations on the road. Others brought butter, eggs and chickens, carrying them in baskets and panniers on horses and ponies, slung one on either side. He had a rival in the person of one Jim Booseley, who was a professional Thames pilot and steered valuable

Longworth Village, about 1910

cargoes down the river from Cricklade to Oxford. He is said to have had a knowledge of every curve, loop, pool and shallow, and was never known to run aground at high or low water.

If Longworth is famed for the sweetness of its orchards and rose-gardens, Kingston Bagpuize looms larger in the eyes of local sportsmen and hunters of the "ruddy reynard." The kennels of the Old Berks Hunt are here; and here are reared many noble hounds that make the meadows ring from Bablock Hythe to Badbury Hill, and from the White Horse to Wallingford and Wittenham. But the beauty of hounds is discovered in the chase, and kennels are no picturesque feature of the Hunt. The gossip of the meet and many a famous death are here related, with numerous merry scenes and incidents that happen every season about the jovial hunting-field.

A tale is told of the haunted Lodge at Longworth and the extra-ordinary behaviour of a certain table, or tripod, that walked by magic across the floors of the rooms and, if removed, was tame and peaceable till it came to a small stream of water, when it compelled the one carrying it to set it down straightway, or replace it within the Lodge. It was believed that the Duxford witch was the cause of the disturbances, and this was the more firmly held because of the table becoming agitated near the stream, since they say that a hare always trembles at the sight of water, especially by moonlight, and this was the form the witch commonly assumed.

"Where have you got that wood, my man?" asked the Squire who held the Lodge of one of his workmen, meeting him one night bearing a heavy faggot.

"At my back, sir!" promptly replied the workman.

"That's not what I asked you. I'll remember you, Denman!" returned the Squire.

"I hope you will, sir! You never did yet," answered the labourer.

True to his promise, the Squire remembered the incident, and at Christmas the labourer was gratified to receive a gift of a ton of coal and a large joint of beef for himself and family.

Old Moll Jones and Nan Garret "starved" birds on the barley lands, and were provided with muzzle-loading guns and powder, but no shot. In the absence of lead they cut wads and rammed a number of small stones into the barrel, and shooting at rooks on the hedgerow, blew the hat off the head of Farmer Brooks, invisible behind the bushes.

"And who provided you with rifles, and powder and shot, I should like to know?" demanded he, angrily.

"Why, our maester did, to be sure!" answered they.

"Then I call it a most capital action." replied he, his rising temper cooled and wrath abated.

In the village were a number of dissenters, who, having no better place of worship, met on the Sabbath in a barn that stood near the roadside. For want of a pulpit the preacher stood in a chaff-basket, and this, by means of ropes passed over a beam, was drawn up to a height of five or six feet from the ground. In this position he delivered his homely sermon, and at the end the basket was lowered and the company dispersed. It chanced one day that an old soldier, home from the wars, with knapsack and bugle, passing along the road, came to the barn, and, entering in, lay down to sleep upon a heap of straw and covered himself with the materials. Unaware of the presence of the stranger, in the afternoon the congregation assembled as usual. In due course the preacher stood in the basket; willing hands drew the ropes and hoisted him up, then they made fast the cords and sat down to hear the discourse.

The subject chanced to be the destruction of Jericho, and the fall of the city walls at the sound of the trumpet. The eyes of Moll Jones' husband Tom opened wide with astonishment, listening to the narrative, and all the company quivered with excitement. The soldier, awakened with the noise, lay listening to the tale, and, with characteristic cunning and resource, conspired to scare the rustics and make the proceedings more realistic. Reaching for his battered bugle, still unobserved, he put it to his lips and blew a series of thrilling blasts. The congregation fled in a panic, leaving the preacher suspended in the basket. As he attempted to descend the basket overturned and he fell sprawling on the floor using language native to the Vale, but rude and unscriptural.

The tradition of how the Thames willows took the side of the King and assisted in the defeat of the imposter, Perkin Warbeck, who personated the Duke of York and laid claim to the throne, and who was finally hanged at Tyburn, though apparently no more than a piece of superstition or a groundless myth, is much nearer the truth than would be commonly supposed. Of willow poles lopped from pollards that grew by the river-side a special charcoal was prepared that entered into the composition of gunpowder, and was most efficacious for the purpose; so that the willow tree came to be more powerful than oak, iron, steel sword, battle-axe or deadly battering-ram. The King's artillery, that swept many a field and broke down fortresses and towers, depended upon the wood of withies for its destructive agency: who would imagine that a plant so innocent in appearance was capable of promoting such terrible scenes of ruin and devastation?

The small village of Fyfield is indirectly connected with the history of Perkin Warbeck, the Pretender: the old Manor House, with its high, timbered walls, and its setting of elms and chestnuts, is pointed out as having been the residence of his widow. After his death on the scaffold, she was married to one Christopher Ashtone, of Fyfield; her tomb is to be seen in the chancel of the church that stands alongside the Manor House.

A fire broke out in the church in the year 1893 and gutted the interior, leaving only the bare walls and a few relics of tombs and monuments, including the figure of a mailed knight with feet resting upon the backs of two hounds crouching, and a cadaver, or shrouded skeleton, reposing beneath. A hospital or almshouse was founded by the knight whose effigy rests in the church, in 1442. A curious charity survives in the nature of a gift of loaves to the aged poor of Fyfield. This takes place every Sunday in the church, and may not be discontinued; there are, at the present time, about a score of recipients.

The fame of Tubney rested principally in its noble wood, and in the possession of a massive elm tree that stood at the junction of the highway, and was known far and wide as "Tubney Tree." The giant elm, the trunk of which was forty-five feet in circumference, had stood on the site for over six centuries, and had served as a place of worship, for the village assembly, and a roadside mart for untold years. Robbers and desperadoes sheltered beneath its boughs at intervals, waiting to molest the drivers of stage-coaches bound for Oxford or Abingdon; and corpses of thieves and highwaymen were buried with little ceremony below the greensward at the junction of the roads.

Osier-cutting

Chapter 9

THE WEIRKEEPER, BESSELSLEIGH AND APPLETON

Though some might be tempted to envy the weirkeeper his apparently indolent existence and fortunate circumstances, he is much more fully occupied than many would imagine. As soon as summer comes and the fishing season opens he must be on the alert from early morning till late evening, keeping watch over the water in his reach. At all times of the day he must be ready to fill the lock and allow pleasure boats and punts to pass up or down the stream, and even bordering on midnight he is occasionally requested to go to the assistance of some belated traveller, who, lost amid the crooks and curves of the lonely meadow, is anxious to pass the lock and proceed on his way romantically by moonlight. He is, of course, under no obligation to render services of this nature at such an hour, but the knowledge of one in distress makes a powerful appeal, and any assistance given is not likely to go unrewarded. It is to his interest to cultivate the goodwill of all who frequent or make use of the river, though the strict and conscientious discharge of his duties is a matter of some seriousness, and must never be neglected.

The prime function of the weirkeeper is implied in his designation. His principal duty is to attend to the lock and weir, to watch over and regulate the flow of water, especially in winter, and to register depths all the year round. In a dry season the whole of the paddles are kept closed, so that little water passes the weir; in winter they are removed and the lock-doors opened to allow the moving torrent a free passage to the lower level. At such times a strange silence is observed in the vicinity of the weir. On the fall of the water the thunder is resumed, but it gradually diminishes until it approaches the clear, sweet musical note so delicious to hear upon a warm summer's evening.

In addition to attending to the water, opening and closing the lock-doors, and taking tolls, the weir-keeper must patrol the bank, and guard the river as far as his reach extends. He must see that the by-laws relating to the taking of fish are properly observed, prevent fishing in the close season, and guard against the setting of night-lines for eels and other kinds by trespassers and poachers. He has the power of search and arrest in suspicious circumstances, and is a recognised instrument of the law where the interests of the river are concerned. In his official punt he moves up and down the stream, and periodically examines the banks and shores for encroachments and other damage. He naturally comes to know where the largest trout and pike are to be found, and is acquainted with the best pools for chub and barbel. Being trained in river lore, and himself an expert angler, he is worthy to be consulted by the most accomplished sportsmen ; it is not to be wondered at that his friendship and assistance are sought by the majority of those who frequent the banks of the river.

Although he possesses numerous advantages, he is bound by several restrictions, except in places such as Rushey, where the weir is a private possession and not subject to the whole of the laws passed by the river authorities. He must not set traps for eels, use nets, or infringe any of the rules more than another person. He is not permitted to cut weeds, reeds or bulrushes for any private purpose, nor must he allow others to do so; all this is considered as pertaining to "river scenery," and as such is jealously regarded. The reeds and bulrushes also afford protection to fish and wild fowl, though the preservation of the beauty of the margin is the principal object in view. Later in the season the weeds will be cut from the bed with a series of scythe-blades, drawn to and fro up-stream with ropes by men upon opposite banks. After drifting down they are removed from the water and allowed to decay in heaps. Here snipes and other wild birds will resort in winter-time, where they will be sure to obtain a feast of small worms and insects.

The loneliness of the weir-keepr's life may be more apparent than real ; but to any who have not an aptness for the duties it might prove tedious, if not intolerable, upon the upper river. The most remote and solitary weirs are Grafton and Radcot; but even there the keepers would be unwilling to confess that they felt dull and deserted, except in flood-time. Provided with good cottages and gardens, they may let rooms to fishermen and others, if they desire; as a rule there is no lack of visitors and pleasure seekers, of one kind or another, all the year round. Usually the weir-keeper has one or two pleasure boats or punts, which he may let for hire, and which bring him in a welcome return. He may also keep poultry and pigs, which provide him with labour and a source of interest, as well as returning him a respectable profit. From the space enclosed within the lock and the weir he may every summer secure a small stack of hay which someone will be glad to purchase. In the autumn anglers who have spare baits will give them to the weir-keeper, and he, by preserving them in perforated boxes, will have them to dispose of in the winter to any who desire a day's pike-fishing, when no baits are otherwise to be obtained.

A footpath through the meadows from the weir climbs the hill to Appleton and Besselsleigh, hidden amid woods and winding ways

Rushy Weir, Buckland: footbridge and lock house from above, about 1872

between the high road and the river. Both are old villages, and both possess interesting historical relics and materials in the remains of their Manor Houses and monuments. The Bessels were famed for feats of arms, and were formidable in battle and tournament. Edward I and his Queen attended a tournament at Besselsleigh, when one of the Bessels fought with a masked knight, who had previously conquered every opponent, and gained the victory. The old Manor House has now disappeared; but the tiny church is scarcely less ancient. If the warrior knight ever possessed a tomb here it is no longer in evidence. The small gallery beneath the bell turret is curious; curious, too, are the high box pews, Jacobean pulpit, and the Cupids, looking down from beneath the roof. With the artificiality and insincerity of many of the eighteenth-century practices we are familiar. It is said that the stall-like pews in the churches of Besselsleigh and Cumnor had padded seats, and curtains to keep out the draught. Later on they were provided with stoves for use in the winter, and worshippers brought poker and tongs to stir up the coals during the sermon.

The woods and grounds of Besselsleigh harboured herds of deer, and provided sport and entertainment for the King's hunters and many lords, knights and learned men from the neighbouring City of Oxford. The marten cat was a resident here, and the aged keeper of Besselsleigh remembered when the last was taken, some sixty years ago: this is the only instance in which I have met anyone who actually remembered the animal in England.

Appleton is larger and more remote than the village of Besselsleigh. It is famed by reason of its old moated Manor House, of the date Richard I, and especially, in recent times, for its beautiful peal of bells and the skill of its ringers. This is principally a result of the patience and energy of a local family who adopted the profession of bell-hangers and bell-tuners. Gifted with remarkable taste and discrimination, a member of the family first overhauled and tuned and afterwards added to the local peal of bells till by their number, quality and agreement they have no equal in the southern part of the country.

The Whites were village blacksmiths and musicians, and they comprised the orchestra that occupied the gallery in the small church at Besselsleigh. It is related how one Chamberlain White, being short of work at the forge, a century and a half ago, set out for Blewbury, where he was offered employment cutting beans in the autumn. Having no hook, he approached the blacksmith at Blewbury, one John Hunt, who was also a bell-founder, and asked him to make one. Hunt excused himself on the ground of inability; but White said that if he would give him a piece of steel he would soon fashion a hook. This he did to the admiration of Hunt, who, recognising his skilful workmanship, found him employment forthwith. It is said that the same Hunt failed in business owing to his miscalculation of metal in the casting of Blewbury tenor bell. Having prepared the mould and heated the metal, that ran short and the bell could not be completed. A second attempt ended with the same ill-success, for similar reasons. When the moulds had been broken and re-fashioned and the metal heated for the third time, Hunt, in desperation, declared that if the material ran short he would jump in the mould and so make good the deficiency. In commemoration of this the bell was said to bear the following inscription:

> "John Hunt made me
> Blewbury tenor for to be;
> Three times run and three times cast,
> Blewbury's tenor's cast at last."

The popular account, however, is fabulous, for the actual inscription on the bell, I believe, is *Nil Desperandum* ('never give up in despair').

Such was the Appleton blacksmith's first contact with bell-founding; but not till some years later did the family become famous for tuning and hanging: there was no actual bell-founding at Appleton. Beginning with the bells of the village, they put them in such excellent condition by tuning and exchanging that their skill was immediately recognised and their services were sought throughout the country by village clergy, and also by the guardians of proud minster churches. The bells of Hereford Cathedral were re-hung and tuned by these village workmen; and Great Tom of Oxford has received attention at their hands. The oldest bells renovated by the Whites were two turret bells of fourteenth century date. Bells of considerable age are rare in this country; comparatively few are found older than the sixteenth century. Out of 698 bells recently examined in the County of Wiltshire only 63 belong to a period earlier than 1500; 23 were cast in the sixteenth century and all the remainder since that time.

The reason why few bells of ancient or mediaeval date are found is to be explained by the fact of their having been seized from the church towers and cast into cannon during the sixteenth and seventeenth centuries. The Duke of Somerset, by the order of Henry VIII, pretending that one small bell was sufficient for summoning people to worship, stripped hundreds of churches of their bells and sent them to the foundries and arsenals. They were also exported in such numbers that an order was issued in 1547 to prohibit the practice lest metal for gun-casting should run short at home. Private persons and church-wardens also occasionally appropriated bells from the tower and sold them for their own profit. It is possible, therefore, that the account of the charmed bell of Kintbury, buried in a well, contains a certain amount of truth. For what would be more natural then for villagers, proud of a fine bell, on hearing of the spoliation of churches, to remove it from the tower and conceal it, rather than allow it to fall into the hands of robbers, privileged or unprivileged?

Oak for the frame and the wheel, but elm for the headstock is the general modern practice in bell-hanging. The reason of the elm for a headstock is that oak is more liable to split in that position; but elm is never found in the framework. Chestnut was occasionally used in frames in days past and proved but little inferior to oak; this is discovered by its colour, since it invariably turns dark with the process of time. Willow has been found in old wheels; but they are usually of oak, where discovered intact. Good bell-metal consists of copper and tin in the proportion of one of tin to three of copper. The idea that silver entered largely into the composition of bells is a fiction, its effect being to deaden the sound, not to sweeten it. Silver in small quantities has doubtless been admitted: there is a tradition to the effect that when the bells of this village where I am writing were cast a benevolent lady shot a lapful of silver coins into the furnace. I have been told, however, that gold and silver would not mingle with the molten metal, but would be poured off with the dross, so that the foundry-men might benefit and the donors of the gold or silver be not a whit the wiser.

The note of a bell, provided the metal be of ordinarily good quality, is determined by its weight and thickness; a thick bell is by nature sharp and a thin bell flat. To render a sharp bell more flat, therefore, in the tuning it is necessary to make it more thin, and this is effected by chipping the interior of the sound-bow. Similarly, to convert a flat into a sharp it is necessary to reduce the edge, or the rim, until the desired effect is attained; but for a bell that is very thin there would be no remedy except to re-cast it and weight it with additional metal. It is in the tuning of a peal that the skill of the workmen is most evident; without a perfect knowledge of technique and a delicate sense of sound an exact agreement would never be produced. There are peals of bells that are not now, and never were, in tune. Where the bells are of miscellaneous date and origin, and have not been properly examined and tested, this is not to be wondered at; and many churchwardens and clergymen have neither the interest nor the energy to give the matter worthy consideration and make their peal of bells more musical.

In change-ringing the men of Appleton hold the world's record, with 21,363 Stedman Caters rung on the village peal of ten bells in 12 hours 25 minutes, in the year 1922. The eighteenth century witnessed many remarkable performances on bells: in the year 1761 no less than 40,320 changes were rung at Leeds, in Kent, by thirteen men, in 27 hours; but since the performance was spread over two days the feat does not equal that of the Appleton ringers.

I have heard of an old custom of ringing church bells with the intent to mitigate the affects of electricity in thunder-weather, by a kind of counter-vibration. But it may be that the object of ringing the bells was merely to give warning to husbandmen to have regard to their cattle and property in the fields, exposed to the danger of lightning.

The old Manor House of Appleton has recently been in the hands of workmen, who have restored the walls and rendered them more secure by the process of under-pinning. To do this the foundations were excavated, the stone removed, and new materials substituted, the whole being cemented and made thoroughly compact to support the heavy mass of masonry superimposed. The removal of an end wall and the stripping of interiors, which was necessary in order to ascertain the safety, or the danger, of different parts of the building, furnished a convenient opportunity for examining the methods of architects and masons of that early period. A curious and surprising feature of the work was the total absence of true mortar, or cement, from foundation to roof. The outer and inner courses of stones were laid with clay, or marl, and the interiors of the walls were dry-filled. Of any elaborate pointing there was no trace; the clay appeared to have been merely "dabbed" between the joints. The theory of builders that damp necessarily penetrates walls and disintegrates mortar would not seem to apply in this case, unless something were mixed with the clay to render it more durable, of which there is no evidence. Since the building has stood for nearly eight hundred years it must be admitted that the architect and masons were justified by the confidence they placed in their methods and materials. Perhaps a secret of the endurance of the walls is to be found in their massiveness and their perfect poise; but a close scrutiny proves that the work was carefully and skilfully executed. The most striking feature of the Manor House is its beautiful round-headed hall doorway. It also contains an original fireplace, a carved oak chimney-piece, and wainscotting. The massive beams that support the roof and ceilings are of oak; the joists are of elm and continue intact after the passage of centuries.

I used to imagine that the mixing of the blood of bulls with mortar in order to make it hard and durable was no more than a legend, but I find that it was a fact beyond all controversy. An old mason of Cumnor has told me that he often used bullocks' blood in bygone days, and local belief in its efficacy is in no wise diminished. A common use for it in the locality was for the formation of floors in cottages. These were composed of gravel dug from the Cumnor pits and mixed with lime; after treading and ramming with the beetle a coating of bullocks' blood was added, which, they say, made a hard and perfect surface. Where bullocks' blood was difficult to obtain buttermilk was used for the same purpose and produced an effect similar, but somewhat inferior to the other.

The master-mason at Appleton has told me that some years ago he was in charge of restoration work in a church in the Midlands and the vicar insisted that the mortar should be mixed with bulls' blood. This was accordingly done; but it would be difficult to say whether the vicar was influenced as much by a belief in the efficacy of the blood as by a desire to have the work carried out in accordance with a cherished local tradition.

Old Job Lane, who was originally a mason, but who threw his hammer and trowel into the river and spent most of his time at the ancient inn that stood below Newbridge, was famed for the possession of an enormous appetite: it is recorded that he once ate thirty fried eggs, a gammon of bacon, 1lb. of tallow candles and a quartern loaf, and drank a four and a half of cider, and completed the feast within an hour. Credulous people imagined that he was short-witted, and two wags of the village, meeting him one day, made a wager with him that he would not go into the churchyard at midnight and lay his hand on a couple of skulls that had been set upon a flat tomb. When evening came the wags, by arrangement, first entered the churchyard, and, crouching behind the tomb, waited for old Job's arrival. At the appointed hour he approached, and, groping in the darkness, seized one of the skulls. "That's mine!" echoed a hollow voice behind the tomb; but old Job, undeterred, groped again and laid his hand upon the second skull. "And that's mine!" echoed again amid the darkness. "Damme! you caan't have two skulls," returned Job, and, thrusting them into his pockets, he set out to claim his reward.

A pathway led through the churchyard, and it happened that when old Farmer Jenkins died and his grave was opened, in dark November, Job Lane, going home from the inn, losing his way, fell into the pit, and, by reason of his condition, could not get out, but lay there all night. In the early hours of the morning Silas Higgins, the cowman, on his way to milking, passing throught the churchyard, being in a careless mood, and remembering that one of his old companions was buried near, unaware of Job's presence and plight, cried foolishly: "How are you going on down there?" Old Job, hearing the inquiry, gave a piteous moan and replied hoarsely: "Wet and cold," which frightened Higgins to such an extent that he ran home and forgot his cows, so that they were not milked till dinner-time.

Afterwards, when Dick Yeats, the rat-catcher, was found dead in the loft above the stable, half eaten by his ferrets, Job discovered his intrepidity by voluntarily sleeping with the corpse; but his spirit was broken and his nerves shattered as the result of an experience he suffered some few months later. A gate leading into a field was said to be haunted, being frequently observed to open and shut of its own accord, so that horses and cattle shied and would not enter the meadow, and workpeople feared to pass that way. Then Job, who was convinced that he had power to appease the spirit, took a jew's harp and set out for the site; but he had scarcely arrived there and begun his melody when he was struck, as it were, with an electric shock, and the jew's harp flew to pieces in his hand.

A relation of his lived in a small stone cottage that he had inherited from his father and grandfather, who had been miserly in their habits; and when he died, through eating, it is said, a new cheese and a peck of green watercresses, old Job, who had tidings of the event, took away a cart-load of copper coins, which proved to be old ounce pennies, of many pounds in value.

Chapter 10

EYNSHAM, BABLOCK HYTHE AND STANTON HARCOURT

There was a custom, observed for many years at Eynsham, of ringing the church bells at four in the morning during summer and harvest, to call mowers, reapers and labourers to work in the fields. Another local custom was the grazing of cattle in the churchyard, and this has not long been discontinued. I have often been told that cattle, and especially mares in foal, dislike grass from churchyards, and refuse to eat it, as though they were aware of a certain flavour given to the herbage by the presence of the mouldering remains of human beings. The farmer whose cattle were driven into the Eynsham enclosure was otherwise persuaded. He declared that the cows were exceedingly fond of the grass, and that the milk and cream were richer and sweeter than when the herd was driven out to pasture on the meadow lands and the common.

At Eynsham one afternoon in July a pair of labourers, turning swaths of hay beside a backwater, saw a large pike sunning itself below the bank, and one of the men, whose ancestors had been accomplished river-poachers, having a wire about his person, immediately fastened it to the end of a rod, slipped it over the pike's head and shoulders, jerked the fish out of the water and secured it. Upon landing the fish they observed something protruding from one side of the mouth; and after stunning it and opening its jaws they perceived it to be the tail of a very large rat which the pike had only partly swallowed. The discovery of a rat in the gullet of a pike is not extraordinary, being really a natural occurrence; but the sight disgusted the labourers, and though they had hoped for a good square meal they could no longer fancy the feast. They accordingly removed the rat, cut the fish, that weighed eleven pounds, into sections and sold it in the streets of Eynsham for a pot of liquor, extolling the prime condition of the fish and giving a guarantee of its sweet and delicate flavour.

The river-poachers of Eynsham and Cumnor, in addition to

Swinford Bridge, Eynsham: looking south-east from toll-house across bridge to Beacon Hill, about 1900

practising with the wire, made frequent use of the cast-net and secured good hauls of fish, especially perch and roach. The success of this mode of fishing depended upon the skill in making the cast. The net, which was of a circular shape, provided with lines, and weighted with plummets, when properly cast, opened to its full extent and enveloped all within its compass, so that weeds and everything were drawn away as it was closed up with the lines. Such poaching was usually done at late evening, or by moonlight; for though no watch was kept on the river, occupiers of the land would not permit the trespass. It was necessary to have a fair knowledge of the waters; in the deepest pools the nets were of little use, as falling a good way short of the bottom.

The record of such practices has almost died out now, and there are not half a dozen men living on the banks of the river who can remember anything about them. I was told by an aged man of Cumnor and by the gamekeeper of Besselsleigh, both above ninety years, of poaching with the cast-net, and they also remembered the curious old inn that stood at Skinner's Weir. Between this and the drinking-house known as "Tumble-Down Dick," which is said to have stood in the lane at the foot of the hill, a certain understanding existed; but it would be unfair to surmise that drinking, poaching and other forms of lawlessness were in anything like general vogue along the riverside at that or any other time.

How the inn called "Tumble-Down Dick" came by its title I am unable to say with certainty. The house was an old one and no living person remembered it by any other name. There is an account of a pair of clowns taking hay from a rick in the farmyard, one of whom met with a misfortune, and this may bear some relation to the case. As Dick was cutting hay for the cows, Tom moved the ladder and he fell, seeing which, Tom bawled: "Dwoant e' come down the ladder, Dick, 'cos 'e ain't there!"

There is, furthermore, the rhyme:

"Richard and Dick went up the hill,
    And truly I engage,
One was old and the other was young,
    And yet they were both of an age."

Richard was the under-carter, and Dick was his old grey horse. There is not a great amount of ingenuity in the lines, and yet I have heard them quoted appreciatively by simple country people, and with them others more droll or humorous, such as:

"A crow flew over the river
With a roll of raw liver,"

to repeat which quickly and without making an error was accounted some proof of lingual dexterity.

The old ferry at Bablock Hythe is a lonely spot in the winter season, but in the spring and summer it is much visited, being private, cool and peaceful. Here the waters of the river are deep, and famed for shoals of roach of a large size; so that in the autumn, when the weeds decay, which is always the best time for roach, those with a taste for the sport wend their way down the hill, or through the meadows, heedless of the weather, and, having made sure of a supply of refreshments from the inn that stands near the ferry, choose a site and prepare baits and tackle. I have never heard local people pronounce Bablock Hythe correctly; the majority say "Babli Coy," which is easier, as they say "Stan 'Arcut" for Stanton Harcourt, and "Aton" for Eaton. The old men of Standlake and Eynsham used to sing me a plaintive ditty, simple in style and epic in length, concerning the fate of a fair maiden, who, betrayed by a heartless lover, drowned herself in the river, and whose body went floating away till it came to "Ferry Hinksey Town," where it was recovered by sympathetic watermen.

There is a happier story connected with the ferry, which I heard at Northmoor. In the year 1762 an Oxford undergraduate, one William Flowers, in the habit of walking in the locality, came to the ferry, and, seeing a maiden in a punt near the opposite shore, beckoned to her to take him across. Then the maid, by name Betty Rudge, daughter of the innkeeper, acceded to his request, and by her beauty and innocence won the heart of the undergraduate, so that he came often to the inn and in course of time asked her to be his wife. Upon her consenting, with the approval of her parents — for Betty, though a good girl, could neither read nor write — he sent her away for three years to be educated. Before the end of the three years, by the death of his relative, he became Viscount Ashbrook; but he married the innkeeper's daughter at Northmoor Church in 1765, and they lived for some time at a house called "The Ark" on the banks of the river, a short way above the ferry.

Shepherds and ploughmen who sally down from the hill or walk across from the village are attracted not so much by the river as by the reputation of the liquor at the inn. The quietude of the site may possibly make an appeal to them; but they say the ale is better at the ferry than it is in the neighbouring village or on the hill-side.

I have heard of a curious error made at the ferry some years ago, which might have been attended with tragic results, but it ended fortunately. A gentleman student at Oxford — an American, and a stranger to the locality — who used to drive two horses and a light chaise, approaching the river from the Cumnor side, mistook the ferry for a ford and drove his horses into the water. They, being in no wise alarmed, took the flood bravely and swam to the opposite shore, drawing the chaise and its occupant and making a landing without difficulty.

The village of Stanton Harcourt, as its name implies, is of Saxon foundation, being so called from the huge "stanes," or stones, that

Bablock Hythe with old ferry, looking west, about 1880

stand amid the cornfields on the south-west side. The stones are probably the remains of monuments once set up by prehistoric people.

The church is partly Norman, to which doorways and windows testify; and there are other rare and beautiful relics, among them a famous Early English chancel screen, partly painted with figures, the portions of an old font, an alms chest, brasses and fragments of thirteenth-century stained glass windows.

In the chancel and the transept are several handsome monuments, but those of the Harcourt mortuary chapel possess the greater interest, both by their superior beauty and by their historical associations.

> "There are twenty of Harcourt's barons bold
> Lie buried within that proud chapelle,"

and, indeed, few churches possess shrines more noble and dignified, or with a more magnificent spirit of solemn and stately repose.

The ancient inn, with its spreading walnut tree and sturdy, iron-bound stocks nearly, was' famed for its generous home-brewed beer. Once I had tasted it and admired its choice flavour, I wanted to know how to make it. To this end I spent an evening with the landlord and he taught me the secret and the whole formula of the trade.

"Many people," said he, "use but three things in brewing — malt, hops and water — and of them make three kinds of liquor: strong beer, fresh beer and sims."

"Strong beer I know, and fresh beer I know, but sims I do not know. What is sims?" I queried.

"It sims like beer, but it isn't," answered he.

"Then," said I, quoting an old rhyme that I once heard at harvest home,

> " 'This puts me in mind of Dame Trot when she began to brew:
> She took half-a-peck of stale malt and half-a-peck of new;
> She made forty gallons of black strap,
> And forty gallons of wivvy wink,
> And forty gallons of terrible drink,'

and this must be some of the terrible drink."

"Brewing is like a fat pig; it's all profit. You can sell everything, even to the skimmings," proceeded the landlord.

"Teach me how to make it," I replied.

"A bushel of malt and one pound of hops will make eighteen gallons of beer and nine gallons of ale; but if you want body in it just do as I tell you. Boil your water for the mash and empty it into the tub, steeping the hops in a separate vessel. When the steam has gone off the tub, so that you can see your face in the water, and not before, put in your malt and stir it, then cover with a sack and leave it for nine hours, giving it a rout now and then. In the meantime, clean out your casks and have your cooling-tub ready. Draw off the sweet-wort, set the grains aside for the ale, put the liquor, with the hops, into the boiler, which must be iron or copper, and not zinc, and simmer for one hour. And now, if you want extra good beer, tap an old sycamore tree with an augur and get a quart of juice and mix it with the liquor; or get a bunch of carrots, parsnips, or beetroot, split them with a knife, and throw them into the boiler. At the end of an hour strain into the cooling-vat, saving the hops, and mix a dozen pounds of coarse brown sugar, or treacle, with the sweet-wort and put in the barm at blood-heat. The following morning take what barm you require, put it into strong bottles and bury it in the earth, where it will keep as long as you please; and remember that barm wants changing for seed, and that a tablespoonful of barm with a little brandy is the best thing in the world for a stoppage and has saved many a man's life. If you wish you can put it in the cask the same night; but it will be better to wait for twenty-four hours, at least. Well cork the barrel and fill to the bung-hole, saving a little to make up for each day's waste. Look at the barrel to see that it ferments. At the end of a fortnight take two handfuls of dry hops and put them into the barrel, stir with a stick and bung up. To make new beer appear old pour a little vinegar into the bung-hole; but to be good and strong it needs to be kept from six to twelve months; that is, from October till October comes again."

There was an old jest which said that the natives of Northmoor and Standlake were born with webbed feet and once possessed tails, like tadpoles. The truth of the matter undoubtedly is that someone or other once observed that the inbaitants needed to be born with webbed feet and to be equipped with tails like tadpoles in order to exist amid local conditions. This has reference to the very low and flat nature of the land lying east of the junction of the Thames and Windrush, which was once a marsh and a waste. The name Standlake, they say, merely perpetuates the fact of a lake having stood here; and Northmoor marks the site of the adjacent moor or swamp. As would be expected, there is a Southmoor; this is on the opposite side of the river, and denotes a waste that formerly stretched away to the banks of the small river Ock.

A feature of the locality is the number of moated dwellings, which may merely point to the solitude of the situation and the survival of the moat as a means of protection when in other parts, more accessible and more frequented, the moats had been filled in, so that no evidence of them any longer remains. Two such houses stand in close proximity, one being the old Northmoor Manor, and the other known as Gaunt House. The old Rectory Farm was moated; so was the ancient inn bearing the sign of the Dun Cow. The church is Early English in style with an old lead-lined font, a narrow gallery, and a quaint bell-loft. It is claimed that a subterranean passage connected Gaunt House with the Northmoor Manor; if such a thing ever existed it could only have been traversed by swimming and diving, for it would certainly have been filled with water for the greater part of the year.

Both houses were said to be haunted and under the domination of a powerful witch, who lived at Northmoor and assumed the shape of a white calf.

The curious excrescences often observed growing upon the trunks of elm trees in the Vale are called locally "witches' butter," and are said to be caused by the churning-stick of the witch, whatever that may be understood to imply. I remember being told not long ago by a member of the medical faculty that the growths bear a relation to the occurrence of cancer among human beings. In a district where they abound, cancer, said he, is almost certain to be prevalent; but I have never taken steps to establish or disprove the truth of the statement.

Perch are fond of assembling at a deep inlet and below locks and weirs, the reason being that they obtain an abundance of food where there is a flow of fresh water. This explains the prevalence of fine perch at the junction of the Windrush, below the walls of Newbridge, where I have stood and watched boys who lived at the inn take excellent fish in June, almost as fast as they could bait their hooks and let them into the water. Perch taken there are invariably in good condition, and they are certainly of superior flavour to others I have tasted caught in pools not far removed, which is to be accounted for by the large volume of fresh water continually pouring in, bearing all kinds of worms and insects. The perch-fisher does not always meet with a uniform amount of success, for perch may behave in an extraordinary manner, avoiding the bait of the angler altogether, or taking it with much greediness. I saw a farm labourer near Tadpole with forty-two perch that he had taken in just over two hours; and I remember that I once took seventeen perch in less than thirty minutes in a small lake. They say that perch in a shoal will sometimes continue biting till every one is taken; and that, I imagine, is what happened in the case referred to, for though I often fished in the same place I never had a bite from a perch there afterwards. I recently saw one take a perch with a live roach while trolling for pike, and I observed that the perch was but little, if any, larger than the bait it attempted to swallow.

The fame of the Windrush as a trout stream is not as high as it has been. In the mill-ponds pike have been allowed to increase, to the detriment of trout; and the fact that from Witney the river flows by three channels, while it affords a greater length of water, it detracts from the value of the stream as a fishing preserve, since pools are less numerous, and less deep, and there would be no protection from the ravages of the otter or the activity of poachers if they should set out with the intent to trespass. The lamprey is a successful bait for trout on the lower Windrush; this abounds in the soft mud of the Thames and its tributaries.

I asked an old poacher of Standlake if he had ever caught trout by the process of tickling, but he replied that he had not done so, and he did not believe that it was reasonably practicable. His own favourite method was that of taking them in holes of the banks, to which the fish resort, especially in wet weather. This may sound rather pleasant; but though I have never thought it worth while to indulge in the practice, I knew those who regularly went to the stream on pouring wet afternoons to trout-catching, which was by taking them with the hands in holes where the fish had gone, literally to shelter from the rain. The old men say that fish, like all other creatures, lie down to rest and to sleep, and perhaps they do, and this may possibly be the secret of the success of the trout-taking; but I give no guarantee that the account is strictly trustworthy.

The current of the Windrush is swift, hence its name; it was therefore well-adapted for the turning of water-wheels and grinding corn, and it is a pity that the power could not now to some extent be utilised. Five mills stood on its banks between Newbridge and Witney; but though they have not been dismantled they do nothing beyond crushing corn for poultry. The mills are blamed at the present day for preventing the escape of water in flood-time; and doubtless, with their bays and pounds, and narrow side-gates, they do help to hold up the water and flood the meadows, many thousands of acres of which are covered after a heavy rainfall. While being conducted over one of the local mills and shown the massive wooden machinery, I was careful to take the opportunity of examining the hand of the miller to see if he were of the honest kind, since they say that every honest miller has a tuft of hair growing from the centre of the palm, but I did not observe that he differed from the generality of men of his profession.

> "Oh the miller, I doubt not, he is a cheat;
> He takes double toll, and he changes the wheat."

I have heard a heartless story of a miller deemed so covetous that, having made a fortune, he drowned himself in his pond, in order, as he hoped, to obtain the first mill in Paradise.

It was customary for the Rector of Standlake to preach a sermon once a year standing at the head of a barrel of beer in an inn named "The Chequers." The reason of the practice was that on the position occupied by the inn there once stood a religious house, and the barrel marked the site of an ancient altar. At the Reformation a sermon was substituted for the Mass; but since the inn has now disappeared the custom has become obsolete.

Chapter 11

FLOODS, GIPSIES AND LOCAL BELIEFS

There used to be an immense number of crayfish in the upper river and about the lower reaches of the Windrush, the Evenlode, the Leach and the Coln. Every·small brook and dyke, in fact, contained an abundance of them; and in the months of August and September, after they had spawned, which was the best time for eating them, the young men of the village went regularly to take them with nets, or with the hand, feeling in all the holes of the bank where the water was shallow. The best results were obtained in old walls of bridges, or locks of the river, or canals; and many a sharp pinch have I felt from the claws of a monster, thrusting my fingers between the stones at the wooden swing-bridge to draw the crayfish from their lurking-place. A hard pinch, though not entirely pleasant, might be a fair token of success, for withdrawing the hand as the claws closed usually enabled one to secure the fish; but it must have been done speedily, for the creature had a habit of loosing its hold and again backing shrewdly between the stones.

The best catch of crayfish I ever saw was on the River Leach, between Lechlade Mill and Little Faringdon; but they had been taken with the hand from holes in the bank one wet afternoon, and several good trout figured among them; they totalled over half a sackful. As boys we used to make "bob-nets," i.e., nets attached to a wire hoop about fifteen inches in diameter, and bait them with a portion of a stale herring. In deep water, such as the Thames, a common method of catching crayfish was to take several large rough faggots, and enclose in the centre of them pieces of stale liver, then, having weighted the faggots with stones, to lower them in a convenient place, such as beneath a bridge, or near the wall of a weir. The faggots were usually left for two or three days; and one might be sure of drawing up several hundreds of fish entangled with the wood, if one was not too dilatory.

Another practice was to obtain the carcase of a sheep, or calf, if possible, and having taken out the entrails, and secured it with a rope, to lower it into a pool, when it would certainly be packed full of fish by the following morning. There is a dark mystery concerning the fate of crayfish, for about twenty years ago they nearly all died in the region of the upper river, owing, it is supposed, to some kind of disease peculiar to crustaceans.

Summer or winter a moderate flood stopped all the mills on the lower Windrush; for when the water is high on both sides of the wheel that ceases to revolve, so that an excessive supply is no better than having the stream low. As a rule, though Thames floods may be deep and extensive — and he who has not seen the river in flood from the top of Faringdon Folly or Beacon Hill has missed a memorable sight — they cause little havoc or damage unless they occur in the summer season. The nearer we approach the river's source, i.e., above Lechlade, the swifter the rise, and the fall: at Duxford, Standlake and Eynsham the rise is more gradual; but when it occurs it signifies that some days, if not weeks, will elapse before the meadows are again visible.

Thames folk say, rather curiously, in respect of floods, "Soon down, soon up"; by which they mean that they prefer to see the water disappear gradually, and not for the river to make a sudden fall, or, they say, it will be sure as suddenly to rise agin. This is exactly the opposite of what we hear of snow; for if that lies a long time before melting, people on every hand are heard to observe "This snow's waiting about for more"; and the frequency with which the prophecy is fulfilled is not to be disputed. Very often a snowstorm passes above the Vale, but falls upon the Downs, and the villager, viewing the gleaming slopes, observes to his neighbour: "Tha bin white-washin' they owl' 'ills again durin' the night. There'll be plenty o' slush for the yeows an' leetle lambs presently."

Whereas a normal flood in winter is harmless, unless it reaches the ploughed fields, in the month of June it may cause very considerable damage, and even totally ruin grass and other crops on the low-lying lands. Wise farmers at such times send their cattle away, especially their milking cows and mares; they say that the scum on the grass "rots" the stomachs of the beasts. Others, before turning out the cows to graze, drench them with a mixture of strong ale, and repeat this every day for a week or a fortnight.

I suppose that Thames weather differs little from what is experienced elsewhere, and local saws are the same as those in use in other quarters. "Wind in the south, in the rain's mouth," is a maxim that is fairly general. Here, in reference to the daily forecast, we say:

"Rain afore seven, dry afore 'leven"; and
"'Tween one and two, see what the day'll do."

"If the oak's out before the ash
We shall only have a splash;
But if the ash is out before the oak
We are bound to have a soak,"

is a rhyme much quoted, but the prophecy, like others, is not always literally fulfilled. It is held that the position of the wind during the three days from March 18 to 21, and the state of the weather at that time, is a fair indication of what may be expected till Midsummer Day; and when the early summer is inclined to be wet and windy labourers adopt a philosophic attitude and say: "Count 't'ull be no better now till aater the turn o' the daays."

Labourers remark that "white rain" gives disease to potatoes; by this I imagine they mean a kind of soft warm thunder-rain, when the drops are very large and lucid.

"A dripping June puts all things in tune," but this is not meant to refer to a wet season, for, as an old labourer only recently remarked to me, "I never knowed a dry summer borrow from a wet un yet, in my time."

"Drat this yer raain! 'T'ull drive I craazy if it don' soon take up an' be fine," remarked John to the old road-mender, meeting him one day in the village.

"Waal, a know, John, 'tis summat to do to put up wi' 't; but if you takes perticler notice you'll see as we mos' 'n ginerally do get some sort o' weather just along now," returned he, pleasantly.

Concerning the report of a pike over forty pounds in weight said to have been taken in a pool above Newbridge, and another monster of almost equal dimensions being somewhere in the waters at the present time, I have made many inquiries of river-men and labourers, landlords of inns, lock-keepers, rough-looking customers and respectable gentlemen, and the result is that I am strongly inclined to believe the account. Young people, I observe, are usually incredulous or sarcastic at the speech of their elders; but I have conversed with many thoughtful and serious old men dwelling on the banks of the river, and they all agree in declaring that large fish have from time to time been taken out of it.

In an inn at Bampton, I heard of a pike of such a size that no one of the party at the time had a wire large enough to slip over its head, and which, when taken, after weeks of search, was "as large as a gate-post, blind on one eye, its mouth full of hooks and broken tackle, and a hundred years old, if it was a day."

"Green" water is considered the best for fishing in the river, and "black" water, i.e., after a flood, the worst; but perch usually bite ravenously after a flood in summer, before the water has become properly normal. River-men say the the flood washes away a great part of the ordinary food of the fish, and in the absence of this it does not hesitate to take the bait. The best perch are usually taken from the deeper waters, and it is wise, if fish of two or three pound weight are desired, to use a ledger or a paternoster. Where the centre of the river is clear, and weeds extend from both sides, the bait is best dropped immediately near the weeds, because the perch will be feeding there. Tench like a quiet pool, preferably a deep backwater; the old disused

A countryman, probably a mole-catcher, about 1881

course of the river at Duxford contains a few fine holes and I know that capital tench have been taken there. The ruffe is sometimes mistaken for a diminutive perch; a local name for this is the "daddy." The prick of its spines is accounted poisonous, so that boys handle it with care, and when they have taken one usually lose no time in returning it to the water.

The gipsies who camped on the common and in the shady lanes round about Harrow Down were skilled fisher folk, but they had no knowledge of angling, being proficient with net, wire and spear. They also made themselves rude boats or canoes, out of willow wood, and fashioned a kind of blunt sword of stout hoop iron. Equipped in this manner they moved up and down the river, and when they saw a large pike or chub they steathily approached it and dealt it a heavy blow with the implement, stunning it or breaking its back with the stroke. The chief of the tribe had a lovely daughter who was crowned "Queen of all the Gipsies," and she married a handsome young farmer, whose father was a wealthy squire and landowner. Both the chief, who was by profession a rat-catcher, and his lady, who told fortunes and was a kind of local physician, went to the wedding and stayed several days at the feast; and while their daughter lived in a grand stone-built house, they remained under the hedge in a smoky little twig tent.

The old woman, who went by the name of "Liney," was almost as dark in the skin as an Indian. She smoked a short black clay pipe, made her own medicines of the marsh mallow, comfrey, nettle and woundwort; and she carried besides a store of badger's fat, or that of the viper, for anointing sores and wounds, in the treatment of which she was considered to be eminently successful. I have heard that she was particularly skilful in curing the mumps, which she did by anointing with badger's fat and gentle massage, taking care always to rub away from the throat, never towards it. At her death — she lived to be one hundred and one — the common was black with mourners, who assembled from every quarter of the Vale, and the proceedings terminated in a feast and wake, which was observed for a week, after which the company dispersed and the relics of the family soon afterwards deserted the district.

As we know, and have somewhere or other mentioned, not gipsies alone had resort to herbs of the hedgerow and other plants for the making of medicines, but every cottager had a knowledge of the value of herbs and simples, the bark of trees, and the fat of animals. An indiscriminate use of them would naturally prove injurious, and so we sometimes hear of such and such a one being half-poisoned, or made very sick by drinking dandelion tea, nettle broth, or a decoction of dock-root or mandrake. The fault was that not one, but perhaps twenty doses were taken, enough reasonably for a week or a fortnight; and we are aware of what might happen if a patient, having obtained a full bottle of medicine from the surgery or the chemist, should swallow the whole the same night without dilution.

Strange and curious, nevertheless, and of dubious virtue were some of the remedies in use along the Thames-side; while others, beyond all doubt, were salutary and valuable. I know a cripple man who suffered severely with rheumatism at one time, and he was much addicted to the use of oak-bark, and professed unbounded faith in the remedy. This he obtained from boughs and trees in the hedgerows or woods, and, having stripped off the inner parts, boiled them and drank the liquor in moderate quantities. His old wife was also in the habit of preparing several kinds of herb teas and liniments, among them those derived from cow-parsley — great chervil — "pellitory of the wall," and ground ivy. For swellings and inflammation she kept a store of hedgehog's fat, the animals from which it was obtained having been roasted and eaten.

I once saw an old man with long snowy locks at Inglesham, gathering ivy from a pollard ash-tree, and when I inquired what he would do with it he informed me that he was about to boil it to make tea, which he described as a famous thing for the liver. I had never heard of the use before, and told him so; but he reminded me that many kinds of birds feed upon the berries, and are always light and merry. His grandmother, said he, had performed the office of nurse to the village, that is, in midwifery, and liked nothing so well as rhubarb tea and elder-water for her patients. Linseed and camomile, boiled in milk, also found favour in her sight; and, instead of smelling-salts, the dried root of the mandrake, carefully pounded, and the flour sifted through fine muslin.

For blood-poisoning, nothing was held more efficacious than boiled carrot, mashed, and made into a poultice; and for burns, scraped potato, applied raw, the juice of which is held capable of immediately allaying inflamation. Primrose ointment was another excellent thing for burns and sores of every description; and for a severe cold on the chest, a tallow plaster, made by saturating thick brown paper with melted tallow and applying it as hot as it was possible for one to bear. Marigold tea was a famous thing for measles, so also was hot beer, intended in its effect to drive out the measles from those afflicted: tea made from garden rue was used for the same purpose. For dysentery, local women were accustomed to make tea from thyme; and I remember that my grandmother, if we chanced to have the ear-ache used to roast a small onion and put it into the ear at bed-time. The old gipsy woman, before mentioned, had a specific for sore eyes, which was spittle, applied with the finger; and I have evidence that this was a remedy very commonly recognised. If you had a portion of dust or a hay-mote in your eye, your nearest neighbour or companion turned up the lid and licked it out with his tongue.

In the winter-time a cow, having given birth to a calf, received as a drench a quart of hot beer; and if she had sore teats they were bathed twice or thrice a day with liquor in which had been boiled a quantity of marsh mallows. Mallows, in fact, were in high favour, being given to horses and all kinds of cattle, and they were good to cure toothache in men and women. For sprains and wounds rain-water and snow-water were held to be efficacious; a "rain-water poultice" was warranted to cure a black eye, and was good to wash the wounds of back-sworders and wrestlers. The old women of the village, they say, used to melt snow and keep it in bottles expressly for this purpose.

Most people will have some knowledge of "tea-kettle broth," which may be taken in the place of a meal at bed-time, or as something to soothe the stomach after a process of purging. This is made merely by pouring boiling water from the kettle upon bread and adding salt and pepper to taste. To improve it still further, a little butter or cream may be added; in any case the dish will be mildly medicinal in its effect upon the stomach.

Local people make use of a series of epithets by which they denote the particular features of the villages and hamlets on the north bank of the river hereabout. I claim nothing for their elegance, nor can I at this time vouch for their literal accuracy, for they are all old, and mainly refer to a condition of things such as existed in all probability before the enclosing of the common lands. They say — or they used to say — "Bampton in the Bush, Ashton in the Rich, Cote in the Ditch, Shifford Gate-Posts, and Muddy Standlake." The first epithet is clear, and needs no explanation; but the others are ambiguous: what they imply I received from a greybeard at Aston, and he had heard them quoted by his grandfather.

"Ashton in the Rich" referred to the prosperous condition of the village of Aston, or Ashton, which was famed for its wealthy yeomen, and also for its valuable ash timber. "Cote in the Ditch" merely signified the low position of the hamlet of Cote; but it might also refer to its famous old moated manor and farm-houses. "Shifford Gate-Posts" testified to the gateway of the old town, of which nothing remained but the posts, a century and a half ago; and "Muddy Standlake" referred to the condition of the streets of that village by reason of its multitude of cows, which were pastured daily on the common that extended alongside the river.

The gravel lands of Aston, by which the local yeomen waxed rich, lay high and dry of the river, were well-drained with streams and dykes, "kind" and early. The native breed of sheep was thrifty, and bore excellent fleeces, and I have always been told that the people were well clothed and well fed, light-hearted, gay and musical. A merry feast, with games and dancing, fell in the middle of July, and the loaves baked and eaten at that festival were to be made of flour ground from wheat harvested and threshed before that date, which affords proof of the earliness of the local season.

Rats and bats abound at Chimney and Shifford, with hedgehog and weasel, nimble stoat, and white and brown owl; and I heard one speak of a polecat lurking in the withy beds in the neighbourhood of the old moated mansion at Cote. I often see the great bat hawking near the river, and I imagine it to be as frequently met with here as the small or common kind. Labourers say that it follows them with the intent to injure their eyes; and I actually heard a report of a bat having struck a young woman in the face, but the contact may have been accidental.

An old man told me once that the bat would suck the blood of sleeping people, entering the bedroom by the open window and lodging on the legs in the summer-time; and he said that the bat would gorge itself with blood, and yet suck it so cleverly as not to wake the sleeping person. I tried many times to obtain further evidence of this: but though I found that most people disliked and feared bats, they were unaware of the blood-sucking. At Highworth, however, a farm labourer told me that a bat one night entered a room of his cottage, where children were sleeping, and split the toenail of a young girl; and he offered to show me the foot of the child, but I begged to be excused from making the examination.

While I was talking to a farmer near his pigsties, a large rat made its appearance at the far end, and the farmer, having his gun, immediately shot it, with the remark that he had been waiting for that particular specimen. Upon taking it up we found that it had but one leg and three stumps, and yet, notwithstanding this fact, it was both in good condition, and ran as nimbly, apparently, as any other of its kind. This had no doubt been in a trap three times and effected its escape by gnawing off the wounded leg above the fracture. Those several adventures had made it "trap-shy," and in the absence of ferrets powder and shot were invoked to secure its destruction.

People in these parts have a simple and curious device for warding off rats from their chicken pens and nurseries, which is to keep guinea-pigs in boxes or hutches and set them at various points about the farmyard. They say that rats dislike the peculiar noise made by the guinea-pig, mistaking it probably for that of the ferret; but they may also be suspicious of the scent of the animal. The acute sense of smell of the rat is not always taken into account by those who would ensnare it with iron gins, and consequently, though the trap be set with care and placed in the run, nothing ever touches it, unless it be a hedgehog, or perhaps a mole, wandering in the darkness. The reason is that the rat can smell the hand that set the trap; so, in order to obviate this and stand a better chance of success, it is expedient to use a pair of leather gloves in the process.

It is known that hedgehogs are fond of apples, and the sweeter and juicier they are the better they will be appreciated. When the fruits fall from the trees in autumn the hedgehog visits the orchard and carries them away to the shed, or the hedgerow, and makes a small store; I once saw a gallon of apples that had been deposited in this manner. They say that the hedgehog sucks the milk of cows and occasionally injures their teats, and there is no doubt whatever about it, though it may not be of frequent occurrence. Local people are invariably well-disposed towards the hedgehog and encourage it in their gardens; and village bakers never lose the opportunity of acquiring one, or several, if possible, for their services in destroying beetles and cockroaches, which are attracted by the flour and the heat of the ovens. But hedgehogs prefer liberty, and will not be compelled to feed at the bidding of a master; and therefore it happens that you may seldom or never keep a hedgehog in your buildings or garden, for it will certainly disappear. I remember a labourer who kept a hedgehog indoors, and, having lost sight of it, he supposed that it had escaped; but it was subsequently discovered on a ledge a considerable way up the chimney.

To skin the hedgehog, labourers used first to scald it in order to remove the bristles, when the remainder of the operation might easily be performed. Another mode of dealing with the hedgehog was to make a wood fire, and, having obtained a fair heap of embers, to bury the body completely in them and allow it to bake, then to remove the skin and entrails and consume as much of the remainder as was required. This, I believe, was the method principally employed by gipsies; but farm labourers preferred to skin them and stuff them with breadcrumbs and thyme. Treated in this manner the dish was savoury and nutritious, as I am able to testify; for I have partaken of both roast hedgehog and roast porcupine, which is of similar flavour, but the flesh is richer and rather more indigestible.

Godstow Bridge

Chapter 12

THE RIVER AND ITS PEOPLE

The course of the river from Newbridge to Tadpole is long and lonely, but the meadows are open and spacious and the air and prospect exhilarating. Looking towards the wooded spur of the hill above the broad fields, with herds of black and white cattle, and troops of horses galloping in the distance, I often feel transferred to a region far more ample than the Thames Valley. I have seen the river rushing down in its sedgy banks with a current almost as swift as a rapid, and the tall white sail of a boat swaying to and fro in the wind, passing momentarily out of view behind the willows, and afterwards sweeping up the long arm northward to approach the lock at the end of the cutting, the white foam racing from the bows and scattering like snow upon the stooping bulrush and hempnettle. The calm summer noon is best; or evening, when the sun sinks behind the pine woods that clothe the distant ridge, and meadow and river lie silent and peaceful beneath the warm light reflected from clouds floating high above the glowing horizon. But it is no test of a river-lover that he should take pleasure in the summer season merely. In black rain, driving sleet and snow I have stood upon the bridge and looked on the water, loitering for no purpose, and yet under a certain compulsion, as though there were an affinity between the river and myself which I dare not disregard nor attempt to put asunder. This spirit, or feeling, whatever it is, I have attempted to analyse; and I have been led to ask myself what is the reason of my behaviour, and whether the experience is real or imaginary. At the end of it all I am driven to confess that I understand but little of the subtle influences by which I am governed, and yet I find myself continually yielding to the same mysterious impulse.

The journey by barge from Oxford to Lechlade was divided into three daily stages of about ten miles each. The first was from Oxford to Bablock Hythe, the second was from Bablock Hythe to Tadpole, and the third brought the vessel and its cargo safely to the Lechlade wharf, above the Ha'penny Bridge. This time-table was subject to certain modifications, since allowance needed to be made for accidents, such as running aground, springing a leak, becoming fixed on a weir and so forth. I have heard of other mishaps, as when a boatman was swept off his deck with the rope and drowned in the boiling surge of the weir; and on another occasion one fell and was crushed to death between the bow of his boat and the wharf as he was drawing alongside with a full freight of corn.

When a boat became fixed in a shallow, word had to be passed to the next weir up-stream and a "flash" of water was asked for. The weir-keeper, therefore, opened his gate for a few moments only, and the "flash," flow, or wave passed down the banks. Waiting its approach, the bargeman, immediately he observed it, prepared to start forward, and in this way the shallow was crossed. If he loitered and was slow in taking advantage of the "flash," he would need to make a second request to the weirkeeper, and this might have caused unpleasantness; for in dry seasons weirkeepers had not water to waste upon such as were idle or dilatory. The water often ran shallow at Radcot, in the summer time, and boats frequently became stranded beneath the arch of the old bridge. The next lock was Grafton, a mile or more distant; but beyond that, to Eaton, a good store of water was usually held, and if the boatman and weirkeeper were acquaintances, a liberal quantity was set free to help the navigator over his difficulties. During the summer bargemen slept on the decks of their craft, or on the banks; but when the conditions were unfavourable they needed to shelter at the tavern. In regard to this the old landlord of the Tadpole Inn had a singular reputation, for he would never under any pretext provide accom- modation for such as were strangers, but left them to shift for themselves as best they were able.

It is a picturesque old cottage at Rushey perched on the small island between the lock and the weir, with its high elms and willows, its lawns and arbour, and walls stuck over with heads of monsters taken from the pools — pike, chub and barbel. A real retreat is this, a fisherman's paradise — full of pleasant sights and sounds, of slumberous waters, blackbirds' songs, the redshank's sweet wild whistle, and the flap of the heron's wings.

In days past the stream was crossed by a ford at Rushey, and the road ran northward to Bampton-in-the-Bush, which is an old-fashioned little town, quite as remote as its name implies, but of a strange and curious interest. In Saxon times it gave its name to a Hundred that contained the towns of Burford and Witney, and from this fact it may be concluded that Bampton, that is, they say, the "tree town," was the most important in the neighbourhood. Its grand old church, with the noble spire, is not to be equalled by any other in the Vale, so that the pride of the inhabitants on that account is to be tolerated. The place was noted for its fellmongery, and no other town in England had such a trade for leather jackets, gloves and breeches as Bampton. We have had some notice before of this great activity with skins and hides, where we spoke of the exploits of the Bampton deer-stealers; and the aged men of

Buckland knew much of the matter, for their fathers and grandfathers had fed the deer that drew the robbers forth to cross the river and carry them away, and, no doubt, had knocked out the brains of many in their attempts to defend the bucks and does. The industry has come to an end in recent years — that is, since the decline of the Buckland herd — and the tan-pits are closed; but the great number of people bearing the surname Tanner is proof of what has been said concerning the matter. A noble castle stood west of the town, and, in the market-place, a venerable hawthorn, said to have been a thousand years old, where for centuries mummers, "pace-eggers," and the Whitsun Morris dancers held their merry games, and several other curious local festivals and ceremonies were observed.

Tradition says that King John built Bampton Castle when he desired to have a residence here during those times in which he came to hunt the deer and wild boars that were plentiful in the Vale. In the age of its Morris dancing Bampton is probably without a rival; and it is claimed for the Whitsun games that they have been observed here for three hundred and eighty years without interruption.

Near the river, there grows a quantity of "black withy," that has no beauty of foliage, though it is tough and strong, and of some service in the manufacture of wicker work. This withy, at the end of June, produces an abundance of seed contained in a kind of pod, which, when ripe, bursts and falls, covering the ground with beautiful white down, very soft and sweet, and delicious to the touch. This willow-cotton, as it is called, used to be gathered in days past and spun by the poor cottagers, and I am told that it was, furthermore, used for pillows and cushions. The black poplar yields a similar cotton. There was a kind of thread that was made of boiled sinews of beasts, and for strong sewing local people used the skin of an eel, cutting it skilfully into very fine shreds. "Patch by patch neighbourly, but patch upon patch beggarly," we say hereabout; and I have heard housewives observe, in repairing a seam that had been rent, "This was sewed with a red-hot needle and burning thread," referring, of course, to the poor quality of the materials employed.

Withy is useful for gates and hurdles. Ash-wood is used also for hurdles, but willow is much lighter for the shepherd to carry; accordingly, in the Vale, since willows are plentiful, shepherding is easier than upon the downs, where, because willows do not grow, the hurdles are made of ash cut in the woods and copses. I have heard of a curious use to which willow wood was put in former times. They say that it was employed in the division of mill-stones from the rude cylinder into which the rock had first been hewn, by the following process. The cylinder was first bored with a series of holes all round where the division was to be made, and then into these holes were fitted pegs of withy wood that had been dried in an oven, after which the whole was well watered, and the withy, in expanding, burst the stone as desired.

Although there is an abundance of "snop" withy in the neighbourhood of the river, it has no great value as fuel, and any cottager would prefer hawthorn, in spite of the inconvenience in handling, since it burns better and gives much more heat than the other. Dwellers by the river would not burn elder-wood, accounting it unlucky to do so, and when I sought a reason for the belief the old man whom I addressed replied that elder was considered not a wood but a weed. Local people are also careful never to burn bones, to do which is considered a sign of death.

The old Vicar of Northmoor was "a good passen," who "never went to see anybody," and, "like Paul Pry, he carried an umbrella wet or dry." In the pulpit he admonished his parishioners and warned them against transgression; otherwise he trespassed on the rights of none, and certainly was never accused of wilful interference, boasting or gluttony of any description. His contemporary of the hill town at the other end of the Vale possessed a reputation about the reverse of this, and yet he was not less genuinely respected; for though meekness and humility may be, in a sense, desirable qualities, the average man of the world shows a more decided preference for the bold and the masterful, so that we say "the bigger the rogue the better his desert," and the higher, for certain, is the esteem in which he is held.

It came to pass, however, that one farmer Smith, after attending the local "Cabbage Feast," and seeing the Vicar demolish a whole leg of mutton, while he himself could only secure the leg and wing of a cockerel, was jealous of the Vicar and would not have paid tithe had he not been aware that in any default of his some part of his estate would be confiscated. In course of time Smith's disaffection became more pronounced, and a rupture was brought about in this manner. For twenty years the parson had kept his hunters in farmer Smith's stables, without paying a penny in fees; but when Smith wished to erect a gravestone above the remains of his mother-in-law he was surprised to receive a note from the Vicar demanding the sum of ten pounds before the work could be proceeded with. Smith thereupon saddled his nag, rode to the Vicarage and expostulated with the parson, who still persisted in claiming the fee as his lawful due and his right. Then Smith cried:

> "Ten pound's a girt sound,
> 'Tis fit to buy an acre o' ground.

but if thee oot have it get they hunters out o' my stable and don't set foot on my premises again."

In this village were two farmers, between whom existed an inveterate and senseless rivalry; one of them, for his magnificent behaviour, was termed "Lord" Pinnegar, and the other, because he occupied the local manor was styled "Squire" Withers. "Lord" Pinnegar was a member of

Sheep-washing in the River Thames at Radcot Bridge

the local troop of Yeoman Cavalry and had attended the annual dinner at Highworth clad in full dress uniform and wearing a sword at his side, as was usual at those functions. Upon returning home, rather the worse for liquor, approaching a tall milestone on Red Down Hill, he saw, or he imagined he saw, in the stone the image of his rival, which moved him to anger. Reining his horse, therefore, opposite the milestone, he began to accuse it of misdemeanour in regard to the sale of butter and cream — both Withers and Pinnegar were dairy farmers and cheese-makers — and, failing to receive a reply, became more passionate and insistent.

Enraged with the silence of his fancied opponent, he cried at length: "If you don't answer I'll chop your head off"; and, still receiving no response, he drew his sword, spurred his horse, and with the cry: "If you're a squire, I'm a lord," charged the stone and dealt it a slashing blow, the mark of which, I am told, is even now visible.

Jack Dawes worked for old farmer White and lived in a small two-roomed cottage that used to stand on the roadside between Radcot Bridge and Faringdon. At Michaelmas time the master gave him the offer of a more commodious dwelling, which he gladly accepted. Accordingly, after milking, Jack went to the door and addressed the farmer.

"I shall want a wagon an' dree 'osses to-day, maaster," said he.

"Why, Jack! but one 'oss 'ull be enough to bring thy bit o' goods up, won't it?" replied the farmer.

"No. I shall want dree 'osses," returned Jack.

"Very well! Take three then, if you want them," said White.

Early in the evening Jack set off with the team and loaded his goods, that scarcely filled the bed of the wagon. On the way he met the master, who was going to Faringdon Fair, and he exclaimed: "Ah, Jack! Thees might just as well have had one 'oss, as I telled tha."

"Aw, maaster! 'Tis no good if 'e don't try to cut some sort of a show; for to be poor and to look poor is the devil all over," replied Jack, sturdily.

Squire Goodlake, the blind Justice of Littleworth, was a pathetic figure as he occupied the magisterial bench at Faringdon; but he was very shrewd and penetrating and grasped all the points of the cases tried in his presence. After listening with patience to the evidence, and himself asking several questions or addressing a remark, he was accustomed to observe: "I see! I see! I see the case quite clearly."

By reason of his infirmity he was conducted round his farms, sitting on horseback, by his steward; but he liked to feel that he had received the respects of his workpeople. Accordingly, after visiting the sheep-fold, he inquired as to the behaviour of the shepherd, and on passing a labourer he was overheard to ask who it was, and then followed the inquiry: "Did he make his obeisance?"

Harry and Dick, knowing that there were full barrels in the dairy, and aware of the fact that master and mistress were from home one

Sunday after dinner, insisted on entering the place to regale themselves with the liquor. Having made the servant girl a party to the conspiracy, they drew a bung, but, as it was thunder weather, fermentation was in progress and the beer "boiled over" on to the floor. Mary thereupon feared that the theft would be detected; but Dick took a mug of ale and dashed it upon the ceiling above the barrel, which led the mistress to infer that the bung had blown out by accident.

It was usual on that farm for ploughboys, after harvest home, to have an eating-match, at the master's expense, the first to finish being pledged to help the others out.

Tom Trinder, the shepherd, of Littleworth, went to kill farmer Whitfield's sheep, one of which he slaughtered every week for the use of Whitfield's household and relatives. Tom was asked into the kitchen and placed near the fire, and while he warmed his fingers the good wife served dinner for the master and family, but, whether by oversight or intention, neglected to offer Tom any food. Then Tom, after a few moment's sober reflection, broke the silence.

"It's a bad job 'bout Harry Luckett's sow down the village," said he.

"Why, what's that, Tom?" asked the good wife quickly.

"A 'ed thirteen purty little pegs an' only got twelve teats to suckle 'em," answered Tom.

"Whatever will they do with the other poor thing?" inquired she.

"He'll hef to take a back saat, same as I got to," Tom replied.

"Oh, dear! And I quite forgot you were sitting there all this time, and nothing to put into your inside. Go and get him a plate, Susan, while I cut him a bit o' meat; and fetch me a dumpling from the pot, for I'm sure he must be shrammed a-cold," exclaimed she, hurriedly.

Old Aaron Grainger, the Kelmscott shepherd, who lived alone in a roomy stone cottage, spent a good many evenings at the tavern and occasionally needed assistance to attain his dwelling after closing time. A young farmer of the village, finding him incapable one night, and thinking to do him a kindly office, took him home and, having seated him in a chair, knelt down and unlaced his boots. He had barely finished this when old Aaron, lifting his crab staff, fetched him a hearty crack on the head, with the remark: "'Tis time you got away home now, mi bwoy!"

There were strange words and curious expressions in use here in former times, but the majority have now disappeared before the march of modern education, which tends to eliminate them from the speech of the people, irrespective of origin, value or other significance. Farm labourers speak of chains as "draggeting," "drugeting" and "kinchating"; to spread (reflexive) is to "rassle"; a lazy person "lollaps about," to be shrewd is to be "deedy," and snail-shells are "guggles." I overheard one remark of a young woman: "She's quite bowsy," meaning that she was unsteady and swaggering in her gait.

Buckland Club Day was about the middle of June, on which day no rain had fallen to spoil the proceedings for over forty years. When I arrived, after walking by the river from Radcot to Rushey, the procession had been formed, the service held in the church, and luncheon was being partaken of at the village inn, while the band played suitable selections, patiently awaiting its own turn for refreshment. It was ideal weather, even for Buckland, which is high, dry and bracing, fanned with the temperate breezes that blow from the far down-lands or above the Vale and the river.

In the evening, after the club-men had paraded the streets and collected subscriptions at the great House and the farms, the festival took the form of a merry fair, with fiddle and folk-dancing, swings, roundabouts, and several other kinds of amusement. It was a large and happy crowd assembled; school children, youths and maidens, shepherds and ploughmen with their buxom wives, and wrinkled age leaning upon the staff, but bright and gay, participating in the fun, for, as one above ninety remarked to me: "I must hae a bit of a gammut wi' the young people."

"'Tis a sight many yer, but not all from Buckland," one observed at my elbow; and, in fact, it would have been difficult to tell from where they had come, but certain it is that no village within a wide radius, and that on both sides of the river, was unrepresented. I remained chatting with the local schoolmaster and the aged gamekeeper, and listened again to the old tales which, in spite of their simplicity, I am never tired of hearing; and I left the meadow as the band was playing an air wedded to the words of a local folk-song:

"O my Billy, O my Bill, O my Bill, O—O!
Give me a needle and some thread
To sew up Billy's breeches."

The day was too far spent for me to return to Rushey and walk through the meadows to Radcot, as I had desired, in consequence of which I took the open road that leads on to Faringdon and, after passing through the town, brings one face to face with the White Horse opposite Badbury Hill and the Coxwell barn. Before I reached the Folly the sun had set over the Cotswolds, lying far beyond and beneath; the twilight was fading, and a deep crimson belt extended along the horizon tapering to a thin line in the extreme north-west. I stood for a long time gazing to where, out of the purple hills, the slender river rises and winds slowly down through the Vale.

THE END

INDEX

References to the River Thames are too numerous to be indexed. Illustrations are indicated in *italics*.